The Dynamics of
Rational Deliberation

The Dynamics of
Rational Deliberation

Brian Skyrms

Harvard University Press
Cambridge, Massachusetts
London, England
1990

Library of Congress Cataloging in Publication Data

Skyrms, Brian.
 The dynamics of rational deliberation / Brian Skyrms.
  p. cm.
 Includes bibliographical references.
 ISBN 0-674-21885-X (alk. paper)
 1. Bayesian statistical decision theory. 2. Game theory.
 I. Title.
 QA279.5.S57 1990   89-38949
 519.5'42—dc20   CIP

Contents

Preface

This book is about rational deliberation conceived of as a dynamic process. Where deliberation generates new information relevant to the decision under consideration, a rational decisionmaker will (processing costs permitting) feed back that information and reconsider. A firm decision is reached at a fixed point of this process—a deliberational equilibrium. Although there may be many situations in which informational feedback may be neglected and an essentially static theory of deliberation will suffice, there are others in which informational feedback plays a crucial role. It is this dynamic aspect of rational deliberation which allows one to embed the theory of games in the Bayesian theory of individual rational decision.

The Bayesian theory of individual rational decision under uncertainty and the theory of games appear to employ different criteria for rational decision. The dominant rationality concept of the theory of individual rational decision is maximization of expected utility. The dominant rationality concept in the theory of noncooperative games is equilibrium (which coincides with maximin in the most thoroughly studied case of zero-sum games with mixed strategies). Some writers view game-theoretic situations as fundamentally different from other decisionmaking situations and consider it appropriate that different standards of rationality operate in decision theory and in game theory. The game-theoretic equilibrium concept, however, gives equivocal guidance to the individual players in non-zero-sum noncooperative games because there are typically many game-theoretic equilibria, and if each player plays his end of some game-theoretic equilibrium or other, it does not follow that the result is a game-theoretic equilibrium. The essential facts about these two theories are laid out in Chapter 1.

If one treats deliberation as a dynamic process that generates relevant information, the expected utility principle can be taken as basic and the equilibrium principle as derivative. A Bayesian deliberator can only choose an act which is at a deliberational equilibrium. Noncooperative games then form a special deliberational situation in which part of one player's deliberation consists of an emulation of another player's deliberations. In such a situation, Nash equilibria of the game can be related to deliberational equilibria of the individual Bayesian players, so that the game-theoretic solution concept is a consequence of the expected utility principle. From an initial state of joint indecision, which is common knowledge, Bayesian deliberators (whose Bayesian character is also common knowledge) reach deliberational equilibria that jointly constitute a game-theoretic equilibrium. From this perspective a multiplicity of game-theoretic equilibria is simply a reflection of the multiplicity of possible initial positions rather than an indication of the inadequacy of the underlying conception of rationality. This fundamental relationship between the Nash equilibrium concept and the concept of Bayesian deliberational equilibrium is developed in Chapter 2.

Within this sort of framework we have a natural classification of game-theoretic equilibria in terms of dynamic stability. There are stable and strongly stable equilibria; saddle-point equilibria; unstable stars, and so forth. There are examples of all these in simple games, and the classification throws some light on recent discussions of refinements of the Nash equilibrium concept. Various Nash equilibria that have been criticized as being intuitively irrational are so unstable that it would almost require a miracle for Bayesian deliberators to converge to them. These matters, as well as questions of the structural stability of the deliberational dynamics, are discussed in Chapter 3.

The sort of dynamical questions discussed in Chapters 2 and 3 can be investigated by computer simulation of systems of deliberators. For small games, simulation is feasible on a personal computer. An appendix to the book lists several programs in BASIC to allow readers to run some simple simulations. There is no better way to get a feeling for questions of accessibility and stability than by running such simulations.

It is essential that the qualitative features of the sort of dynamical model I have sketched be grounded on first principles of Bayesian decision theory. First principles must tell us (1) that if costs are negligible a Bayesian decisionmaker should feed back relevant information and (2) how the new information should effect belief revision. The second question calls for a treatment of *dynamic coherence* of rules for belief revision in the light of new evidence. The first calls for an analysis of *the expected utility of cost-free information*. These questions are complicated by the kind of informational feedback we are considering. Information is generated by analysis of the problem. We are in the realm of what I. J. Good calls "dynamic probability." It is at least arguable that the new information is not within the domain of the decisionmaker's probability measure, which means that straightforward conditioning is not available as a means for belief change. Consequently, a proper treatment of questions (1) and (2) may require an extension of classical Bayesian methods and results. Such an extension is carried out in Chapters 4 and 5.

Chapter 4 discusses the expected utility of cost-free information. There is a classic theorem discussed by Good, Savage, and others to the effect that the utility of free information is never negative, and it is positive if there is any positive probability that the new information can affect the subsequent choice of action. As an interesting historical sidelight, I have discovered that unpublished notes of F. P. Ramsey in the Ramsey archives have a version of this result. (As this book goes to press, I have learned that Nils-Eric Sahlin will publish a transcription of this manuscript with an introductory note in the *British Journal for Philosophy of Science*.) The standard version of the theorem assumes belief change by conditioning, but we would like results for more general kinds of dynamically coherent belief change. Chapter 4 establishes a theorem for a kind of *generalized learning situation* that is much more widely applicable than simple conditioning.

Chapter 5 deals with coherent belief change. The stringency of the requirements for dynamic coherence depends on the kind of epistemic situation in which the decisionmaker finds herself. In certain tightly circumscribed situations, dynamic coherence requires belief change by classical conditioning. When more general epistemic situations are considered, the requirements for dynamic coherence are relaxed. It turns out, however, that a quite general requirement for coherence is the key requirement for a *generalized learning situation* in the sense used in the analysis of the value of knowledge in Chapter 4. Taken together, these two chapters provide a principled foundation for the informational feedback which makes deliberational dynamics interesting. They are also— I hope—of interest for their own sake.

The theory of dynamic deliberation not only provides a setting in which classical game theory can be grounded, but also suggests ways in which the classical theory can be generalized. The strong assumptions of common knowledge that are required to get classical game theory out of deliberational dynamics can be relaxed. One interesting way to do this is to introduce possible beliefs that players may, in commonly recurring situations, play in terms of simple habits that are themselves chosen by more elaborate rational deliberation. Chapter 6 shows how just a small doubt that this could be so is enough to introduce phenomena unknown in classical game theory. I speculate that these phenomena may be useful in modeling the rational emergence of a social contract. The final chapter sums up and surveys some open questions.

The techniques discussed in this book have wide relevance, from the modeling of the arms race to the analysis of rational roots of convention and the social contract. Accordingly, I have tried to make the exposition accessible to the intelligent reader who is not a specialist in decision theory or game theory. The essential elements of these theories are introduced in Chapter 1 and further developed along the way. I hope, however, that specialists too will find something of interest in the non-standard point of view that I develop here.

Many friends and colleagues helped me think about the issues treated in this book. In particular, I would like to thank Ernest Adams, Brad Armendt, John Broome, Ellery Eells, Bill Harper, John Harsanyi, Dick Jeffrey, David Lewis, Patrick Maher, Michael Teit Nielsen, Kurt Norlin, Greg Kavka, Larry Samuelson, Bas van Fraassen, and Peter Woodruff for stimulating discussions.

The University of California provided sabbatical leave and the John Simon Guggenheim Foundation, the National Science Foundation, and the Humanities Council of Princeton University generous support during the time when most of this book was written.

The diagram from the Ramsey manuscript is reproduced with the kind permission of the Ramsey family and of the Ramsey archives at the University of Pittsburgh.

Thanks to Lindsay Waters and Kate Schmit of Harvard University Press for seeing the manuscript into production.

This book could not have been written without the support of my family, to whom it is dedicated.

The Dynamics of
Rational Deliberation

1 Principles of Rational Decision

So also, the games in themselves merit to be studied
and if some penetrating mathematician meditated
upon them he would find many important results, for
man has never shown more ingenuity than in his plays.

—G. W. Leibniz (quoted in Ore, 1960)

Two Paradigms of Rational Decision

There are two well-developed theories of rational decisionmaking: the
theory of coherent individual decision of Ramsey, de Finetti, and Savage, which is based on the principle of *maximum expected utility*, and the
theory of games of von Neumann and Morgenstern, which is based on
the concept of *equilibrium*.[1] In the most satisfactory part of the theory of
games, the theory of zero-sum two-person games, von Neumann and
Morgenstern showed that a game-theoretic equilibrium corresponds to
each player playing his or her *security* strategy—the strategy which maximizes the minimum possible gain (the *maximin* strategy).

> *Example: Justice as Fairness 1.* A group of ten people, of which you
> are one, is to divide one million dollars. All agree that a just distribution scheme is one that would be chosen by a rational, self-interested agent if he or she were to be one of the recipients but
> had no information as to which one. Accordingly, each person is
> assigned a numeral from 1 to 10 by lot and you are chosen to
> divide the money by numeral among the members. We assume,
> for present purposes, that utility is proportional to money. If you
> choose by *maximin*, then you will evaluate each distribution
> scheme according to the least amount of money you could receive
> under that scheme. Your unique *security* strategy consists in
> choosing to divide the money equally. If you choose to *maximize
> your expected utility*, you evaluate each distribution scheme
> according to the average of the payoffs to each of the ten num-

bers, weighted by the probability that you have that number. As it is part of the conception of fairness that you have equal probability of holding any number, all distribution schemes look equally good. If, for example, the entire million is to be given to number one and you have a one in ten chance of being number one, your expected payoff is one hundred thousand dollars. This is just the payoff that you would get if the million were shared equally.

What is the proper relationship between the rationality concepts of expected utility theory and game theory? The two theories have developed in the absence of a univocal answer to this question. Luce and Raiffa (1957) suggest in one place that for a decisionmaker facing a situation of risk (where the chances of factors other than the decisionmaker's own choice are known), the proper rule is to maximize expected utility, but in situations of uncertainty (where the chances are not known) one should choose one's security strategy. But this suggestion makes nonsense of the theory of subjective probability which they develop later and which is meant to apply under uncertainty. Shubik (1982, p. 2) makes the cut in a different place:

The general *n*-person game postulates a separate "free will" for each of the contending parties and is therefore fundamentally indeterminate. To be sure, there are limiting cases, which game-theorists call "inessential games," in which the indeterminacy can be resolved satisfactorily by applying the familiar principle of self-seeking utility maximization or individual rationality. But there is no principle of societal rationality, of comparable resolving power, that can cope with the "essential" game, and none is in sight. Instead, deep-seated paradoxes, challenging our intuitive ideas of what kind of behavior should be called "rational," crop up on all sides.

Can the elusive concept of free will bear the weight put on it here? Must we decide such issues before we know how to interact rationally with a person—or an automaton? Would it not be preferable to have a unified theory of rational action, such that in game situations each player can treat the others as part of nature?

To complicate matters further, both classical game theory and decision theory have been vigorously criticized, notably by Herbert Simon (1957, 1972, 1986), for ignoring computational, procedural, and other bounding aspects of the process of reasoning. I believe that such considerations hold part of the key to the correct view of the relation of game theory to individual decision theory.

Deliberation can be modeled as a dynamic process with informational feedback, a process that is carried out by deliberators motivated by considerations of expected utility and having finite computational resources. Consideration of games played by such bounded Bayesian deliberators grounds and illuminates equilibrium concepts of classical game theory under certain special assumptions, and suggests how that theory must be modified in situations where these assumptions fail.

This chapter will provide an introduction to some essential concepts of game theory and expected utility theory. Chapters 2 and 3 will show how models of dynamic deliberation can provide a bridge between them.

Expected Utility

The origin of the concept of an *expected value* is contemporaneous with the origin of mathematical probability theory itself. The *utility* concept was introduced later, and went through a considerable evolution before taking its present form.

The mathematical theory of probability was conceived as an instrument for evaluating gambles in games of chance. It was assumed that the natural measure of value of a gamble was the *expectation* of the payoff—with the payoff of each outcome being measured in terms of liquid assets: gold or coin of the realm. The expected value is just the sum over outcomes of the probability of the outcome times the payoff associated with that outcome. For example, consider two gambles on independent flips of a fair coin with the following payoffs:

Gamble 1: 4 ducats if heads; 0 if tails
Gamble 2: 7 ducats if two heads (HH) on two flips; 0 otherwise

Evaluating by expected payoff in ducats, gamble 1 has an expected payoff of $(\frac{1}{2})(4) + (\frac{1}{2})(0) = 2$; gamble 2 has an expected payoff of $(\frac{1}{4})(7) + (\frac{3}{4})(0) = \frac{7}{4}$; and gamble 1 is to be preferred to gamble 2.

This expected value or "moral hope" was from the beginning taken as the correct quantity for assessing gambles. Intellectual effort was focused more on the question of computing the probabilities than on the philosophical justification of the expectation principle. Later on, with the law of large numbers, a frequentist gloss became available: the expected payoff is almost surely the average payoff one would achieve in a very long series of independent trials of the gamble.

The move from expected ducats to expected *utility* was precipitated by a puzzle, known as the *St. Petersburg* paradox after the journal in which Daniel Bernoulli published a landmark discussion of the problem in 1783. In the St. Petersburg game, a fair coin is to be flipped until it comes up heads. If it comes up heads on the nth toss, you will be paid 2^n ducats. There is no limit to the number of tosses. What is the value of this game?

The St. Petersburg Game		
Possible outcome	Probability	Payoff
H	½	2 ducats
TH	¼	4 ducats
TTH	⅛	8 ducats
•	•	•
•	•	•
•	•	•

The expected payoff is the infinite sum: (½)(2) + (¼)(4) + (⅛)(8) . . . = 1 + 1 + 1 . . ., which exceeds any finite value. Should everyone be willing to pay any amount whatsoever to get into this game? Would you? Bernoulli's rationale for a negative answer (following Gabriel Cramer)[2] is that *value* is not properly measured in monetary units, but rather in terms of a theoretical quantity, *utility*. Money, and most other real goods, have declining marginal utility: an extra ducat on top of a 10-ducat gain adds more utility than an extra ducat on top of a 1,000-ducat gain. Bernoulli even suggests a typical utility function: utility = log(money). The St. Petersburg game has finite expected utility given the logarithmic utility function.[3]

> *Example: Justice as Fairness 2.* Again, a group of ten people of which you are one is to divide a million dollars. You are to select a distribution scheme by number, as before, which will maximize your own expected utility under the fairness assumption that all numbers are equally likely to be your number and under the Bernoullian assumption that utility = log(money). The unique maximal distribution scheme here is the egalitarian one with everyone getting $100,000 or 5 utiles (log of 100,000 is 5). The scheme which gives all the money ($1,000,000 or 6 utiles) to number one has an expected utility for you of only ⁶⁄₁₀ of a utile. Any utility function with strictly declining marginal utility will give the result that equal shares maximize your expected utility. The concave shape of the utility function here gives the egalitarian conclusions

which depended on preference for security (on the *maximin* decision rule) in the previous example, *Justice as Fairness 1.*[4]

The utility hypothesis did not come to Bernoulli—or Cramer—from out of a vacuum. Utilitarian ideas were in the air, floated by (among others) Francis Hutcheson, professor of moral philosophy at Glasgow and teacher of both Adam Smith and David Hume.[5] Questions about the nature of utility did not much occupy probabilists following Bernoulli but they remained within the province of economists and moral philosophers, who discussed them from an ethical and psychological point of view.

It was generally assumed that utility was a psychological quantity, and that there was no difficulty in principle in comparing the utilities of different individuals. Thus, we have Alfred Marshall's remark (quoted in Savage, 1954) that the declining marginal utility of money is well illustrated by the fact that the rich man will take a taxi while the poor man will walk. It is here assumed as a matter of course that the disutility of

Utility

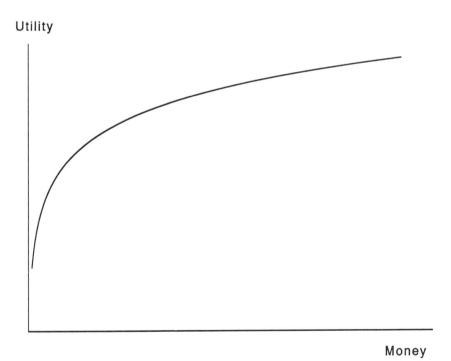

Money

Figure 1.1.   Bernoulli's utility function

walking is approximately the same for the rich and the poor, and so it must exceed the marginal utility of cab fare for the rich but not the poor. It is easy to appreciate how, in the hands of James Mill, Jeremy Bentham, and John Stuart Mill, utilitarianism could have generated a powerful movement for radical social reform.

> *Example: Justice as Fairness Meets Utilitarianism.* You believe in the version of justice as fairness that takes maximization of expected utility as the principle of individual rational decision. You have a friend, a utilitarian, who believes in maximizing total utility of the group. Each of you is to come up with a just plan to distribute one million dollars among 10 people of three different types: 3 of type 1, 4 of type 2, and 3 of type 3. You both believe that utility is an empirical psychological property and that the types in question are so specified as to determine the individual's utility function for money. You agree what the utility functions are for each type.[6] Then you and your friend will agree on the correct distribution scheme. You maximize your expected utility under the fictitious supposition that you have an equal chance of being any one of the ten, that is, that you have 0.3 probability of being of type 1, and so on. Then the quantity that your distribution scheme must maximize is just one tenth of the quantity that your friend's scheme is maximizing.

By the end of the nineteenth century, the sort of conception of utility that we find in the English utilitarians came under positivistic attack, notably by Vilfredo Pareto. If utility was to be interpreted in terms of consumers' behavior, rather than in the manner of introspective psychology, then interpersonal comparisons of utility seemed to make no sense. Indeed, even with respect to one consumer the measurement of utility on a numerical scale appeared to be unjustified. Consumers simply made their choices, and the operational part of utility talk seemed to consist solely of preference ordering.

In his manual of political economy (1927) Pareto used the ordinal indifference curve approach developed by Francis Ysidro Edgeworth. But while Edgeworth thought that utility was measurable and that the indifference curves derived from utility functions, Pareto took them as primitive. The entire theory, he wrote, "rests on no more than a fact of experience, that is on the determination of the quantities of goods which constitute combinations between which the individual is indifferent." This acerbic footnote follows: "This cannot be understood by literary economists and metaphysicians. Nevertheless, they will want to interfere by giving their opinions; and the reader with some knowledge of mathematics can amuse himself by perusing the foolish trash they will put out on the subject."

To some extent, Pareto's position was anticipated by William Stanley Jevons. In his *Theory of Political Economy* (1871) Jevons addressed these skeptical remarks to the question of interpersonal comparisons of utility: "The susceptibility (to pleasure) of one mind may, for all we know, be a thousand times greater than that of another. But, provided that the susceptibility was different in a like ratio in all directions, we should never be able to discover the difference. Every mind is inscrutable to every other mind."

Lionel Robbins' influential discussions in the thirties (1932, 1938) echoed Jevons'. In 1938, he noted how his faith in utilitarian welfare economics had been shaken:

I am not clear how these doubts first suggested themselves; but I well remember how they were brought to a head by my reading somewhere—I think in the works of Sir Henry Maine—the story of how an Indian official had attempted to explain to a high cast Brahmin the sanctions of the Benthamite system. "But that," said the Brahmin, "cannot possibly be right. I am ten times as capable of happiness as that untouchable over there." I had no sympathy with the Brahmin. But I could not escape the conviction that, if I chose to regard men as equally capable of satisfaction and he to regard them as differing according to a hierarchical schedule, the difference between us was not one which could be resolved by the same methods of demonstration as were available in other fields of social judgement.

Lord Robbins needn't have gone to India for his illustration. Consider the following specimen of nineteenth-century chauvinism from Edgeworth's *Mathematical Psychics* (1881, pp. 77–78):

But equality is not the whole of distributive justice . . . in the minds of many good men among the moderns and the wisest of the ancients, there appears a deeper sentiment in favor of aristocratic privilege—the privilege of man above brute, of civilized above savage, of birth, of talent, and of the male sex. This sentiment of right has a ground of utilitarianism in supposed differences of *capacity* . . .

If we suppose that capacity for pleasure is an attribute of skill and talent . . . we may see a reason deeper than Economics may afford for the larger pay, though often more agreeable work, of the aristocracy of skill and talent. The aristocracy of sex is similarly grounded upon the supposed superior capacity of the man for happiness . . . upon the sentiment—

> Woman is the lesser man, and her passions unto mine
> Are as moonlight unto sunlight and as water unto wine.

Illustration: Pareto Optimality. If we agree with Pareto that utility has only a personal and ordinal significance, what is left of utilitarianism as a social philosophy? One can still express certain qualitative features that every utilitarian measure of social welfare would have. We say that a social state S2 *weakly Pareto dominates* a state S1 when some member of society prefers S2 to S1 and no member prefers S1 to S2. S2 *strongly Pareto dominates* S1 if and only if all members of society prefer S2 to S1. The judgment that a social state is preferable to one which it strongly Pareto dominates is an ordinally expressible remainder of the utilitarian doctrine that social utility is the sum of individual utilities. The stronger principle that a social state is preferable to one which it weakly Pareto dominates is motivated by the additional utilitarian principle that everyone counts equally. The ordinal remainder of this principle is, roughly, that everyone counts for something. We will say that a Pareto optimal social state is one which is not weakly Pareto dominated by any other.

The concept of utility was partly rescued from Paretian skepticism by Frank Ramsey in 1926[7] and by John von Neumann and Oskar Morgenstern in 1944. Ramsey's analysis went deeper than that of von Neumann and Morgenstern, but was for a long time little known among economists.[8] When von Neumann and Morgenstern independently rediscovered one of Ramsey's key ideas and published it in *Theory of Games and Economic Behavior,* they carried cardinal utility back into respectability.

The idea in question was to consider preferences not only for goods or prospects, but also for *gambles* over goods. If you know only that my preference order for desserts is

Raspberries and cream
Chocolate mousse
Blueberry pie
Cheesecake

you cannot sensibly answer the question as to whether the *difference* in utility between the first two items is equal to the difference in utility between the second two. But if you are, in addition, told that I am indifferent between a gamble which gives me raspberries and cream (RC) if heads; cheesecake (Ch) if tails, and one which gives me chocolate mousse (CM) if heads; blueberry pie (BP) if tails, then I can conclude that these differences are equal:

$$\text{Utility Gamble 1} = \text{Utility Gamble 2}$$

$$\tfrac{1}{2}U(\text{RC}) + \tfrac{1}{2}U(\text{Ch}) = \tfrac{1}{2}U(\text{CM}) + \tfrac{1}{2}U(\text{BP})$$

$$U(\text{RC}) - U(\text{CM}) = U(\text{BP}) - U(\text{Ch})$$

Pareto had already remarked that if a natural criterion for equality of differences of utility could be found, then utility could be measured on a numerical scale. Given a conventional choice of the zero point and the size of a unit "utile," the utility values would be unique.[9]

The extension of the preference ordering to gambles provided the requisite criterion for quantifying utility. Cardinal utility was, after all, justified in a way strictly in accord with the Paretian methodology. Given von Neumann–Morgenstern utility, Bernoulli's idea about the declining marginal utility of money again makes perfect sense. It is an empirical claim about utility differences for a given individual, and it reduces to a claim about that individual's preferences over gambles. The interpersonal comparisons of utility assumed by the classical English utilitarians, however, are not rescued by the von Neumann–Morgenstern construction. Since the data do not determine the choice of zero point and unit, quantities such as (1) the sum of utilities over different persons and (2) the utility of that member of the group who is worst off in terms of utility are not given any determinate sense.

> *Example: Personal Justice.* Ten followers of von Neumann and Morgenstern are deciding how to distribute one million dollars among them. Each is an expected utility maximizer. Each attempts to find a just distribution scheme among numbers 1 to 10, where players will be assigned numbers later by fair lottery. Each seeks a distribution scheme that maximizes expected utility according to his or her *own* utility function. So each player has a personal conception of justice, and no interpersonal comparison of utilities is involved. Nevertheless, if each player's utility function exhibits a declining marginal utility for money then all players will agree that the egalitarian distribution scheme is the fair one.[10]

Von Neumann and Morgenstern quantified utility by bringing in known chances. But at least some thinkers with empiricist worries about utility also have empiricist worries about chance. This wider skepticism raises questions about the availability of probability to quantify utility. Ramsey had already answered this question in 1926 by constructing both personal utility and personal probability out of preferences over gambles.

The key move is to find subjective surrogates for the *chances* that von Neumann and Morgenstern used to scale the decisionmaker's utilities. Ramsey started by identifying propositions that have no values in and of themselves to the decisionmaker, and whose truth or falsity does not modify the value of payoffs. He calls these propositions "ethically neutral." A proposition, p, is ethically neutral with respect to a collection of payoffs, B, for an agent if she is indifferent between B with p true and B with p false. A proposition, p, is ethically neutral for an agent if it is ethically neutral for her with respect to maximal collections of payoffs.[11] The nice thing about ethically neutral propositions is that the expected utility of gambles on them depends only on their probability and on the utility of the contemplated payoffs. The utility of the ethically neutral propositions themselves is not a complicating factor. In our illustration of the von Neumann–Morgenstern utility scale, I tacitly assumed that the propositions describing the outcome of the coin flip (H or T) were ethically neutral.

We can identify an ethically neutral proposition, H, for which the decisionmaker has personal probability (degree of belief) ½ when there are two payoffs, A and B, such that she prefers A to B but is indifferent between the two gambles: (1) Get A if H is true, B if H is false; (2) get B if H is true, A if H is false. For the purpose of scaling the decisionmaker's utilities, such a proposition is just as good as the proposition that a fair coin comes up heads.

The procedure just described extends in a straightforward way to identify more surrogates for chance. Consider a wheel of fortune with 100 possible outcomes which are ethically neutral. The decisionmaker prefers A to B but is indifferent between (1) A if outcome i, B otherwise, and (2) A if outcome j, B otherwise, for all possible outcomes i and j. Then the decisionmaker regards the 100 possible outcomes as equiprobable, and the disjunction of N outcomes as having probability of $N/100$. For a richer assortment of surrogate chances consider a wheel of fortune with more sides, or consider sequences of outcomes for repeated flips of a coin. A rich enough preference ordering has enough ethically neutral propositions to approximate the external scaling probabilities used by von Neumann and Morgenstern to any desired degree of precision.

These are the key ideas of the procedure by which Ramsey extracted from a rich and coherent preference ordering over gambles both a subjective utility and a subjective degree of belief such that the preference ordering agrees with the ordering by magnitude of expected utility. Utility now has shed the psychological and moral associations with which it was associated in the eighteenth and nineteenth centuries. The theory of expected utility is now a part of *logic:* the logic of coherent preference.

Ramsey proved a *representation theorem* to the effect that any coherent preference ordering over a rich enough set of gambles has associated with it a unique probability and a utility unique up to choice of zero point and magnitude of the unit utile, such that the ordering by expected utility agrees with the preference ordering. If we hold that rational preferences over a meager set of gambles (a) should be coherent and (b) should be embeddable in a coherent set of preferences over an enriched set of gambles, we keep the existence of a probability-utility representation whereby rational preferences over the meager set of gambles goes by expected utility, although we lose uniqueness. In this sense, we can say that the only normative content implied by the use of an expected utility model is that preferences should be coherent.[12]

If one has some sort of coherent moral preferences for society, these preferences must as well admit of an expected utility representation. So coherent social preferences over a rich set of prospects give rise to a corresponding social utility function unique up to choice of a conventional zero point and unit of measurement. When does the social utility have a utilitarian representation? That is, when is it the case that there are choices of zero points and units of measurement for individual utility scales and for the social utility scale, such that social utility is the sum of individual utilities? John Harsanyi answered this question in 1955 by proving the appropriate representation theorem. Neglecting technical details, the theorem says that coherent social preferences which satisfy the Pareto condition[13] with respect to individual preferences have a utilitarian representation. So, it seems that the moral content of modern utilitarianism consists of nothing more and nothing less than the Pareto condition.[14]

Rawls (1971) identified two great traditions in Western ethics: the social contract tradition, whose essential leading idea is justice as fairness, and the utilitarian tradition. When seen in the light of modern utility theory, there is considerable convergence between these traditions. As Harsanyi (1955) pointed out, under certain conditions justice as fairness *entails* utilitarianism. Suppose (1) you derive your social utility ordering by applying the expected utility version of justice as fairness to a society with categories and (2) your preferences conditional on being in a category coincide with the preferences of anyone in that category.[15] Then you are a utilitarian.

It is evident that the whole question of utilitarianism has been profoundly transformed by the evolution of the utility concept. Contemporary philosophy has been a little slow in catching up; a considerable amount of contemporary discussion of the ethics of utilitarianism remains stuck in the nineteenth century. We cannot pursue these implications of the modern utility concept for social philosophy here. The interested reader must be content with a reference to the literature.[16] Returning to our central topic of maximization of expected utility in individual decision, I would like to end this section with a question. *If expected utility theory presupposes only coherent preferences, how could it fail to be applicable in game-theoretic situations?*

The Theory of Games

The theory of games is almost entirely a creation of the twentieth century. Game-theoretic problems were considered in the 1920s by Borel (1924) and von Neumann (1928), and the subject emerged full-blown in von Neumann and Morgenstern's *Theory of Games and Economic Behavior* in 1944.

Von Neumann and Morgenstern argue that there is a difference in principle between rational decisionmaking for a single individual, such as Robinson Crusoe, acting against nature, and for a member of a group of interacting rational individuals (1947, pp. 11–12):

The difference between Crusoe's perspective and that of a participant in a social economy can also be illustrated in this way: Apart from those variables which his will controls, Crusoe is given a number of data which are "dead"; they are the unalterable physical background of the situation . . . Not a single datum with which he has to deal reflects another person's will or intention of an economic kind—based on motives of the same nature as his own. A participant in a social exchange economy, on the other hand, faces data of this last type as well: they are the product of other participants' actions and volitions . . . His actions will be influenced by his expectation of these, and they in turn reflect the other participants' expectation of his actions.

The difficulty that is here supposed to arise in the case of the social exchange economy is not so much the "free will" of the other participants as the role of mutual expectations, expectations of expectations, and so forth that can exist in a community of utility maximizers. These may seem to threaten a kind of self-reference in which the mutually interacting optimization problems of the various actors are not capable of joint solution. This is really the problem to which the theory of games is addressed. It will become clearer when we discuss von Neumann and Morgenstern's justification of their concept of a solution for a game.

First, however, let me introduce a few of the concepts of the theory. In the simplest sort of situation, a *normal-form* game, the players all choose simultaneously and independently among their respective possible acts, and the payoffs are determined by the combination of acts chosen. A game is called *zero-sum* if (for some scaling of the players' utilities) the total payoff for every possible combination of acts is zero.

The simplest zero-sum games are those involving only two players, and it is here that the von Neumann–Morgenstern theory has its greatest success. Such a game can be specified by a payoff matrix for one player, since the second player's preferences can be represented by payoffs which are just the negative of those of the first player. Here is an example:

Row's payoff matrix

	C1	C2	C3
R3	1	−1	−1
R2	1	0	1
R1	−1	−1	1

If Row does his act 3 and Column does her act 1, then Row gets payoff 1 and Column therefore gets payoff −1; whereas if they both do their respective act 2, they both get payoff 0. A simultaneous choice of acts by all players is called a *Nash equilibrium* if no player can improve his or her payoff by a unilateral defection to a different act. In other words, at a Nash equilibrium, *each player maximizes his or her utility conditional on the other player's act.* For example, [R1, C1] is not a Nash equilibrium, because if Column plays 1 then Row is better off playing either 2 or 3. Likewise, [R3, C1] is not a Nash equilibrium because if Row plays 3, Column would do better playing 2 or 3. (Remember that Row's losses are Column's gains.) You can verify that [R2, C2] is the unique Nash equilibrium of the game. If Column plays 2 Row can do no better than to play 2 himself (indeed in this case the alternatives are strictly worse) and Column is in a similar situation when Row plays 2. In a famous passage, von Neumann and Morgenstern (1947, p. 148) argue for the centrality of the Nash equilibrium concept:

Let us now imagine that there exists a complete theory of the zero-sum two-person game which tells a player what to do, and which is absolutely convincing. If the players knew such a theory then each player would have to assume that his strategy has been "found out" by his opponent. The opponent knows the theory, and he knows that the player would be unwise not to follow it . . . a satisfactory theory can exist only if we are able to harmonize the two extremes . . . strategies of player 1 "found out" or of player 2 "found out."

The harmony in question is Nash equilibrium, and the argument is supposed to show that an adequate theory of rational behavior in game-theoretic situations will have the consequences that if each player makes a rational choice, the result will be a Nash equilibrium. Then, if there is such an adequate theory of rational behavior, in any game like our example in which a unique Nash equilibrium exists the rational choice for each player must be to choose the act that is a constituent of the unique Nash equilibrium. In this way, if we have existence and uniqueness of Nash equilibria in general, we can turn the Nash equilibrium concept itself into a theory of rational choice.

Let us pause to consider this argument in the light of subjective expected utility theory. It is far from airtight. Here I want to emphasize one rather large and important gap. Suppose that there is a theory of rationality which is absolutely convincing, and suppose not only that both players know it but that it is common knowledge. (Each knows that the other knows it and that the other knows that he knows it, and so forth.)[17] Suppose that the calculation needed to extract the relevant information is finite, and that it is moreover small enough to take virtually no effort on the part of the players. Does it follow that each player can find out the other player's strategy? Only if the *inputs* to the theory are themselves common knowledge among the players. Von Neumann and Morgenstern are assuming that the *payoff matrix* is common knowledge to the players, but presumably the players' subjective probabilities might be private. Then each player might quite reasonably act to maximize subjective expected utility, believing that he will *not* be found out, with the result *not* being a Nash equilibrium.

For a rather crude illustration of this possibility, suppose in the foregoing example that Row plays 3 because he is almost sure that Column will play 1, thinking that Column is almost sure that he will play 1 in response to the mistaken belief that Column will play 3, etc. And suppose that Column plays 3 because she is almost sure that Row will play 3, because she thinks that Row thinks that she will play 1, etc. Each maximizes expected utility with the result being [R3, C3], which is not an equilibrium. For simplicity, this example uses degrees of belief that are nearly zero or one, but more complex and interesting examples of the phenomenon are possible. It has been recently studied by Bernheim (1984) and Pearce (1984), who call it *rationalizable strategic behavior.*

In two-person games, there is a relatively simple way to identify the rationalizable acts. An act is *strongly dominated* for a player if she has some other act that gives a better payoff no matter what the other player does. For example, in the zero-sum game for which Row's payoff matrix is as follows, Row's act 2 *strongly dominates* Row's act 1, but Column has no strongly dominated acts.[18]

	C1	C2
R2	1	2
R1	0	0

It is clear that no strongly dominated act is rationalizable, since no beliefs about the other player's acts can make it look as attractive as the act which dominates it. Conversely, Pearce (1984) and Bernheim (1984) showed that in two-person games those acts which remain after iterated deletion of strongly dominated strategies are all rationalizable. This principle extends to *n*-person games, if we do not require that one player's beliefs make other players' actions probabilistically independent.[19] Thus, in a game like our first example, where no strategies are strongly dominated, all strategies are rationalizable.

Von Neumann and Morgenstern neglected the possibility of rationalizable nonequilibrium strategies, even though they developed a theory of personal utility, because they never took the extra step with Ramsey to subjective probability. They assume that the information in the payoff matrix is the complete input for a theory of rational decision—an attitude that is perhaps still the prevalent one in game theory. I can find no principled argument for this assumption, and the theory of personal probability as developed by Ramsey, de Finetti, and Savage appears to contradict it.

In order for the von Neumann–Morgenstern argument for Nash equilibrium to work, all the inputs for rational decision must be common knowledge; otherwise the hypothesis that the other player can find out your strategy and make a best reply lacks a foundation. Therefore let us suppose that each player's prior personal probabilities are common knowledge, as is both the payoff matrix and the fact that the players are expected utility maximizers. Does the argument for Nash equilibrium now succeed? To see that it does not, let us modify our example as follows:

	C1	C2	C3
R3	1	0	−1
R2	0	0	0
R1	−1	0	1

[R2, C2] is still the *unique* Nash equilibrium. Now suppose that each player's prior probabilities over the other player's actions are [⅓, ⅓, ⅓] and that this is common knowledge, as is the payoff matrix and the fact that the players are subjective expected utility maximizers. These assumptions are compatible with any play by any player (with no prospect of being found out) and thus with any outcome of the game. Here uniqueness of the Nash equilibrium does not entail uniqueness in the recommendations of the underlying theory of individual rational behavior, so even common knowledge of the prior probabilities does not guarantee that a player's choice of action will be found out. It is apparent that we must build in even stronger assumptions about common knowledge and tell a more complicated story in order to make the argument for Nash equilibria valid. I will return to this question in the next chapter. For the moment, let us take the Nash equilibrium concept with a grain of salt, and proceed.

In the case of two-person zero-sum games, von Neumann and Morgenstern were able to establish a deep connection between security (maximin gain) strategies on the parts of the individual players and Nash equilibria of the game. Suppose that you and I are playing such a game, and our strategies form a Nash equilibrium. Then by the definition of *equilibrium*, neither of us would profit by a unilateral change of strategy. Since the game is zero-sum, my profit is your loss and conversely. So neither of us can lose by the other's unilateral change of strategy. In other words, we are both playing security strategies. So, in this special case, it is a necessary condition for a Nash equilibrium that each player play his or her security strategy.

Is it a sufficient condition? The *prima facie* answer is *no*. Consider the game of Matching Pennies. You either hide a penny in your hand, or not. I guess whether you did. If I guess correctly, I give you a penny, otherwise you give me a penny. Inspection of the payoff matrix will disclose that there *is* no Nash equilibrium:

Matching Pennies

	C1	C2
R2	1	−1
R1	−1	1

At each combination of acts, unilateral deviation will pay one of the players. Each act is a security strategy for each player.

The picture changes radically, however, if one follows Borel (1924) in allowing *mixed strategies*. Each player turns his or her choice of an act over to a chance device, with the operative choice being the choice of the chances. (The chance devices of different players operate independently.) So, in Matching Pennies, Row can choose any number between zero and one as the chance of R2; likewise for Column. Any point in the unit square thus represents mixed strategies for Row and Column. The payoffs for a combination of mixed strategies are the expected utilities, using the chance probabilities to compute the expectation. Figure 1.2 shows Row's payoffs for mixed strategies in Matching Pennies, plotted as a surface above the unit square. Enlarging the set of objects of choice to include mixed strategies has created an equilibrium: the combination of mixed strategies in which each player gives equal chances to each of her alternatives. This consists of the *security* mixed strategy for each player, where each player has an expected payoff of zero. Von Neumann proved in 1928 that it is true in general for finite two-person zero-sum games that if mixed strategies are included, there is always a Nash equilibrium and it will be attained if both players play security strategies.

So we always have *existence* of an equilibrium. But it may fail to be *unique*. There may be many Nash equilibria in a finite two-person zero-sum game with mixed strategies—but the failure of uniqueness is relatively painless. This is because the equilibria are *interchangeable*, in the

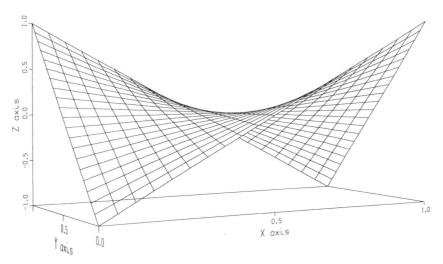

Figure 1.2. Payoff surface for mixed strategies in Matching Pennies

following sense: (i) if I play my end of one equilibrium, and you play your end of another, then the combination of our plays is a third equilibrium, because any combination of security strategies is an equilibrium and (ii) all equilibria have the same value for each player, namely that player's security level.

If one is willing to buy the rather shaky argument advanced by von Neumann and Morgenstern for the equilibrium concept, the problem of rationality has been solved for this special class of games. Rational action consists here in choosing a security strategy. That all players do so is a necessary and sufficient condition for their combined play to be at a Nash equilibrium (that is just as good as any other equilibrium). It is on this basis that the idea of a security strategy was rather widely applied in the heady decade following the publication of *Theory of Games and Economic Behavior*. Everyone knew, of course, that the tight connection between security and equilibrium did not hold for games in general, but the significance of that fact was not always fully appreciated.

When we pass from finite two-person, zero-sum games to finite *n*-person non-zero-sum games, the connection between security and equilibrium is broken and the picture becomes immensely more complicated. One remarkable fact is that here mixed strategies still guarantee the existence of equilibria. This fact was demonstrated by John Nash (1951), after whom they are named.

We now assume that there are a finite number of players, each with a finite number of strategies. Each player's payoff is a function of the choices of strategy of all players. There need be no special relationship between payoffs of different players. Two-person zero-sum games model situations of strict competition, but this larger class of games can model a whole spectrum of payoff profiles from strict competition to pure cooperation.

As an illustration of the difficulties introduced by even the simplest non-zero-sum games, consider the game of Chicken:

Chicken

		Column	
		Don't swerve	Swerve
Row	Don't swerve	$-10, -10$	$5, -5$
	Swerve	$-5, 5$	$0, 0$

The name comes from the image of two teenagers driving down the center of the road on a straight course toward a head-on collision; the first one who swerves is "chicken." The ordered pairs in the payoff matrix list the payoff for Row first and the payoff for Column second. If one swerves and the other doesn't the first loses face and the second gains it. If both swerve their relative status is unchanged. If neither swerves the result is worse than losing face. The story is slightly misleading here since, as before, we want to think of the players as making independent decisions at a given time. So let's suppose that the drivers must make an irreversible decision at the start by pushing a button in their computerized hot rods and then ride it out.

There are two pure Nash equilibria in this game: [Row swerves, Column doesn't] and [Column swerves, Row doesn't], as well as an equilibrium in mixed strategies where each flips a fair coin to decide if she will swerve.[20] We do not have interchangeability. If each picks her end of that Nash equilibrium that she prefers, neither will swerve, since each prefers the pure equilibrium in which the other swerves. This would lead to a definitely nonequilibrium outcome. And the connection with security strategy is broken because each player's security strategy is not to swerve—so the result of both players going for security is again nonequilibrium.

Although uniqueness fails rather dramatically, we do still have existence of equilibria. Nash proved this by exhibiting a continuous function[21] which maps the space of mixed strategies (of all players) into itself for a non-zero-sum game. This function leads each player to put more weight on strategies which look better than the *status quo*. By a well-known theorem of Brower, this function has a fixed point: a mixed strategy that gets mapped onto itself. At such a fixed point, no pure strategy looks better to any player than the mixed strategy associated with that point. This point is therefore a Nash equilibrium.

Nash also investigated special classes of non-zero-sum games where interchangeability of equilibrium points does hold. It is evident, however, that in the general case the status of the equilibrium concept as a touchstone of rationality is here even shakier than in the case of zero-sum game theory. In games with multiple equilibria, even if your opponent knows that you will pick your end of an equilibrium, he cannot figure out your strategy. And if he cannot figure out your strategy and the equilibria are not interchangeable, what is your rationale for even picking an equilibrium in the first place?

Since the pressing problem is too many rather than too few equilibria, there has been reason to look for stronger solution concepts that are met by only some subset of the Nash equilibria. And, indeed, some Nash equilibria seem to look better than others. Consider the following game,[22] supposing you are Row:

	C1	C2
R2	0,0	0,0
R1	1,1	0,0

In this game there are two Nash equilibria, one at [R1, C1] and one at [R2, C2]. Each is a genuine equilibrium; if Column plays her end of the equilibrium you can do no better than to play yours. But if you have even the slightest doubt that she will play C2, R1 will have greater expected utility.[23] And if you reason this way, isn't it likely that Column—being in a symmetric situation—will do so as well?

The two equilibria in this game are distinguished by Selten's (1975) notion of a *perfect* equilibrium. A *completely mixed* strategy is a mixed strategy in which every pure strategy gets some positive probability. If your opponents play mixed strategies, one of your strategies is a *best reply* if it maximizes expected utility where the expected utility is calculated using your opponents' mixing probabilities. An ε-*perfect equilibrium* is a completely mixed strategy (for all players) in which any pure strategy which is not a best reply has weight less than ε. A *perfect equilibrium* is a limit as ε approaches 0 of ε-perfect equilibria. Every perfect equilibrium is a Nash equilibrium, but the converse is not true. In the example, [R1, C1] is a perfect equilibrium, but [R2, C2] is not since for any completely mixed strategy, R1 is Row's unique best reply and C1 is Column's unique best reply.

Selten (1975, p. 35) views the model as embodying "A Model of Slight Mistakes": "There cannot be any mistakes if the players are absolutely rational. Nevertheless, a satisfactory interpretation of equilibrium points in extensive games seems to require that the possibility of mistakes is not completely excluded. This can be achieved by a point of view which looks at complete rationality as a limiting case of incomplete rationality." Myerson (1978, p. 74) commented: "The essential idea behind Selten's perfect equilibria is that no strategy should ever be given zero probability, since there is always a small chance that any strategy might be chosen, if only by mistake." For this reason, Selten's concept is often called "trembling hand" perfection.

Myerson pushed the idea one step further. The previous example can be converted to the next by giving each player a third unattractive alternative:

	C1	C2	C3
R3	−9, −9	−7, −7	−7, −7
R2	0,0	0,0	−7, −7
R1	1,1	0,0	−9, −9

Now there are three Nash equilibria: [R1, C1], [R2, C2], [R3, C3]. There are two perfect equilibria for now not only [R1, C1] but also [R2, C2] is a perfect equilibrium. (To see this consider a path of convergence along which R1, R3, C1, C3 are equiprobable and grow smaller while R2 and C2 are equiprobable and converge to 1.) Yet [R1, C1] still may seem the "best" equilibrium for much the same reason as before. Is one inclined to think that a "tremble" to R3 or to C3 is not really as likely as one to R2 or C2? To capture this intuition, Myerson introduced the notion of a *proper* equilibrium.

An *ε-proper equilibrium* is a completely mixed strategy such that if a pure strategy, A1, is a better response than a pure strategy, A2, then the probability ratio $p(A2)/p(A1)$ is less than ε. A *proper equilibrium* is a limit of a sequence of ε-proper equilibria as ε approaches zero. Every proper equilibrium is a perfect equilibrium but not conversely. In the example, [R1, C1] is proper; [R2, C2] is perfect but not proper; [R3, C3] is a Nash equilibrium but not a perfect one.

Selten and Myerson proved that perfect and indeed proper equilibria *exist* in every game of the kind under consideration. But the problem of nonuniqueness persists. For example, in the game of Chicken, all equilibria are perfect and proper. Considering the symmetry of games like Chicken, it seems unrealistic to expect a stronger equilibrium concept to deliver both existence and uniqueness.[24] Therefore it seems that the situation for non-zero-sum game theory can never be as simple and elegant as in the von Neumann–Morgenstern theory for zero-sum games.

There is a further complication in game theory which I have postponed discussing until now. That is the status of games in *extensive form*. Here we generalize from the simple model where all players simultaneously and independently make their choices to a model which allows a sequence of moves by different players in varying states of information about the moves already made by other players. Von Neumann and Morgenstern have an argument to the effect that all the complexity of the extensive-form model can, in the end, be reduced to the simple normal-form model of one round of simultaneous independent choices. But, as we shall see, this argument has been seriously challenged.

Following Kuhn (1953), we will model the temporal, causal, and informational structure of a game in extensive form as a tree. A simple example is shown in Figure 1.3. Player A moves first, choosing either act A1 or A2. Then player B either finds herself at the top node, in which case she knows that A has played A1, or at the bottom node, in which case she knows that A has played A2. In either case, she must choose between B1 and B2. Then the game is over; the course of play has traversed a path through the tree; and the payoffs at the end of that path are received.

The foregoing is a game of *perfect information*. Each player at each choice point knows whatever preceding choices have been made. The Kuhn model also allows for games where this may not be the case. Consider the tree in Figure 1.4. Here player A begins by choosing A1, A2, or A3. Then B must move. If A chose A1, B knows it. But otherwise, B knows only that A chose either A2 or A3. This is indicated by the dotted line between A2 and A3. The set containing the nodes which these two

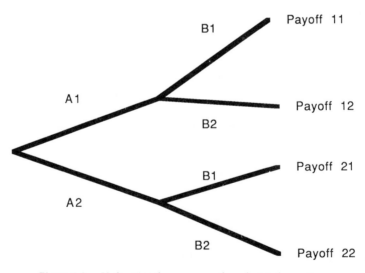

Figure 1.3.   Kuhn tree for a game of perfect information

acts lead to is known as B's *information set* at each of these nodes. A player's knowledge of preceding play by other players may thus be limited by his information set. We do, however, assume perfect recall: a player remembers whatever he knew earlier in the course of play.

A player's *strategy* for an extensive-form game is a comprehensive contingency plan: a function that maps each information set at which he could find himself into a choice of action. If each player thought about how to play the game and independently chose such a strategy, these strategies would jointly determine the course of play. For this reason, von Neumann and Morgenstern argued that a game in extensive form was equivalent to the normal-form game where players choose between its strategies: the *strategic normal-form game* for the original extensive-form game.

The adequacy of the strategic normal-form representation of extensive-form games was generally taken for granted until questioned by

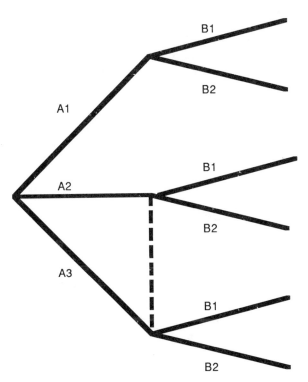

Figure 1.4. Extensive-form game with information set

Selten (1965).[25] Consider the game tree in Figure 1.5, which is the strategic normal form of the game:

	B1 if A2	B2 if A2
A1	0,0	0,0
A2	1,1	$-1,-1$

Since A moves first, he has only two strategies. B has two strategies, depending on what she plans to do if A does A2. If we look at the matrix of the normal form, we find two Nash equilibria: [A2, B1 if A2] and [A1, B2 if A2]. But if we look back at the game tree, we see that the second equilibrium is quite wacky. B would be foolish to choose B2 if A had chosen A2, since choosing B1 would surely give her a greater payoff. (Here B's maximizing expected utility does not depend on B's particular subjective probabilities, because B knows with certainty at the choice point at issue that B1 will give a greater payoff.) Thus the strategy B2 if A2 is not a credible option for B. Seeing this, A will choose A2 and B will choose B1. The point becomes more vivid in the setting of questions of nuclear deterrence. Hermann Kahn (1984, p. 59) reports a typical beginning to a discussion of the policy of mutually assured destruction (MAD):

One Gedanken experiment that I have used many times and in many variations over the last twenty-five or thirty years begins with the statement: "Let us assume that the president of the United States has just been informed that a

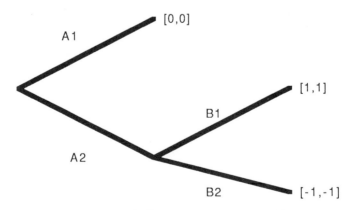

Figure 1.5. A challenge to strategic normal form

multimegaton bomb has been dropped on New York City. What do you think that he would do?" When this was first asked in the mid-1950s, the usual answer was, "Press every button for launching nuclear forces and go home." . . . the dialogue between the audience and myself continued more or less as follows . . .

    Kahn: "What happens next?"
    Audience: "The Soviets do the same!"
    Kahn: "And then what happens?"
    Audience: "Nothing. Both sides have been destroyed."
    Kahn: "Why then did the American President do this?"

A general rethinking of the issue would follow, and the audience would conclude that perhaps the president should not launch an immediate all-out retaliatory attack.

What the audience is beginning to see, in our terms, is that there is an essential difference between the strategic normal-form representation of MAD, which treats it as equivalent to Dr. Strangelove's doomsday machine, and the extensive-form representation, which pays attention to the causal and informational context of the decisions involved in implementing the policy. Even in a situation in which a doomsday machine would be an effective deterrent a policy of mutually assured destruction would not be, because it rests on a noncredible threat. The threat is not credible because in the relevant situation it would not be in the best interests of the nation to carry it out.[26]

It is evident that the strategic normal form of an extensive-form game may fail to capture important causal and informational structure, and consequently that the Nash equilibrium concept applied to strategic normal form may be inadequate. In an important paper, Kreps and Wilson (1982b) proposed to remedy the situation by an application of expected utility theory. A strategy (for all players) is *sequentially rational* if the strategy of each player, starting at each information set, maximizes expected utility according to her beliefs and the strategies of all the other players.

But what of information sets to which players initially assign probability zero? What should a player's beliefs be conditional on reaching such an information set? Kreps and Wilson put a "consistency" condition on these conditional probabilities. They must be obtainable as a limit of well-defined conditional probabilities in a sequence of assessments (degree of belief, strategy pairs) which give each information set nonzero probability. A *sequential* equilibrium is then defined as an assessment which is both consistent and sequentially rational. The fishy equilibrium in the example of Figure 1.5 cannot be sequential.

The attentive reader has perhaps noticed that the fishy equilibrium is also not *perfect* in the sense of Selten, and indeed his concept of perfect equilibrium was introduced with these problems of extensive-form games in mind. Selten's notion is somewhat stronger than that of Kreps and Wilson. It can be thought of as adding to the requirement of sequential rationality an additional requirement of a certain kind of robustness under "trembles." Stronger kinds of robustness conditions have been suggested—for example, the "persistent" equilibria of Kalai and Samet (1984) and the various types of structural stability investigated by Kohlberg and Mertens (1980). For most of these refinements of the Nash equilibrium concept, it can be shown that at least one such refined equilibrium exists in every finite non-zero-sum game. None of them, however, is strong enough to guarantee uniqueness, and thus none solves the problem of multiple equilibria in non-zero-sum games.

Integrating the Two Paradigms

The theory of subjective probability and utility provides a foundation for a univocal rationality principle: *maximize expected utility*. The analysis initiated by Ramsey shows that the normative content of this theory is just that preferences should be *coherent*. There is nothing in the foundations of expected utility theory to limit its applicability in the sort of situations studied by the theory of games.

In the theory of noncooperative games, rational action is discussed in terms of a cluster of equilibrium concepts. The central notion is that of a *Nash equilibrium*, and the concept of a *security strategy* derives its license from its connection with Nash equilibria in the special case of two-person zero-sum games. The concept of a Nash equilibrium rests on that of expected utility. A Nash equilibrium is just a combination of strategies for each player such that if each player has found out the other players' strategies each is maximizing expected utility.

But the rationale for assuming that each player will have found out the other players' strategies is murky. Von Neumann and Morgenstern's argument for this assumption appears to fail even in the case of two-person zero-sum games. And it is in worse trouble in the non-zero-sum case as a result of multiple, noninterchangeable equilibria. Doubts about the von Neumann–Morgenstern argument are, in a way, behind both proposals to weaken (to rationalizability) and to strengthen (to perfect or proper equilibrium) the concept of Nash equilibrium. In games in extensive form the expected utility principle applied at the players' choice points comes in conflict with the Nash equilibrium principle applied to overall strategies. The disparity between these two principles here provides a further motivation for refinements of the Nash equilibrium concept.

All this suggests that the picture of expected utility theory and game theory as separate theories dealing with separate domains is wildly inaccurate. Instead, game theory is and should be founded on expected utility theory, but the details of the foundation are open to serious question. If anything like classical game theory is to emerge, it must be under stronger assumptions than just common knowledge of Bayesian rationality (that is, expected utility maximization). The strength of assumptions needed to derive classical game theory, and the effect on game theory of weakening those assumptions, are subjects which merit investigation.

2 Dynamic Deliberation: Equilibria

> A static theory deals with equilibria. The essential
> characteristic of an equilibrium is that it has no
> tendency to change, i.e. that it is not conducive to
> dynamic developments. An analysis of this feature is,
> of course, inconceivable without the use of certain
> rudimentary dynamic concepts.
>
> —John von Neumann and Oskar Morgenstern (1947, p. 45)

Deliberational Dynamics and Game Theory

Let us suppose that one deliberates by calculating expected utility. In the simplest cases, deliberation is trivial; one calculates expected utility and maximizes. But in more interesting cases, the very process of deliberation may generate information that is relevant to the evaluation of the expected utilities. Then, processing costs permitting, a Bayesian deliberator will feed back that information, modify his probabilities of states of the world, and recalculate expected utilities in light of the new knowledge.[1]

In the presence of informational feedback Bayesian deliberation becomes a dynamical process. The decisionmaker starts in a state of indecision; calculates expected utility; moves in the direction of maximum expected utility; feeds back the information generated by his move and recalculates; and so forth. In this process, his probabilities of doing the various acts evolve until, at the time of decision, his probability of doing the selected act becomes virtually one.

The theory of dynamic deliberation carries with it an *equilibrium* principle for individual decision. The decisionmaker cannot decide to do an act that is not an equilibrium of the deliberational process.[2] If he is about to choose a nonequilibrium act, deliberation carries him away from that decision. This sort of equilibrium requirement for individual decision can be seen as *a consequence of the expected utility principle*. It is usually neglected only because the process of informational feedback in deliberation is usually neglected. In cases in which there is no informational feedback, simple choice of the act with initial maximum expected utility automatically fulfills the equilibrium requirement.

One sort of situation where such informational feedback is relevant is that envisioned by von Neumann and Morgenstern in their indirect argument for the Nash equilibrium concept. Each player calculates the *prima facie* optimum act; but then there is sufficient common knowledge for each player to work out the others' calculations, feed back this information, and recalculate; but then each knows that this will have happened, works out these calculations, feeds back this information, and so forth.

We know from the discussion in Chapter 1 that sufficient common knowledge to make sense of this story must include considerably more than the common knowledge of rationality assumed by von Neumann and Morgenstern. We will see in this chapter how, under suitably strengthened assumptions of common knowledge, *a joint deliberational equilibrium on the part of all the players corresponds to a Nash equilibrium point of the game.* This is the sort of justification that von Neumann and Morgenstern desired, and it is based on the expected utility principle. Furthermore, strengthening the assumptions slightly to make the players qualitatively "more Bayesian" leads in a natural way to refinements of the Nash equilibrium. There is also an important connection with *correlated equilibria.*

Deliberational Equilibria

Let us model the deliberational situation in an abstract and fairly general way. A Bayesian has to choose between a finite number of acts: A_1 . . . A_n. Calculation takes time for her, although its cost is negligible. We assume that she is certain that deliberation will end and she will choose some act (perhaps a mixed one) at that time. Her *state of indecision* will be a probability vector assigning probabilities to each of the n acts, which sum to one. These are to be interpreted as her probabilities now that she will do the act in question at the end of deliberation. A state of indecision, P, carries with it an expected utility, the expectation according to the probability vector $\mathbf{P} = \langle p_1 \ldots p_n \rangle$ of the expected utilities of the acts A_1 . . . A_n. The expected utility of a state of indecision is thus computed just as that of the corresponding mixed act. Indeed, the adoption of a mixed strategy can be thought of as a way to turn the state of indecision for its constituent pure acts to stone. We will call the mixed act corresponding to a state of indecision the state's *default mixed act.*[3]

A person's state of indecision will evolve during deliberation. In the first place, on completing the calculation of expected utility, she will believe more strongly that she will ultimately do that act (or one of those acts) that are ranked more highly than her current state of indecision. If her calculation yields one act with maximum expected utility, will she not simply become sure that she will do that act? She will not *on pain of incoherence* if she believes that she is in an informational feedback situation and if she assigns any positive probability at all to the possibility that informational feedback may lead her ultimately to a different decision. (I will return to this topic, in more detail, in Chapter 4.) So, she will typically in one step of the process move in the direction of the currently perceived good, but not all the way to decision.

We assume that she moves according to some simple dynamical rule for "making up one's mind," as opposed to performing an elaborate calculation at each step. This rule should, however, be "qualitatively Bayesian" in various ways. It should reflect her knowledge that she is an expected utility maximizer and the status of her present expected utility values as her expectation of her final utility values.

For the moment, we will assume that we have a dynamical rule that *seeks the good*,[4] in the following modest sense:

1. the rule raises the probability of an act only if that act has utility greater than that of the status quo;
2. the rule raises the sum of the probabilities of all acts with utility greater than that of the status quo (if any).

All dynamical rules that seek the good have the same fixed points: those states in which the expected utility of the status quo is maximal.

As a concrete example of such a rule we can take the function that Nash (1951) used to prove the existence of equilibria for finite non-zero-sum games. Define the *covetability* of an act, A, to a person in a state of indecision, P, as the difference in expected utility between the act and the state of indecision if the act is preferable to the state of indecision, and as zero if the state of indecision is preferable to the act, or cov (A) = max$[U(A) - U(P), 0]$. Then the Nash map takes the decisionmaker from state of indecision P to state of indecision P', where each component p_i of **P** is changed to:

$$p'_i = \frac{p_i + \text{cov}(A_i)}{1 + \Sigma_i \text{cov}(A_i)}$$

Here a bold revision is hedged by averaging with the status quo.

We can get a whole family of Nash maps by allowing different weights for the average:

$$p'_i = \frac{kp_i + \text{cov}(A_i)}{k + \Sigma_i \text{cov}(A_i)}$$

The constant k $(k > 0)$ is an index of caution. The higher k is, the more slowly the decisionmaker moves in the direction of acts that look more attractive than the status quo. In continuous time, one has the corresponding Nash flows:

$$\frac{dp(A)}{dt} = \frac{\text{cov}(A) - p(A)\Sigma_j \text{cov}(A_j)}{k + \Sigma_j \text{cov}(A_j)}$$

The Nash rules are not the only rules which seek the good,[5] and we shall see later that a more refined Bayesian analysis may lead elsewhere. But we will use the rules as a source of easily realized concrete examples. The Appendix shows how to implement the Nash dynamics on a personal computer, and the interested reader is urged to try it out on various games.

The decisionmaker's calculation of expected utility and subsequent application of the dynamical rule constitutes new information. The new information may affect the expected utilities of the pure acts by affecting the probabilities of the states of nature, which together with the act determine the payoff. In the typical game-theoretical contexts, states of nature consist of the possible actions of the opposing players. For simplicity, we will assume here a finite number of states of nature.

The decisionmaker's *personal state* is then, for our purposes, determined by two things: her state of indecision and the probabilities that she assigns to states of nature. Her personal state space is the product space of her space of indecision and her space of states of nature. Deliberation defines a dynamics on this space. We could model the dynamics as either discrete or continuous, but for the moment we will focus on discrete dynamics. We assume a dynamical function, ϕ, which maps a personal state $\langle x,y \rangle$ into a new personal state $\langle x',y' \rangle$ in one unit of time. The dynamical function, ϕ, has two associated rules: (1) the adaptive dynamical rule,[6] D, which maps $\langle x,y \rangle$ onto x' and (2) the informational feedback process, I, which maps $\langle x,y \rangle$ onto y' [where $\langle x',y' \rangle = \phi\langle x,y \rangle$].

A personal state $\langle x,y \rangle$ is a *deliberational equilibrium* of the dynamics, ϕ, if and only if $\phi\langle x,y \rangle = \langle x,y \rangle$. If D and I are continuous, then ϕ is continuous and it follows from the Brower fixed point theorem that a deliberational equilibrium exists. Let N be the Nash dynamics for some $k > 0$. Then if the informational feedback process, I, is continuous, the dynamical function $\langle N,I \rangle$ is continuous and has a deliberational equilibrium. Then, since N *seeks the good*, for any continuous informational feedback process, I, $\langle N,I \rangle$ has a deliberational equilibrium $\langle x,y \rangle$ whose corresponding mixed act maximizes expected utility in state $\langle x,y \rangle$. This is a point from which process I does not move y and process N does not move x.

But if process N does not move x, then no other process which seeks the good will either (whether or not it is continuous). So, we have—*à la Nash*—a general existence result for deliberational equilibria:

> If D seeks the good and I is continuous, then there is a deliberational equilibrium, $\langle x,y \rangle$, for $\langle D,I \rangle$. If D' also seeks the good, then $\langle x,y \rangle$ is also a deliberational equilibrium for $\langle D',I \rangle$. The default mixed act corresponding to x maximizes expected utility at $\langle x,y \rangle$.

Games Played by Bayesian Deliberators

Suppose that two (or more) Bayesian deliberators are deliberating about what action to take in a noncooperative non-zero-sum matrix game. We assume that each player has only one choice to make, and that the choices are causally independent in that there is no way for one player's decision to *influence* the decisions of the other players. Then, from the point of view of decision theory, for each player the decisions of the other players constitute the relevant *state of the world* which, together with her decision, determines the *consequence* in accordance with the payoff matrix.

Suppose, in addition, that each player has an adaptive rule, D, which seeks the good (each one need not have the same rule) and that what kind of Bayesian deliberator each player is is common knowledge. Suppose also that each player's initial state of indecision is common knowledge, and that other players take a given player's state of indecision as their own best estimate of what that player will ultimately do. Then initially there is a probability assignment to all the acts for all the players that is shared by all the players and is common knowledge.[7]

Under these strong assumptions of common knowledge, an interesting informational feedback process becomes available. Starting from the initial position, player 1 calculates expected utility and moves by her adaptive rule to a new state of indecision. She knows that the other players are Bayesian deliberators who have just carried out a similar process, and she knows their initial states of indecision and their updating rules. So she can simply go through their calculations to see their new states of indecision and update her probabilities of their acts accordingly. We will call this sort of informational feedback process *updating by emulation*. Suppose that all the players update by emulation. Then, in this ideal case, the new state is common knowledge as well and the process can be repeated.

Since the joint state of all players is common knowledge at all times, the von Neumann–Morgenstern reasoning applies:

> In a game played by Bayesian deliberators with a common prior, an adaptive rule that seeks the good, and a feedback process that updates by emulation,[8] with common knowledge of all the foregoing, each player is at a deliberational equilibrium at a state of the system if and only if the assignment of the default mixed acts to each player constitutes a Nash equilibrium of the game.

There is an alternative interpretation of the mathematics of this model, which fits nicely with an alternative interpretation of mixed equilibria. In this interpretation, the application of the "adaptive rule" represents not a given player's rule for changing beliefs in her probabilities of her own actions, but rather the other players' shared inductive rule for modifying predictions of her action.[9] Her updating by emulation then tells her what other players have as shared probabilities for her actions. The requirement that dynamical rules "seek the good" is then a somewhat more modest and perhaps more credible version of "best-response" reasoning.

The notion of a "default mixed act" falls away if we adopt a reinterpretation of mixed equilibria suggested by Aumann.[10] He advocates a point of view in which the probabilities in a player's mixed strategy are thought of as shared probabilities of the other players' strategies.[11] Mixed equilibria are then thought of as equilibria in beliefs. If we adopt this point of view together with the reinterpretation of deliberational dynamics, we can conclude that in the situation envisioned above the players are at a joint deliberational equilibrium just in case their beliefs constitute an equilibrium in this sense.

Equilibrium Selection

It is worth taking a closer look at the way in which dynamic deliberation, in the sort of setting under consideration, deals with the problem of multiple equilibria in non-zero-sum games. Consider the following game:

Battle of the Sexes

	C1	C2
R1	2,1	0,0
R2	0,0	1,2

A woman, Row, and a man, Column, are each deciding where to go for an evening's entertainment. The woman would rather go to event 1 and the man to event 2, but each would prefer to go to the event where he or she will meet the other. (Back in the 1950s, the conventional way of telling this story made event 1 an opera and event 2 a prizefight!) This game is a nice mixture of competitive and cooperative motivations. There is an equilibrium at [R1, C1], which the woman prefers, one at [R2, C2], which is favored by the man, and a mixed equilibrium with each tossing a fair coin.

  Suppose that they start deliberating with a commonly known probability of 0.8 that the woman will choose R1 and 0.6 that the man will choose C2. Notice that if each were simply to maximize expected utilities on these probabilities, without informational feedback, the woman would choose R2 and the man C1, with the result that they will both end up with a payoff of zero. Now suppose that it is common knowledge that they are Nash deliberators (with a fairly high index of caution, which is also common knowledge). Then deliberation will carry them along the orbit indicated in Figure 2.1 to [R1, C1]. Equilibrium selection is effected by the dynamics in virtue of the strong assumptions of common knowledge in force. That strong assumptions are required to overcome the difficulties of classical non-zero-sum game theory should not come as a surprise. We will be interested in subsequent chapters in investigating the results of weakening these assumptions in various ways, but in this chapter we will be interested in principled Bayesian reasons for slight modifications and strengthenings of the condition that the dynamics "seeks the good."

The Bayes Dynamics

A Bayesian updates by Bayes' rule. Thus, if the new information that a player gets by emulating other players' calculations, updating his probabilities on their actions, and recalculating his expected utilities is e, then his new probabilities that he will in the end do an act A, $p_2(A)$, in terms of his old probabilities, $p_1(A)$, should be:

$$B: \quad p_2(A) = p_1(A)\frac{p(e|A)}{\sum_i p(A_i)p(e|A_i)}$$

where $\{A_i\}$ is a partition of alternative acts.[12]

Our story has been that the deliberator does not have the appropriate proposition, e, in a large probability space that defines the likelihood, $p(e|A)$. Instead, our "bounded Bayesian" deliberator uses a simple dynamical rule at this stage of deliberation. But such a simple dynamical

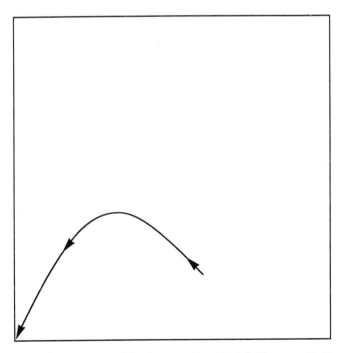

Figure 2.1.   Battle of the Sexes: orbit of [0.2,0.6] goes to [0,0]

rule can still, in a sense, be more or less Bayesian according to which qualitative features of a full Bayesian analysis it retains.

For instance, one can argue that updating by Bayes' rule (on evidence with positive prior probability) cannot raise zero probabilities. In this respect, the Nash dynamics is un-Bayesian because it can and does raise zero probabilities. Thus, no hypothesis one could make about the likelihoods, $p(e_i|A)$, could embed the Nash dynamics in a larger setting in which it coincided with Bayes' rule. In a way, the Nash dynamics tries too hard. If a deliberator starts out with probability one that he will do an act that has utility less than that of the status quo, Nash dynamics will pull that probability down and raise the zero probabilities of competing acts (as will every rule which "seeks the good"). From the standpoint of adaptive behavior this effort seems laudable, but with respect to coherent updating it may leave something to be desired.[13]

Indeed, one can argue that if a deliberator is absolutely sure which act he is going to do he needn't deliberate, and if he is absolutely sure he won't do one of a set of alternative acts his deliberations should concern only the others. Putting it the other way around, if a decisionmaker thinks that there is any chance that deliberation might change his probabilities of an act, he should have given the act a probability different from zero or one. According to this account, deliberation should start at some point in the *interior* of the space of indecision, and the desideratum that a dynamic rule should seek the good should be restricted to moving probabilities that are properly movable. Notice that when deliberation originates in the interior of the space of indecision, the Nash dynamics stays in the interior so it will never get a chance to display unruly behavior with respect to probabilities of zero and one.

The Nash dynamics can lead to un-Bayesian updating in another, more subtle way when there are more than two possible acts under consideration. If two or more acts have utility less than that of the status quo, (SQ), they all get the same covetability—namely, zero—even if their expected utilities are quite different. (Remember that the $cov(A) = \max[0, U(A) - U(SQ)]$.) This does not square well with the Bayesian story we give to motivate dynamic rules seeking the good on the interior of the space of indecision.

Our deliberator supposes that her calculations yielding new expected utilities give new information about what she will finally do because she believes that she will move in the direction of the apparent good until the moment of truth. It is possible—perhaps likely—that deliberation will have reached an equilibrium by the moment of truth, in which case her decision will be a best response. On the other hand, in the absence of special knowledge, it is no more likely if the moment of truth arrives before equilibrium that she will make a worse response rather than a better one. The present expected utilities just calculated may not be the ones which will obtain at the moment of truth, but they are in a sense the decisionmaker's best estimate of them.[14]

On the basis of such general considerations, the decisionmaker acts as if the likelihood, $p(e|A)$, is an increasing function of the newly calculated expected utility of A. We could call this the assumption of a *tendency toward better response*. The reasoning deserves to be looked at in more detail, and we will do so later. For the moment, I just want to point out that to the extent the assumption supports pumping up the probability of what looks best, it also supports pumping up the ratios of the probabilities of second to third place, and so on. By Bayes' theorem:

$$\frac{p_2(A)}{p_2(B)} = \frac{p_1(A)}{p_1(B)} \cdot \frac{p_1(e|A)}{p_1(e|B)}$$

If the likelihood is an increasing function of the expected utility of an act, then the Bayes dynamics will modify the probabilities of those acts with expected utility less than that of the status quo in a way that the Nash dynamics does not.

It would be nice to have a concrete example of this sort of Bayesian dynamics. The simplest way to make the likelihood an increasing function of the expected utility is to set the likelihood equal to the expected utility (with respect to some appropriate utility scale). This gives:

$$D: \qquad p_2(A) = p_1(A)\frac{U(A)}{U(SQ)}$$

where utility should be measured on a scale which is nonnegative, and positive on the interior of the space of indecision.[15]

Readers familiar with the evolutionary game theory of Maynard Smith (1982) will recognize this as a dynamics that Nature implements through the process of evolution. (The payoffs are in terms of reproductive fitness.) For this reason we will call it the Darwin map. It's nice to know that Mother Nature is a rough-and-ready Bayesian.

The continuous counterpart of the Darwin map is the Darwin flow:

$$\frac{dp(A)}{dt} = k\frac{U(A) - U(SQ)}{U(SQ)}$$

The Appendix shows how to implement the Darwin dynamics on a personal computer. One can, of course, construct all sorts of other Bayesian dynamics with more or less plausibility by setting the likelihood equal to other continuous monotonic functions of the utility.

The connection between deliberational dynamics and the Nash equilibrium concept becomes slightly more complicated if we accept these Bayesian modifications of our viewpoint. Since Bayesian dynamics seeks the good on the interior of the space of indecision, the connection between deliberational equilibria and Nash equilibria remains the same for points in the interior. But with respect to points not in the interior, we must focus on limiting behavior. If Darwin dynamics starting in the interior converges to a point, then that point corresponds to a Nash equilibrium of the game.

Refinements of the Nash Equilibrium for the Normal Form

Models of dynamic deliberation provide a setting which may make more sense of the project of refining the Nash equilibrium concept than does the metaphor of the trembling hand. If we think of perfection as being motivated by considerations of a slight probability of irrationality on the part of other players, we will have trouble making sense of the concept. If the probability of irrational play *really is zero*, why not stick with the Nash equilibrium? If it really isn't zero, we open up a Pandora's box whose contents cannot be adequately dealt with by the concept of perfection. The situation is even more paradoxical with respect to *proper* equilibria. Here the "trembles" must be considered more likely in the direction of least loss, an assumption that requires a kind of rational control of irrationality. In models of dynamic deliberation, however, there is no irrationality—only uncertainty—as the players deliberate. From this point of view, we see the examples used to motivate refinements of the Nash equilibrium in a new light.

Let us begin by reconsidering a matrix game used in Chapter 1 to motivate Selten's notion of a perfect equilibrium:

	C1	C2
R2	0,0	0,0
R1	1,1	0,0

We can get an idea of the deliberational dynamic structure under Nash deliberation by examining the orbits plotted in Figure 2.2. Every point

in the interior of the space of indecision is carried by dynamic deliberation to the perfect equilibrium [R1, C1]. This is not a peculiarity of the
Nash dynamics, but is true for any dynamics which seeks the good. Of
course, if the players are both absolutely sure that [R2, C2] will be
played, then act 2 has maximal expected utility for each player. But in
this case, deliberation does not make sense. If, as I argued in the previous section, Bayesian deliberation must start in the interior of the
space of indecision, *dynamic deliberation cannot lead to* [R2, C2].

Thus there is a natural motivation for a refinement of the Nash equilibrium concept in the theory of deliberational dynamics—that is, *an
equilibrium which one can converge to by deliberation starting at a completely
mixed state of indecision.* Let us call such an equilibrium *accessible.* In the
foregoing example the odd equilibrium [R2, C2] is not accessible under
Nash or Darwin deliberation. Does Selten's concept of perfection coincide with some variety of accessibility?

Now let us consider the following example of the kind Myerson (1978)
used:

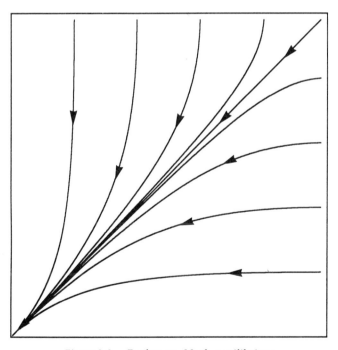

Figure 2.2.   Perfect vs. Nash equilibrium

	C1	C2	C3
R3	−9, −9	−4, −4	−4, −4
R2	0,0	0,0	−4, −4
R1	1,1	0,0	−9, −9

Nash deliberation can lead to both the proper equilibrium at [R1, C1] and the improper equilibrium at [R2, C2]. Figure 2.3 shows the orbit starting at $p(R1) = 0.01$, $p(R2) = 0.5$, $p(R3) = 0.49$, $p(C1) = 0.01$, $p(C2) = 0.5$, $p(C3) = 0.49$ converging to the improper equilibrium at [R2, C2]. (Because of the symmetry of the game and the starting points, Row's orbit on the subspace with vertices R1, R2, and R3 is identical to

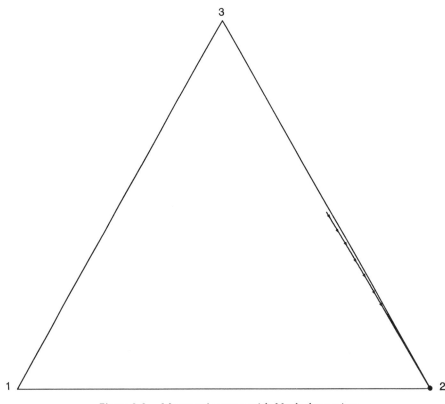

Figure 2.3.   Myerson's game with Nash dynamics:
orbit of [(0.01,0.5,0.49),(0.01,0.5,0.49)]
converges to a perfect but improper equilibrium

Column's orbit on the subspace with vertices C1, C2, and C3.) Convergence to [R2, C2] is possible because the Nash dynamics is not affected by the relative attractiveness of acts with expected utility less than that of the status quo. Compare the orbit of the same point under Darwin deliberation (with the utilities appropriately rescaled), shown in Figure 2.4. As the probability of act 2 increases for a given player, the relative attractiveness of act 1 over act 3 increases for the other player. When the relative probability of act 1 over act 3 for a player gets large enough, act 1 becomes more attractive to the other player than act 2. The orbit then "turns the corner" and heads for the proper equilibrium.[16] Thus we have a natural motivation in deliberational dynamics for another refinement: equilibrium that can be reached by the Bayes dynamics starting

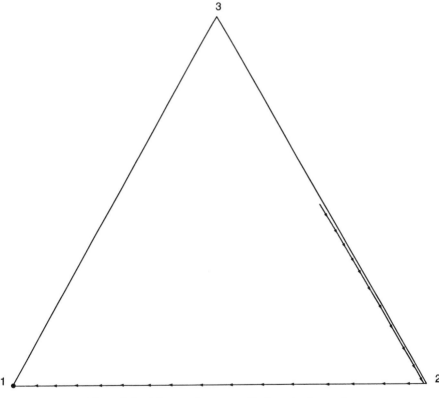

Figure 2.4.   Myerson's game with Darwin dynamics:
orbit of [(0.01,0.5,0.49),(0.01,0.5,0.49)]
converges to a proper equilibrium

from a completely mixed point. Does Myerson's concept of proper equilibrium coincide with accessibility under a Bayes dynamics?

Analysis by Larry Samuelson (1988)[17] shows that our Bayesian accessibility concepts do not coincide with the refinements of the Nash equilibrium that have been proposed by Selten and Myerson. Darwin deliberation can lead to an equilibrium that is not only improper but also imperfect. Consider the following game:

	C1	C2
R2	0,0	0,0
R1	1,1	$-1,-1$

As shown in Figure 2.5, the orbit starting at $p(R2) = 0.5$, $p(C2) = 0.99$ is carried to an imperfect equilibrium by Darwin deliberation. The reason is that although C1 looks better than the status quo to Column at any completely mixed strategy, the velocity $dp(C1)/dt$ depends on *how much* better it looks. Along the orbit leading to the imperfect equilibri-

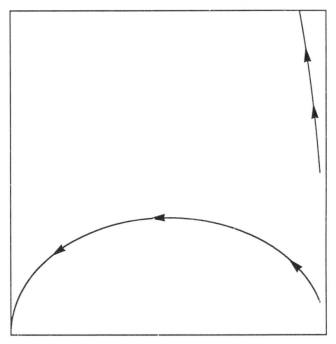

Figure 2.5.   Darwin can lead to an imperfect equilibrium

um, R2 looks better than R1 to Row, and it looks enough better so that the orbit converges to the imperfect mixed equilibrium shown.

Compare this outcome with the results of Nash deliberation for the same game shown in Figure 2.6. The orbit of $p(R2) = 0.05$, $p(C2) = 0.99$ goes nicely to the perfect equilibrium, as do the other cases shown. Notice, however, that this is due to the un-Bayesian nature of Nash deliberation. The covetability of C2 is identically zero throughout the interior of the space, even though C2 looks as nearly as good as C1 when $p(R2)$ is near one.

This example suggests that there may be a class of adaptive rules such that for rules in that class the deliberationally accessible equilibria are just the perfect ones. In fact, for two-person games Samuelson (1988) has isolated such a class of rules. A key feature of this class is *ordinality*: the velocity of probability change of a strategy depends only on the ordinal ranking among strategies according to their expected utilities.

It is, however, not clear to me that the orbit of the Darwin deliberator in this example is in any way unreasonable. In this respect, this example

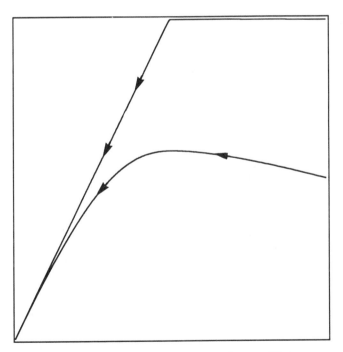

Figure 2.6.   Nash converging to a perfect equilibrium

is quite different from the one given earlier. I will be bold enough to suggest that perhaps the correct response to this sort of example may be to reconsider the motivation for the definitions of perfect and proper equilibrium. In each of these definitions, it is required that the relative probabilities of a better and a worse prospect change in a way that is not sensitive to the magnitude of the difference. From the standpoint of dynamic Bayesian deliberation, the ordinal nature of these definitions is hard to justify.

The model of the dynamic deliberator may make more sense out of the program of refining the Nash equilibrium concept than does the metaphor of the trembling hand, but it also suggests that important boundaries are to be drawn in somewhat different places.

Refinements of the Nash Equilibrium for the Extensive Form

Dynamic deliberation for games in extensive form is a straightforward generalization of deliberational dynamics for games in normal form. The essential difference is that at an information set, the player's expected utilities are calculated using probabilities *conditional on being at that information set*.[18] This is simply a matter of respecting the informational structure that is specified in the game tree, but it clearly leads to deliberational inequivalences between an extensive form game and its strategic normal form.

To illustrate the process, let us reconsider the simple extensive-form game from Chapter 1 (Figure 2.7). Let us compare deliberation in the extensive form with deliberation in the strategic normal form:

	B1 if A2	B2 if A2
A1	0,0	0,0
A2	1,1	−1,−1

This is a familiar matrix. There are two Nash equilibria, a sensible one [A2, B1 if A2] and a questionable one [A1, B2 if A2]. For deliberation under Nash dynamics on the strategic normal form, both coincide with deliberational equilibria with the sensible one being strongly stable and the questionable one being unstable. But under Nash deliberation on the extensive form game, the questionable Nash equilibrium [A1, B2 if A2] is not a deliberational equilibrium at all. The reason is that the probability that A does A2 *conditional on B's information set where he chooses between B1 and B2* must be one, no matter what the unconditional probabilities are. Using these conditional probabilities, B is faced with a choice of payoffs between 1 and −1. Deliberation on the strategic normal form uses the unconditional probabilities and ignores the informational structure of the tree.

This difference between deliberation on the strategic normal form and that on the extensive form is evident in a more subtle way when we consider accessibility from a completely mixed point under Darwin deliberation. This is the normal-form matrix that I used to make Samuelson's point. There are imperfect mixed equilibria, such as [A1, $p(B2|A2) = 0.96$], that are accessible under the Darwin dynamics. These equilibria are *not* accessible under Darwin dynamics for deliberational dynamics based on the true extensive form. Figure 2.8 shows the phase portraits for this game under Darwin deliberation for (A) the strategic normal form and (B) the extensive form. The difference between them is this: in simultaneous deliberation about strategies (Figure 2.8A), B's expected utility for the strategy B2 if A2 is a weighted average of B's payoff from this strategy if A does A1 and B's payoff from the strategy if A does A2; in extensive-form deliberation (Figure 2.8B), B uses his expected utilities *at his information set* so that the utility of B1 if A2 is 1 and the utility of B2 if A2 is −1 throughout deliberation. It is true that B1 if A2 looks better than B2 if A2 to both deliberators, but the *magnitude* of the difference shrinks to zero for deliberation in the normal form but remains constant for deliberation in the extensive form. Deliberation with a dynamical rule like Darwin, for which these relative magnitudes are crucial, puts the difference between extensive form and strategic normal form in the spotlight.

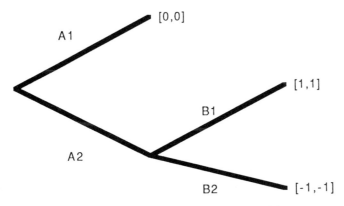

Figure 2.7.   A challenge to strategic normal form

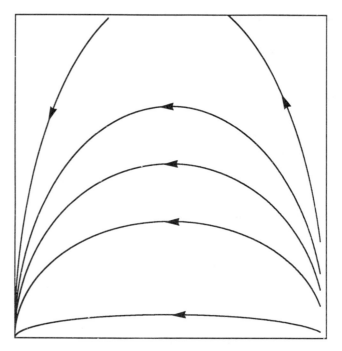

Figure 2.8A.   Darwin dynamics on strategic normal form

As another illustration of the same sort of phenomenon, consider the sinister toy example of nuclear deterrence presented in Figure 2.9. At the onset, A can either attack or not. Then B can retaliate or not. If A attacks and B retaliates, A is devastated by B (A's payoff is −10) and B is devastated by A and suffers additional loss from the fallout from his own strike (B's payoff is −11). If A attacks and B doesn't retaliate, A gains an advantage (+1) and B is devastated (−10). If A doesn't attack and B "retaliates" anyway, A is devastated (−10) and B gains a slight advantage but perhaps also invites retaliation from A—let us say B's payoff is −5. If A doesn't attack and B doesn't retaliate, both get a payoff of 0. In strategic normal form there are three pure Nash equilibria: MAD—A doesn't attack and B retaliates if and only if attacked; First strike 1—A attacks and B does not retaliate whether attacked or not; and First strike 2—A attacks and B retaliates if and only if not attacked. But strategic normal form conceals the fact that MAD rests on a noncredible threat. Deliberation on the extensive-form game will lead from a state of initial uncertainty to First strike. Once we see retaliation as a non-

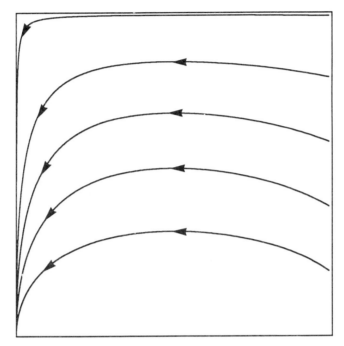

Figure 2.8B.   Darwin dynamics on extensive form

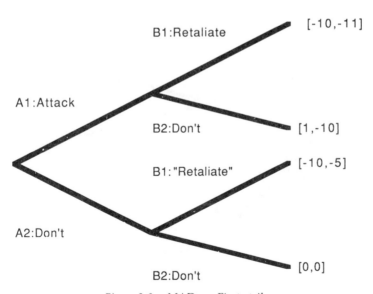

Figure 2.9.   MAD vs. First strike

credible threat we might reconsider the payoffs when A doesn't attack and B "retaliates" anyway. B's payoff here should be just +1 for the advantage gained. I invite you to explore the deliberational dynamics of this modified game and to think of further modifications or alternatives to it.

Things become more interesting in games where some information sets are not unit sets. In some such games the same point can be made without worrying about the probabilities on the information set. Consider the game due to Kreps and Wilson (1982b, p. 871) given in Figure 2.10. One Nash equilibrium has A playing A1 and B having the strategy of play B2 if he finds himself at the information set where A has played either A2 or A3. B's strategy is not credible. No matter how B's probabilities might tilt between A2 and A3 at this information set, B will be better off choosing B1 than B2, since B1 gives him a better payoff than B2 in any case. Thus B would play B1 at this information set, and A, realizing this, will play A2 and assure herself a payoff of 12. This more credible equilibrium [A2, B1 if A2 or A3] is *sequential* in the sense of Kreps and Wilson, whereas the noncredible one is not.[19] The non-

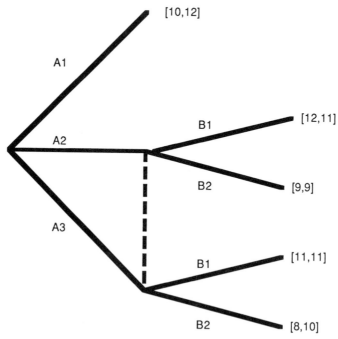

Figure 2.10. Sequential equilibrium vs. [subgame perfect] Nash equilibrium

credible equilibrium has B's agent at the information set [A2 or A3] make a choice that cannot maximize expected utility for any probability over [A1, A2]. As is to be expected, deliberational dynamics will never lead to the "bad" equilibrium and will always lead to the "good" one.

The power of dynamic deliberation is underutilized in the foregoing examples, because although A has to worry about what B will do, B doesn't really have to worry about what A has done. Things are different in the example due to Kohlberg and Mertens (1986) in Figure 2.11. Here A must worry about what B will do at information set [A2 or A3], and B must worry about what A has done to get him in that information set. There is an equilibrium at [A1, B2 if A2 or A3], and one at [A2, B1 if A2 or A3]. Both equilibria are sequential, but there is nevertheless something wrong about the first one. If A plays A2, A will get a better payoff than if A plays A3, no matter what B does. A can figure this out and B can figure out that A can figure it out. So B should make his probability of A2 conditional on A2 or A3 high, which will lead him to play B1 if he finds himself at the information set [A2 or A3]. A should be able to figure *this* out, and so will play A2 to secure a payoff of 16.

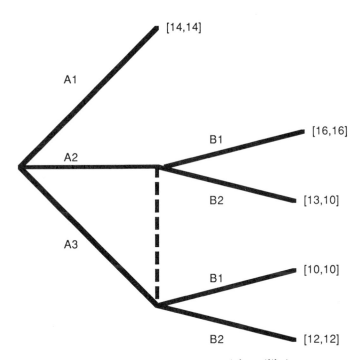

Figure 2.11. Proper vs. sequential equilibrium

This sort of reasoning can be implemented by deliberational dynamics provided we implement some version of the *Bayes dynamics* with the assumption of a *tendency toward better response*.[20] Figure 2.12 shows the action of the Darwin deliberation when this game is started near the "bad" sequential equilibrium. This is most striking when viewed in real time. The players appear to sit on the bad equilibrium for a long time, mulling it over, and then they suddenly start moving to the good *proper sequential equilibrium*. What is really happening is that very near the "bad" equilibrium, the ratios of the very tiny probabilities of A2 and A3 are being adjusted until [B1 if A2 or A3] begins to look better to B than the alternative. Probabilities are adjusted until A2 looks best and then the system moves rapidly toward the proper equilibrium.

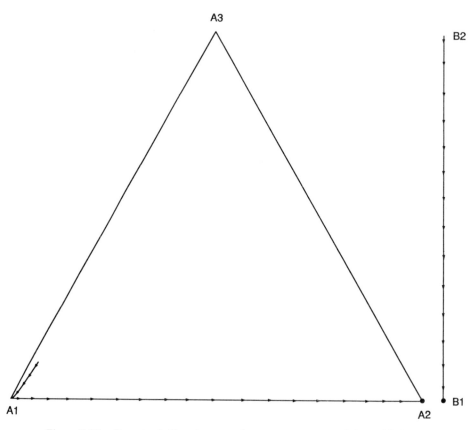

Figure 2.12. Darwin deliberators opt for a proper sequential equilibrium

So far so good, but Kohlberg and Mertens have an example in which the supposedly bad equilibrium is sequential and proper. In this example, Bayesian deliberational dynamics can lead to the "bad" equilibrium. I believe, however, that the arguments given here against the "bad" equilibrium are not conclusive, and that whether it is bad or not depends on the prior probabilities at the start of deliberation or on the mode of deliberation. The example is given in Figure 2.13. There is a perfect sequential equilibrium at [A1, B2 if A2 or A3] and another at [A2, B1 if A2 or A3]. Kohlberg and Mertens argue as follows: A1 strictly dominates A3 (in other words, no matter what B does, A1 gives B a greater payoff than A3). Therefore, B should know that A will play A2 or A3 only if she plays A2. Accordingly, B will play B1 rather than B2, and knowing this A will play A2 rather than A1.

Notice the difference between the reasoning in this example and that given in the preceding one. In the example given in Figure 2.12 it was argued that upon reflection we would have to conclude that the probability of A2 conditional on A2 or A3 should be high because A2 strictly dominates A3. In this example it is being argued that the same condi-

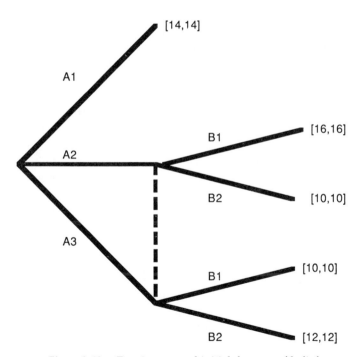

Figure 2.13. Dominance and initial degrees of belief

tional probability should be high because *A1* dominates A3. This argument is a *non sequitur* unless it can be supplemented with some extra assumptions.

Darwin deliberation can take players to either equilibrium. Questions of timing here are crucial. *If* before deliberation begins player A has been looking for strictly dominated strategies, and giving them probabilities that are virtually zero and very small relative to the probabilities of all other strategies, then deliberation will begin with $p(A2|A2$ or $A3)$ large. In this case, deliberational dynamics will lead to the "good" equilibrium at [A2, B1 if A2 or A3]. On the other hand, the players may have started deliberation without noticing dominance or they may for some reason have started deliberation with A2 having a very small probability (or both these conditions may hold), so that initially $p(A3|A2$ or $A3)$ is large. Suppose also that for whatever reasons, the players' initial $p(B2|A2$ or $A3)$ is large. Then during deliberation dominance will be reflected by the ratio $p(A1)/p(A3)$ getting large, but at the same time the magnitudes of the expected utilities will also lead to $p(A1)/p(A2)$ getting larger. In this case deliberation will lead to the "bad" equilibrium at [A1, B2 if A2 or A3]. Figure 2.14 shows the two kinds of orbit.

On the other hand, rather than pushing these considerations into the predeliberational beliefs, one might focus on deliberators who build temporal precedence of considerations of dominance into the deliberational rules. For example, the players might begin deliberation with a routine for iterated elimination of strictly dominated strategies and then proceed to apply Nash or Darwin deliberation to the remaining problem. Such deliberators would go through essentially the same reasoning as Kohlberg and Mertens and end up at the preferred equilibrium. This sort of two-stage procedure constitutes one reasonable way for deliberation to proceed; but is it the *only* reasonable way for deliberation to proceed? If not, the Kohlberg-Mertens reasoning applies only to a proper subclass of rational deliberators.

Correlated Equilibria

I will close this chapter with a discussion of the relation of dynamic deliberation to a rather different equilibrium concept, Aumann's (1974) notion of a *correlated equilibrium*. Two different points of view may be adopted in discussions of "solution concepts" for games. One is the point of view of the players themselves as rational actors. The other is that of a disinterested rational observer or theorist. I have so far discussed deliberational dynamics from the viewpoint of the deliberators themselves, but the subject has interesting consequences for the external point of view as well. I shall illustrate these consequences in two cases where the external point of view is taken by a philosopher or social theorist: the question of the possibility of convention and the question of the nature of the "state of nature." In each case, rational deliberation generates correlation. This phenomenon can be described generally using the notion of a *correlated equilibrium*.

How is convention possible? Quine (1936) challenged conventionalist accounts of language to provide a satisfactory account of how the relevant conventions are set up and maintained that does not presuppose linguistic communication or competency. David Lewis (1969) replied that convention is possible without communication. The mutual expec-

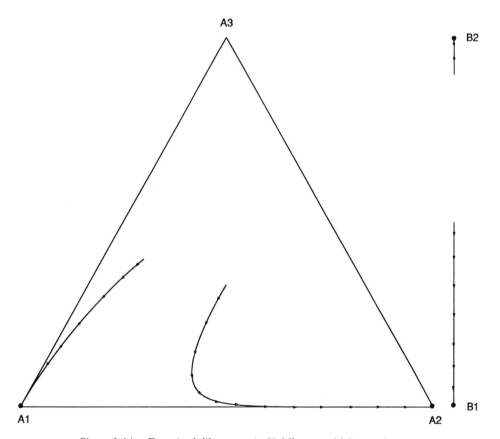

Figure 2.14. Darwin deliberators in Kohlberg and Mertens' game

tations of rational agents can explain the maintenance of a convention at a game-theoretic equilibrium. Consider the pure coordination game:

The Winding Road

	Left	Right
Left	1,1	0,0
Right	0,0	1,1

Two cars approach a blind curve from opposite directions. Each would prefer that they are both driving on the left or both driving on the right. There are two pure equilibria, equally attractive, but if Row goes for one of them and Column goes for the other, they will end up in trouble. If, however, Row believes Column expects him to drive on the left and believes that Column believes him to believe this, and so on, and Column believes likewise about Row, and each believes that the other is rational and that the other believes that he is, then they each have good reason to drive on the left.

The question as to how convention without communication is possible between rational agents has two parts: (1) How can convention without communication be sustained? and (2) How can convention without communication be generated? Lewis gave the answer to the first question in terms of equilibrium (or stable equilibrium) and common knowledge of rationality. His discussion of the second question—following Schelling (1960)—is framed in terms of salience, where a salient coordination equilibrium is "one which stands out from the others in some conspicuous respect." Salience could derive from preplay communication among the players, but it could also arise in other ways. It could arise by precedent. In fact, since salience is a psychological rather than a logical notion, the ways in which salience may arise are as various as the possible psychologies of the players.

The informal discussions of salience by Lewis and Schelling are convincing regarding the plausibility of real-world coordination by salience, but I believe that they give only a partial answer to the second question. Here, deliberational dynamics has something to contribute.

Let us model The Winding Road as a game played by Nash deliberators. (The results would be essentially the same here if we used Darwin deliberation.) Row and Column each have predeliberational probabilities of driving on the left or right. They can be anything at all. At the onset of deliberation each player's initial probabilities of driving left or right are announced and become common knowledge. (This idealization will be weakened later.) You—the philosopher—have some probability distribution over the space of Row's and Column's initial probabilities. You needn't think it likely that they are anywhere near an equilibrium. In fact, we will suppose only that your probability distribution is reasonably smooth (that is, it is absolutely continuous with respect to Lebesgue measure on the unit square), otherwise it can be anything at all. Then you should believe with probability one that the deliberators will converge to one of the pure Nash equilibria, as is evident from Figure 2.15.

It is not surprising here that the players should be led to the state of mutually reinforcing expectations that attend a Nash equilibrium. Coordination is effected by rational deliberation. Precedent and other forms of initial salience may influence the deliberators' initial probabilities, and thus may play a role in determining *which* equilibrium is selected. The answer to the question of how convention can be generated for Bayesian deliberators has both methodological and psychological aspects.

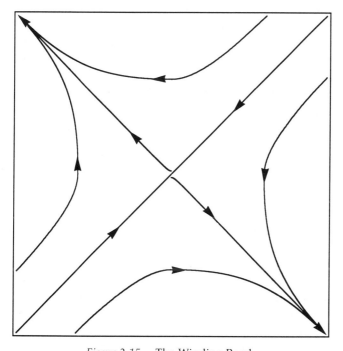

Figure 2.15. The Winding Road

Of course, Bayesian players are not always so lucky as to be involved in pure coordination games. People have conflicting desires and limited altruism. They are roughly equal in their mental and physical powers. Elements of competition intrude. Thomas Hobbes argued that as a consequence rational self-interested decisionmakers in a state of nature, unrestrained by the power of a sovereign, will be engaged in a "war of all against all."

After Darwin, Hobbesian philosophy enjoyed a resurgence. Karl Marx wrote to Engels: "It is remarkable how Darwin has discerned anew among beasts and plants his English society . . . It is Hobbes' *bellum omnium contra omnes.*"[21] Marx was being somewhat unfair to Darwin, but "Darwin's Bulldog" lived up to the caricature. In an essay entitled "The Struggle for Existence" (1888), T. H. Huxley popularized Hobbesian Darwinism. Primitive man "fights out the struggle for existence to the bitter end, like any other animal . . . Life was a continual free fight, and beyond the limited and temporary relations of the family, the Hobbesian war of each against all was the normal state of existence" (p. 165). This picture seemed so perverted to Prince Petr Kropotkin that he was moved to write *Mutual Aid* (1902), describing cooperation among animals and also among men in all stages of civilization.

In a fine critical study, Gregory Kavka (1983) found Hobbes' argument inconclusive although, as he points out, many other commentators appear to regard it as obviously correct. Kavka and Gauthier (1969) modeled conflict in the state of nature in terms of Prisoner's Dilemma, but I think the game of Chicken models Hobbes' premises at least as well.

Chicken

	Don't swerve	Swerve
Don't swerve	$-10, -10$	$5, -5$
Swerve	$-5, 5$	$0, 0$

Each player would like to profit from his opponent's loss. Each would like, at the outset, to appear more aggressive than his opponent. But aggression on the part of both creates an intolerable situation. There are two Nash equilibria in pure strategies: Row swerves and Column doesn't and Column swerves and Row doesn't. There is also a mixed equilibrium where each player has equal chances of swerving and not swerving. If the players are Bayesian deliberators coordination can again be achieved by deliberation, just as in the coordination game. As shown in Figure 2.16, for Nash deliberators every initial point leads to a Nash equilibrium, and almost every initial point leads to a pure Nash equilibrium.

In this example, it is easy to say which initial points go to which equilibrium. For almost every initial point, one player is initially more likely to swerve and if so that player ends up swerving while the other player does not. In the case in which both players are initially equally likely to swerve, they are carried to a mixed equilibrium where each adopts a random strategy of swerving with chance of 0.5. Here there is a genuine Hobbesian incentive for initial bellicosity. (There is none in Prisoner's Dilemma.) Nevertheless, crashes are almost always avoided as a result of rational deliberation.

Did Hobbes attempt to derive a Prisoner's Dilemma conclusion from Chicken premises? It would be premature to draw this conclusion from such an oversimplified model of the state of nature. A number of complications need to be introduced before we could begin to do Hobbes justice (see Chapter 6). One can find materials for more realistic models

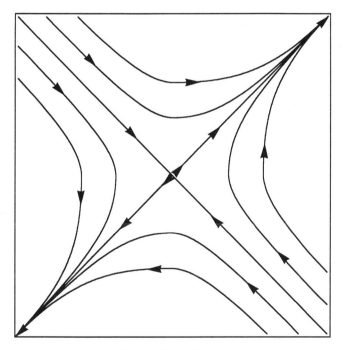

Figure 2.16.   Chicken

in ethological descriptions of varieties of animal conflict. Of particular interest is the prevalence of ritualized aggression in which little real damage is done (Lorenz, 1966; Eibl-Eibesfeld, 1970). This *is* part of the state of nature, and it does not agree with Hobbes' description. Kropotkin's remark of 1902 is even more suitable now: "science has made some progress since Hobbes' time, and we have safer ground to stand upon than the speculations of Hobbes and Rousseau."

One might argue that the rationality of humans invalidates the analogy, but the analyses of evolutionary game theory do not support this objection (see Maynard Smith and Price, 1973; Parker, 1974; Maynard Smith, 1982). For these sorts of game-theoretic models, Bayesian deliberators of the kind considered here will decide by deliberational dynamics in a way analogous to the way that Mother Nature decides by evolution. In the games considered by Maynard Smith and Price, self-interested rational deliberators will play in a decidedly un-Hobbesian way. In general, we must agree with the carefully considered conclusion of Kavka (1986, p. 122) that "which strategy is better overall probably cannot be determined a priori for all state of nature situations. Instead, it will depend on the value of a number of important variables and parameters, which will vary according to the version of the state of nature in question."

These considerations, however incomplete they may be with respect to Hobbes, nevertheless make the general point that deliberation may play a role in the genesis of coordination in situations with a considerable amount of competition as well as in pure coordination games. There is a general conception under which all these cases fall. It is a notion usually discussed in *cooperative* game theory—a *correlated equilibrium.* Aumann (1974) suggested that mixed strategies, where the chance devices used by different players are assumed independent, be treated as a special case of *correlated* strategies, where the chance devices may have any joint probability distribution at all.

You might think of a referee observing the outcome of some random process—say, the toss of a many-sided die—and communicating to each player the aspect of the process that is *that player's* random variable. For example, one player might get to know the color of the face, another the number of spots showing. Any correlation of colors and spots in the random device is allowed.

A *random strategy* for player i can be thought of as a probability assignment to his space of possible actions, A_i, namely, a random variable mapping some probability space into A_1. A *joint correlated strategy* can be thought of as any probability assignment on the product space of the action spaces of all players, $A_1 \times A_2 \times \ldots \times A_n$, or a mapping of a probability space into sequences of actions. A correlated strategy can obviously be specified by giving the underlying joint probability space together with a sequence of random variables on it: $f_1, f_2, \ldots f_n$, where f_i maps the probability space into the action space of player i. In the special case of ordinary mixed strategies, the probability on the product space is the product measure and the random strategies are independent. An *i-deviation* from a correlated strategy C consists of the same probability space and the same random variables f_i except that each f_i is replaced by some random variable $g(f_i)$ taking values in A_i. An *i*-deviation represents player i unilaterally deviating from the original joint correlated strategy so that when the original strategy tells him to do one thing he does something else, while all other players stick to the original correlated strategy. A *correlated equilibrium* is a joint correlated strategy such that for each player i expected utility on the joint correlated equilibrium strategy is greater than or equal to his expected utility on any *i*-deviation from it (the expectation being taken according to the underlying probability space). Thus, a correlated equilibrium is a joint correlated strategy from which no player has anything to gain by unilateral deviation.

In certain situations, it might be to all the players' mutual advantage to agree on a joint correlated equilibrium strategy and then either hire a referee or construct a machine to carry out the random experiment and communicate to each player the action selected for him. On the face of it, it might appear that "for strategies to be correlated there must be some mechanism for communicating and contracting between the players" (Shubik, 1982, p. 247). But, as we have seen in several examples, rational deliberation can play a powerful role in establishing correlation. Let us consider in a general way the sort of situation sketched at the beginning of this section.

An observer, Theo, knows that n players will be induced to play a certain n-person noncooperative game. Theo knows that the players are all Bayesian dynamic deliberators with a common dynamics and that this fact will be common knowledge to the players at the onset of deliberation, as will their prior probabilities. Theo has analyzed the game and knows that in it (as in every example we have seen so far) the dynamics always converges to a Nash equilibrium. Theo may or may not know who the players are. He does not know what their initial probabilities for their possible actions will be, but rather has his own probability measure over the possible initial states of indecision of the system. Although the interpretation of the mathematics is quite different, we nevertheless see that with respect to Theo's probability measure *the players are at a correlated equilibrium.*

When the true initial state of indecision is selected, a recommendation for action is delivered up to each player by deliberational dynamics. Since the dynamics leads from each initial state to a Nash equilibrium, no player has anything to gain by deviating from that recommendation. Thus no *i*-deviation from the joint correlated strategy defined by Theo's probability is preferable to it for player *i*, so that joint correlated strategy is, by definition, a correlated equilibrium. This is true no matter what Theo's probability measure over the space of initial states of indecision. *This correlated equilibrium is a general result of the players' common knowledge and Bayesian dynamic deliberation.*

The same result may be obtained without the outside observer if prior to deliberation the players themselves share the role of Theo. For example, Sue and Dora are going to fly to the small country of Freedonia for a vacation and each plans to rent a car. They are to pick up cars at a deserted airport in Freedonia. Sue thinks it likely that Freedonians drive on the left; Dora thinks it likely that Freedonians drive on the right. There may be no one else in Freedonia then because it is a special holiday, and there are no road signs in Freedonia. Sue and Dora prepare to be involved in a game of The Winding Road with one another. They agree that before leaving the airport they will share their then current probabilities of opting for Left or Right and then go their separate ways, deliberate, and do the best they can.

This example brings us close to the point of view of Aumann (1987), who argued that correlated equilibrium is a consequence of a common prior probability together with common knowledge of Bayesian rationality. The latter is taken to be common knowledge that the players will each arrive at a decision that maximizes that player's expected utility. The former includes prior probabilities over what each player will ultimately choose and is, then, itself interpreted as the probability setting up the correlated strategy, with the joint maximization of expected utility assuring that it is an equilibrium.

Aumann's viewpoint is somewhat different from the one presented here in that he does not consider the process of deliberation, but only its result. So there is no analysis of how the players jointly arrive at decisions where each maximizes his expected utility. In contrast, we made additional assumptions to get stronger conclusions. We assumed common knowledge of the dynamical law of deliberation, which is a stronger common-knowledge assumption than that used by Aumann. This is what enables accurate updating by emulation and assures that a state at which each player is at a deliberational equilibrium corresponds to a Nash equilibrium for the game. Consequently, our predeliberational correlated equilibria are mixtures of Nash equilibria. As such they are a proper subclass of Aumann's correlated equilibria, that have especially tight correlation. Considerations of deliberational dynamics add a further dimension to the theory of correlated equilibria and provide an account of one way in which correlated equilibria can be generated.

Equilibria and Rationality

We saw in Chapter 1 that it was hard to justify the Nash equilibrium concept, even for two-person zero-sum games, without making further assumptions. In this chapter we have considered some very simple models of bounded Bayesian deliberators who, under quite strong conditions of prior common knowledge, are at a joint deliberational equilibrium if and only if they are at a Nash equilibrium. Refinements of the deliberational dynamics in a qualitatively Bayesian direction leads naturally to refinements of the Nash equilibrium concept. There is also an important connection between deliberational dynamics and Aumann's concept of a correlated equilibrium. These results about equilibria come from strong assumptions, and one would like to know more about how sensitive they are to small changes in those assumptions.

3 Dynamic Deliberation: Stability

Since in applications of dynamical systems, one
cannot pinpoint a state exactly, but only
approximately, an equilibrium must be stable to be
physically meaningful.

—M. W. Hirsch and S. Smale (1974)

The existence of joint deliberational equilibria corresponds to a consistent solution to the joint decision problem of many players. In the last chapter I discussed conditions under which joint deliberational equilibria exist, under which conditions they correspond to Nash equilibria of a game, and under which conditions they are reachable by Bayesian deliberation starting at a completely mixed point of indecision. The last consideration gives one natural principled motivation for refinements of the Nash equilibrium concept.

Given the strong simplifying assumptions of this discussion, it is natural to raise the question of robustness—of sensitivity to small changes in various aspects of the model. This sort of consideration is a different kind of motivation for refinements of the Nash equilibrium, one aspect of which is dramatized in the metaphor of the "trembling hand." Within the framework of dynamic deliberation, questions of stability and robustness can be categorized and investigated with standard tools of the theory of dynamical systems. In this chapter, I will give some indications of the directions that such analyses can take.

Dynamic Stability of Equilibria

An equilibrium point, e, is stable under the dynamics if points nearby remain close for all time under the action of the dynamics.[1] It is strongly stable (or asymptotically stable) if there is a neighborhood of e such that the trajectories of all points in that neighborhood converge to e. The basin of attraction of a strongly stable equilibrium is the union of all trajectories that converge to it. An equilibrium is unstable if it is not stable. A dynamically unstable equilibrium is the natural focus for worries about the "trembling hand," since in this case there is a neighborhood, N, of e such that for every neighborhood, N', inside N, the trajectory of some point originating in N' leads outside N. Thus, for a dynamically unstable equilibrium, confining the "trembles" to an arbitrarily small N' cannot guarantee that the trajectory stays within N.

Let us reconsider the game of Chicken with the Nash dynamics from this perspective. (I will turn to the effects of varying the dynamics later in this chapter.) The phase portrait is given in Figure 3.1: the lower right corner represents probability one that both players swerve; the upper left represents probability one that neither swerves. The lower left and upper right corners correspond to the two Nash equilibria in pure strategies: Row swerves and Column doesn't; Column swerves and Row doesn't. These are both strongly stable equilibria. The first has as its basin of attraction every point to the lower left of the diagonal and the second has as its basin of attraction every point to the upper right.

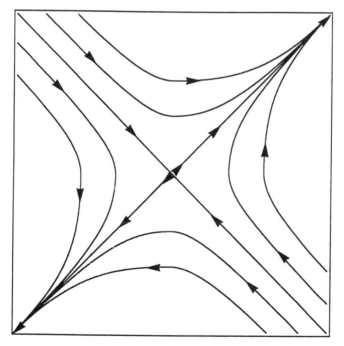

Figure 3.1. The Nash dynamics of Chicken with two stable pure equilibria and an unstable mixed equilibrium

The mixed equilibrium at [0.5,0.5] is unstable. It is called a saddle-point equilibrium, since the dynamics carries every point on the diagonal to it and every point off the diagonal away from it. Notice that this is perfect equilibrium, but it is far from being robust under trembles unless the trembles are somehow conceived as confined to the diagonal.

Pure equilibria can be dynamically unstable. Recall Myerson's game:

Myerson's game

	C1	C2	C3
R3	$-9,-9$	$-7,-7$	$-7,-7$
R2	0,0	0,0	$-7,-7$
R1	1,1	0,0	$-9,-9$

Of the three Nash equilibria in pure strategies [R1, C1], [R2, C2], and [R3, C3], both [R2, C2] and [R3, C3] are dynamically unstable under both the Nash and Darwin dynamics while the proper equilibrium at [R1, C1] is strongly stable.[2]

Mixed equilibria can be dynamically stable, and even strongly stable. As an example we can take Matching Pennies under the Nash dynamics.

Matching Pennies

	C1	C2
R2	1,0	0,1
R1	0,1	1,0

Here the unique Nash equilibrium of the game is in mixed strategies at [0.5,0.5]. This is a strongly stable equilibrium under the Nash dynamics,[3] with the whole space as its basin of attraction. Trajectories spiral in as they converge to this point. A typical example is shown in Figure 3.2.

The general phenomenon just described does not depend on there being no Nash equilibria in pure strategies. Consider the following example of Moulin (1986):

Moulin's game

	C1	C2	C3
R3	1,3	2,0	3,1
R2	0,2	2,2	0,2
R1	3,1	2,0	1,3

There is a unique Nash equilibrium in pure strategies [R2, C2], but for each player act 2 is weakly dominated by both act 1 and act 3. If a player does not assign probability one to the other player's doing act 2, his own acts 1 and 3 both look better than his act 2. Consequently, [R2, C2] is highly unstable. Under Nash dynamics, every point in the interior of the space of indecision goes to the mixed equilibrium, where each player gives probability 0.5 of playing act 1 and of playing act 3. The orbits of Row [0.3, 0.7, 0] and Column [0, 0.7, 0.3] are shown in Figure 3.3.

The last two examples point up a difference between a static and a dynamic view of stability. In static discussions of game theory, it is often remarked that mixed equilibria are intrinsically unstable because if your opponent plays the equilibrium strategy you can do just as well by play-ing any pure strategy with positive weight in your mixed equilibrium strategy as by playing the mixed equilibrium itself. The situation changes if you and your opponent are treated as dynamic deliberators. In this case mixed equilibria may or may not be dynamically stable, and each case must be evaluated on its own merits.

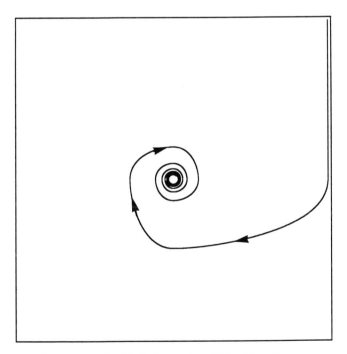

Figure 3.2. The Nash dynamics of Matching Pennies with a stable mixed equilibrium

Imprecise Priors and Elicitation through Deliberation

Our idealized model of games played by Bayesian deliberators makes the unrealistic assumption that at the onset of deliberation precise states of indecision of the players are common knowledge. It is of interest to explore the consequences of weakening this assumption, and it can be weakened in various ways. The prior states of indecision might not be common knowledge or they might not be precise or both. I will postpone discussion of the relaxation of the common-knowledge assumption and concentrate here on imprecise states of indecision.

There are various ways in which imprecise states of indecision might be modeled. Here I will discuss the computationally simplest alternative. Instead of taking a player's state of indecision to be a probability measure over his space of final actions, I will present it as a convex set

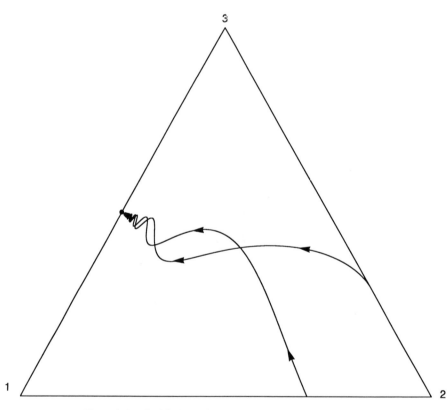

Figure 3.3.   Stable mixed equilibrium in Moulin's game

of probability measures (as suggested by Good, 1950; Smith, 1961; Kyburg, 1961; Levi, 1974). I will focus on the simplest case of two-person games, where each player has only two possible actions and a player's state of indecision is given by a closed interval. If, for example, Row's probability of act 2 is to lie in the interval between Row's upper probability of act 2 = 0.7 and Row's lower probability of act 2 = 0.6, then the extreme probability measure corresponding to Row's upper probability of act 2 is $p(A2) = 0.7$, $p(A1) = 0.3$, and the extreme measure corresponding to Row's lower probability of act 2 is $p(A2) = 0.6$, $p(A1) = 0.4$. The convex set in question is composed of all probability measures over the space [A1,A2] that can be realized as a weighted average of the extreme measures.

How should Row calculate expected utilities given Column's probability interval? He should have a set of expected utilities, one corresponding to each possible point probability consistent with Column's probability interval. Because of the nature of the expectation, however, Row need only compute the expected utilities relative to the endpoints of Column's interval with assurance that the other point utilities lie between the endpoints.

How should Row modify his probability sets in the light of new expected utility sets? He should have new probability sets corresponding to every point reached by applying his dynamical law to a point chosen from the expected utility set and a point chosen from his old probability set. But for the Nash dynamics, and a large class of reasonable dynamical laws to which it belongs, it is a consequence of the form of the dynamical law that if the old probability of an act, A, is in the interval between the upper and lower probabilities of the act [call the two extremes $p_1(A)$ and $p_3(A)$ and the point in between $p_2(A)$], and if the old utility of the act is in the interval of utilities corresponding to the probability interval [call the utilities $U_1(A)$, $U_2(A)$, and $U_3(A)$], then the new probability, p', is in a new probability interval [that is, $p'_2(A)$ is between $p'_1(A)$ and $p'_3(A)$]. It is a consequence of these observations that Row can achieve the results of point deliberation on every pair consisting of one point from his interval and one from Column's interval by performing four point computations on pairs consisting of one endpoint from his interval and one from Column's interval. The new maximum and minimum probabilities of A among the four possibilities form the endpoints of his new probability for A. The general points made above continue to hold good *mutatis mutandis* for numbers of acts greater than two, with intervals being generalized to convex sets of probability measures and endpoints being generalized to extreme points. With regard to computational tractability, deliberational dynamics, as so far developed, has a certain affinity for convex set representations of imprecise probabilities.

In the case of two players each of whom must choose between two acts, a state of indecision in the interval-valued sense is now represented as a rectangle in the old space of indecision—the product of Row's and Column's intervals. Points are considered degenerate intervals, and point states of indecision are special cases of rectangles of indecision. At the other extreme a player's interval may be the whole interval [0,1], in which case we will say that he is totally bewildered, and where the state of indecision is the whole space, we will say that the players are in a state of mutual total bewilderment. A rectangle of indecision that the dynamics maps onto itself is a dynamical equilibrium state.

The area of a rectangle of indecision need not be preserved by deliberational dynamics. For example, players may start out with nondegenerate interval-valued probabilities and be carried by deliberation to point probabilities. One might call such a process elicitation of point probabilities through deliberation. It is illustrated in Figure 3.4 in terms of the

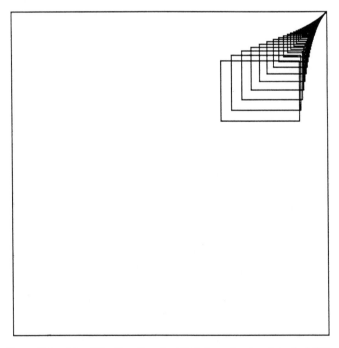

Figure 3.4.   The Winding Road with interval-valued probabilities

Nash dynamics applied to a pure coordination game, The Winding Road. Row starts with a probability interval of [0.6, 0.8] and Column starts with a probability interval of [0.6, 0.9]. They each converge to a point probability of one (of driving on the right).

The same process in the case of a game with elements of both competition and coordination is illustrated in Figure 3.5. Here, in the game of Chicken, we have the orbit of [0.4,0.1], [0.4,0.1] converging to [0,0] and that of [0.9,0.6], [0.9,0.6] converging to [1,1]. The effect is illustrated in the extreme in Figure 3.6, where an initial state of mutual total bewilderment is carried to the point equilibrium [Defect, Defect] by the Nash dynamics in Prisoner's Dilemma.

It is evident that much of our analyses of these games is robust under generalization to interval-valued probabilities. Let us look at the matter a little more closely. Let us say that a point equilibrium is here robust under imprecision if there is a nondegenerate rectangle of indecision that contains the point and converges to it. Figure 3.6 shows that [Defect, Defect] in Prisoner's Dilemma is robust under imprecision. [Right, Right] and [Left, Left] in The Winding Road and [Row swerves,

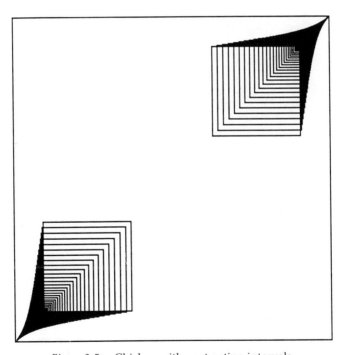

Figure 3.5.   Chicken with contracting intervals

Column doesn't] and [Column swerves, Row doesn't] in Chicken are all robust under imprecision. However, the mixed equilibria in these games are not. For example, consider the mixed point equilibrium at [0.5,0.5] in Chicken. The orbit of the small rectangle, [0.51,0.49], [0.51,0.49], explodes to a state of mutual total bewilderment, as does any rectangle that straddles the separatrix of the point dynamics (the diagonal from upper left to lower right). The orbits of nondegenerate rectangles that include the mixed point equilibrium but do not straddle the separatrix suffer a more modest explosion, as shown in Figure 3.7, where an initial rectangle of [0.5,0.4], [0.5,0.4] is carried to an equilibrium rectangle of [0.5,0], [0.5,0].

In the examples given so far the point equilibria that were robust under imprecision were ones which were strongly stable in the point dynamics. One might suspect that these notions coincide, but this conjecture is shown false by the simple example of Matching Pennies. Recall that this game has only one Nash equilibrium point at [0.5,0.5] and that for point probabilities under the Nash dynamics this point is a

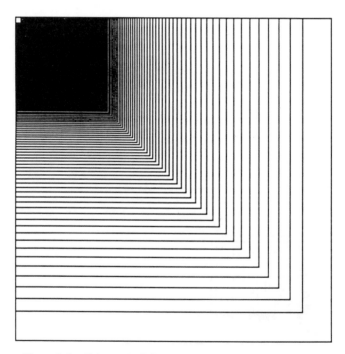

Figure 3.6. Prisoner's Dilemma with contracting intervals

strongly stable equilibrium that is an attractor for every point in the space. If, however, we start with nondegenerate rectangles rather than points in the joint space of indecision, the situation is reversed. Every nondegenerate interval explodes to a state of mutual total bewilderment. This is illustrated in Figure 3.8 for an initial rectangle of [0.51,0.49], [0.51,0.49]. Other nondegenerate rectangles do no better. Robustness under imprecision is a stronger variety of stability for equilibrium points than strong stability is in the point dynamics.

The analysis of Matching Pennies for point states of indecision does not deserve to be called robust under imprecision. What about our analyses of The Winding Road and Chicken? In each of these cases, the pure Nash equilibria are robust under imprecision. Any rectangle that does not touch the separatrix diagonal has an orbit that converges to one of the pure Nash equilibrium points. On the other hand, the mixed Nash equilibrium point is not robust under imprecision and interaction with the diagonal leads to trouble. How much of the space leads to trouble depends on how imprecise the players' priors are. One can get some

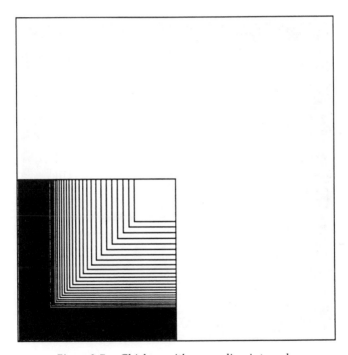

Figure 3.7.   Chicken with expanding intervals

idea of the magnitude of the difficulties by putting a grid over the space of indecision. In a regular grid with 0.1 spacing, ten of the squares straddle the diagonal and eighteen more touch it, for a total of 28 percent troublemakers. For a spacing of 0.05 about 15 percent are troublemakers, and for a spacing of 0.01 the proportion of troublemakers drops to about 2 percent.

When analyzed in terms of point priors, The Winding Road and Chicken were both seen to be situations in which coordination could arise spontaneously. In fact, in that setting, it seemed to require a miracle for coordination *not* to occur. The conclusion that coordination can occur spontaneously in such situations continues to hold good for imprecise priors. But the modeling of this section, although still far from realistic, does give us some reason to expect trouble near the diagonal. (Exactly what sort of trouble it is depends on what, if anything, bewildered players are supposed to do. See the discussion of interval-valued probabilities in Chapter 5.) Coordination does not appear quite so effortless, and it would be to everyone's mutual advantage to set up the pre-

Figure 3.8. Intervals explode in Matching Pennies

deliberational environment to keep players away from the diagonal. For The Winding Road, a liberal use of street signs might do the trick. Or consider The Intersection, a sort of attenuated game of Chicken discussed in Moulin (1986):

The Intersection

	Go	Stop
Go	−10, −10	1, −.1
Stop	−.1, 1	0,0

A stoplight in the predeliberational environment is a reasonably effective means for keeping the players away from the diagonal.

Analysis of robustness under imprecision could be developed further, and imprecision could be modeled in other—perhaps more realistic— ways. In what follows I will for the most part deal with simpler models with point probability states of indecision, but I wish to point out that additional questions of robustness under imprecision are always in order.

Structural Stability I

Another kind of dynamic stability is of interest. That is the stability of the location and type of equilibrium points as differential equations are varied. One way of varying the differential equations keeps the fundamental dynamical law the same but varies the payoffs of the game. I will illustrate with game-theoretic models of the arms race. Political philosophers often model the arms race as Prisoner's Dilemma, with the following payoffs:

Prisoner's Dilemma

	Defect	Don't defect
Defect	−5, −5	5, −10
Don't defect	−10, 5	0,0

Deliberational dynamics inexorably carries every point in the space to the tragic strong equilibrium of both sides deciding to arm (Figure 3.9). But, at least in some arms races, some generals and some politicians may think that the proper model of the arms race is not Prisoner's Dilemma but, rather, Chicken. The disagreement is about the relative values of D and R in the payoff matrix:

	C1	C2
R2	D,D	5,R
R1	R,5	0,0

With $D = -5$ and $R = -10$ we have Prisoner's Dilemma; with $D = -10$ and $R = -5$ we have Chicken. With $D = R = -10$ we have a structurally unstable transition game, which has the following payoff matrix and which is plotted in Figure 3.10.

	C1	C2
R2	$-10, -10$	$5, -10$
R1	$-10,5$	0,0

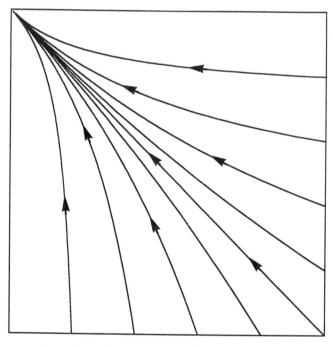

Figure 3.9.   Nash dynamics of Prisoner's Dilemma

Figure 3.10 looks much like the portrait of Prisoner's Dilemma in Figure 3.9, but there are some subtle changes: there are additional (unstable) equilibria in pure acts at [0,0] and [1,1] and additional (unstable) equilibria in mixed acts at $x = 0$, $y < 1$ and at $y = 1$, $x > 0$. These equilibria are indicated in the figure by the bold lines. The equilibrium at [0,1] is still stable, but it is no longer strongly stable for it is not an attractor for orbits of the aforementioned mixed equilibrium points. If D is allowed to creep a little below R, then we have The Birth of Chicken (Figure 3.11), whose payoff matrix is:

The Birth of Chicken

	Don't swerve	Swerve
Don't swerve	$-10.5, -10.5$	$5, -10$
Swerve	$-10, 5$	$0, 0$

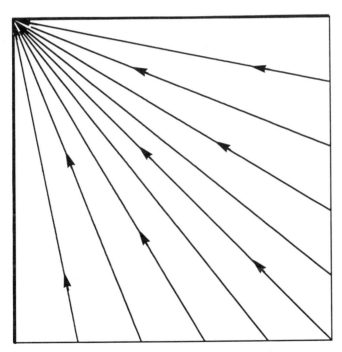

Figure 3.10.   Transition from Prisoner's Dilemma to Chicken

There is now a dramatic change. The equilibrium point formerly at [0,1] moves down the diagonal and changes from a stable equilibrium to a hyperbolic one. The equilibria at [0,0] and [1,1] change from unstable to strongly stable. They are now attractors for the orbits of almost all points in the space. The former mixed equilibria on $x = 0$ and on $y = 1$ have vanished. We have passed through the "better R than D" bifurcation. The equilibrium points as a function of decreasing D are plotted in Figure 3.12.

Other transitions are of interest. Consider a Dove's model of the arms race. The Dove may well believe that the payoff in the case of mutual disarmament is greater than the payoff in the case in which her country arms and the other doesn't. After all, arming diverts economic resources and may tempt her own country's political leaders into adventures they had best not undertake. Thus, she thinks that in the payoff matrix

	C1	C2
R2	D,D	$5,R$
R1	$R,5$	P,P

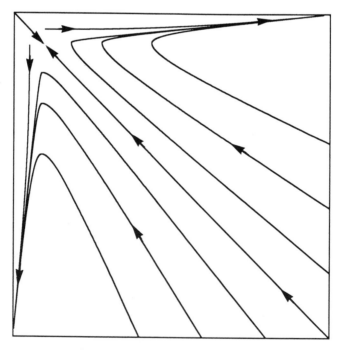

Figure 3.11.   The Birth of Chicken

P should be greater than 5. Figure 3.13 shows the transition from Prisoner's Dilemma to the Dove model with $D = -5$, $R = -10$, $P = 5.5$. A tiny window of hope has opened in the lower right corner. It is bounded by a saddle-point equilibrium on the [0,1]–[1,0] diagonal. Orbits of points in its interior are attracted to a new stable equilibrium in the lower right corner. If the players come to this game with enough prior goodwill to put the initial point in the window, they will be carried to this equilibrium. This Dove game is also a test of will.

All of these games (and other variations that may suggest themselves to you) may be more or less reasonable models for arms races in various specific situations. For those who would model the arms race in this way it is of real interest to investigate the dramatic changes in deliberational equilibria that can occur as the payoffs are continuously varied. In the first place, doing so would give important information as to the robustness of the model. And if the model is accurate, neighborhoods of structural instability may represent situations of great risk or great opportunity.

One useful concept of structural stability was introduced into the

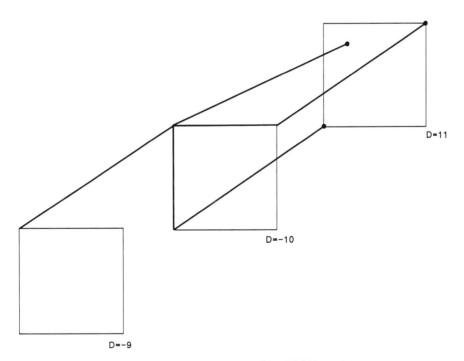

Figure 3.12. The "better *R* than *D*" bifurcation

game-theoretic literature by Kohlberg and Mertens (1986), who call a Nash equilibrium of a game hyperstable if it is robust under small variations in the payoffs. Hyperstability can be studied without reference to the particular dynamics since it depends only on how the Nash equilibria move, and Kohlberg and Mertens did not consider dynamics.[4] But from the point of view of deliberational dynamics, hyperstability can be viewed as a concept for classifying joint deliberational equilibria.

More precisely, a Nash equilibrium, N, is hyperstable if for every ε there is a δ such that if the pure strategy payoffs are perturbed by less than δ there is a Nash equilibrium in the open ball with radius ε centered at N. Not every game has a hyperstable equilibrium, but almost all do. That is, except for a set of Lebesgue measure zero in the space of pure strategy payoffs, every normal-form game has a hyperstable equilibrium. If a game has only a finite number of equilibria, then one of them is hyperstable. This sort of structural stability is not unrelated to previous concerns. Hyperstable equilibria are always proper and perfect (see Kohlberg and Mertens, 1986; Leal, 1986).

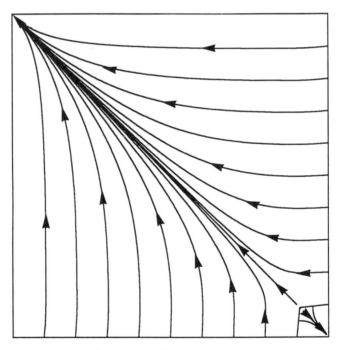

Figure 3.13. The Birth of Dove

For example, consider Samuelson's game, in which Darwin can converge to imperfect equilibria:

	C1	C2
R2	11,11	11,11
R1	12,10	9,8

The imperfect equilibria at $p(R2) = 1$, $p(C2) > 0.25$ are not hyperstable, because they cease to be equilibria in the perturbed game:

	C1	C2
R2	11,11 + ε	11,11
R1	12,10	9,8

The perfect equilibrium at $p(R1) = p(C1) = 1$ is hyperstable. In fact, small perturbations in the pure strategy payoffs do not move it at all.

For a somewhat different kind of example, let us reconsider Matching Pennies. Here there is only one Nash equilibrium: the mixed strategy where each player gives each of his pure strategies probability 0.5. This equilibrium is hyperstable. Here small perturbations in the payoffs can move the equilibrium, but arbitrarily small perturbations move the equilibrium an arbitrarily small amount.

Considerations of hyperstability, however, tell only part of the story about the structural stability of equilibria. Recall the transition game between Prisoner's Dilemma and Chicken:

	C1	C2
R2	$-10, -10$	$5, -10$
R1	$-10, 5$	$0, 0$

The Nash equilibria consist of all points with $p(C1) = 1$ and all points with $p(R2) = 1$. Consideration of perturbations in the direction of Prisoner's Dilemma and of Chicken is sufficient to show that equilibria other than $E = [p(R2) = 1, p(C1) = 1]$ are not hyperstable. In the direction of Prisoner's Dilemma, E does not move; in the direction of Chicken it moves a little bit in response to small perturbations. However, this leaves out the fact that E changes its dynamic stability status, under the Nash dynamics, from strongly stable in Prisoner's Dilemma to stable but not strongly stable, in the transition game, to an unstable saddle point in Chicken. Furthermore, consideration of asymmetric perturbations shows that E is not hyperstable either. For any positive ε, the perturbed game given by

	C1	C2
R2	$-10, -10 + \varepsilon$	$5, -10$
R1	$-10 + \varepsilon, 5$	$0, 0$

has a unique Nash equilibrium at $p(R1) = p(C1) = 1$. So the short story regarding structural stability for the transition game is that there are no hyperstable equilibria but, as we have seen, there is a much richer long story to be told.

Structural Stability II

One can investigate structural stability at a more radical level. Instead of simply changing the payoffs, one can change the dynamical law. Then one can investigate which features of the dynamics are robust under changes of the dynamical laws. For example, let us look once more at Matching Pennies. In the Nash flow:

$$\frac{dp(A)}{dt} = \frac{cov(A) - p(A)\Sigma_i cov(A_i)}{1 + \Sigma_i cov(A_i)}$$

In the closely related Brown–von Neumann flow:

$$\frac{dp(A)}{dt} = cov(A)^2 - p(A)\Sigma_i cov(A_i)^2$$

And in the Darwin flow:

$$\frac{dp(A)}{dt} = p(A)\frac{EU(A) - EU(SQ)}{EU(SQ)}$$

The unique mixed equilibrium at $[p(R2) = 0.5, p(C2) = 0.5]$ is a strongly stable spiral attractor, having the whole space as its basin of attraction. If we move to the Aristotelian flow for 2×2 games (Skyrms, 1986), such that

$$\frac{dp(A2)}{dt} = EU(A2) - EU(A1)$$

the vector field changes character, as illustrated in Figure 3.14. The Nash equilibrium is still stable, but it is no longer strongly stable. The deliberators jointly form a harmonic oscillator. The closed orbits are not structurally stable.[5] Slight variations in the dynamics can turn them into outward or inward spirals.[6]

Some games are more sensitive to changes in the dynamics than others. Consider a game like Chicken. The vector field looks qualitatively the same as that illustrated in Figure 3.1 for a wide variety of dynamical rules.[7] The curvature of the orbits may vary, but the destinations of the points remain the same. Every point to the lower left of the diagonal goes to the Nash equilibrium at the lower left corner; every point to the upper right goes to the upper right corner. Every point on the (anti) diagonal (except perhaps endpoints) goes to the saddle-point equilibri-

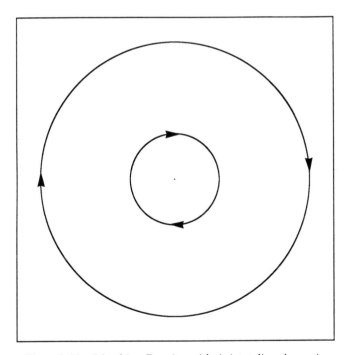

Figure 3.14.   Matching Pennies with Aristotelian dynamics

um at [0.5,0.5]. We can argue that any reasonable autonomous dynamics will give this sort of picture.

If the dynamics seeks the good then the qualitative direction of the flow in the four quadrants of the space of indecision is as indicated in Figure 3.15. Suppose $dp(A_i)/dt$ is a continuous function of the expected utilities and probabilities of the A_i, which assumes the value zero only if $U(A_i) = U(SQ)$ or $p(A_i) = 1$ or 0. Consider a point, p, in the interior of the lower left quadrant, as in Figure 3.16. The point must move into the rectangle *APBE* and cannot ever get out. Draw a horizontal line *DC* at $p(R1) = 1 - \varepsilon$. Within the rectangle *APCD*, $dp(R1)/dt$ is always positive since on *APBE* it is zero only at *E*. By continuity (a continuous function defined on a compact set assumes a maximum and a minimum), $dp(R1)/dt$ is bounded away from zero on *APCD*. So in some finite amount of time the trajectory of p moves into *DCBE*, from which it cannot escape. A similar argument with respect to $dp(C1)/dt$ gets the point to within ε of $p(C1) = 1$. Since ε is arbitrary the trajectory must converge to the equilibrium, *E*. The situation in the upper right quadrant is similar. The equilibria [Row swerves, Column doesn't] and [Column swerves, Row doesn't] are thus as stable as you please in all the ways we have discussed.

Suppose that a point is on the diagonal from upper left to lower right. Then by symmetry, $dp(R2)/dt = dp(C1)/dt$, and by a continuity argument similar to the one above every point except endpoints must converge to

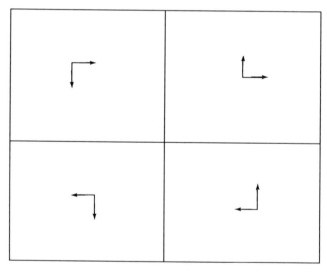

Figure 3.15.   Four quadrants in Chicken

the mixed Nash equilibrium at [0.5,0.5]. The situation in the rest of the upper left and lower right quadrants is only slightly more sensitive. Consider the triangle consisting of the space below the diagonal in the upper left quadrant. Drop a vertical line from the diagonal, as shown in Figure 3.17. On the diagonal, $dp(R1)/dt = dp(C2)/dt > 0$. At $p(R1) = 0.5$,

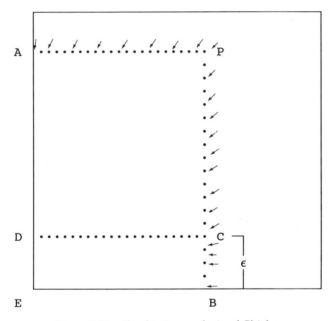

Figure 3.16. Qualitative analysis of Chicken

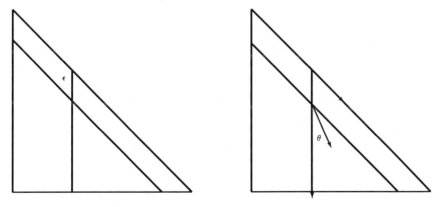

Figure 3.17. Below the diagonal in the upper left quadrant

$dp(C2)/dt = 0$ while $dp(R1)/dt$ is positive. Let us make the additional assumption that the direction of the velocity vector as measured by the indicated angle θ varies continuously and monotonically along this line. Then, for any point in this region, we can draw a line between it and the diagonal such that at that line the vector field always points inward. Since the downward velocity $dp(R1)/dt$ is positive throughout the smaller triangle thus formed, it must by continuity be bounded away from zero and in some finite time the trajectory of the point must emerge into the lower left quadrant, and so be delivered to the lower left equilibrium. The remaining cases are similar. Thus the whole qualitative analysis of Chicken is extremely robust over variations in the deliberational dynamics.

However, there is one sense in which Prisoner's Dilemma is even more robust than Chicken. In the discussion of Chicken, we allowed the dynamical laws to vary among a wide class but we assumed that in any particular situation whatever dynamics was being used was common to the players and common knowledge between them. This extends even to the index of caution. If Row is a Nash deliberator and Column a Darwin deliberator, or even if both are Nash deliberators but one has a greater index of caution, and if these facts are common knowledge, then orbits that originate on the diagonal will not stay on it.

In Prisoner's Dilemma, however, it doesn't matter. Suppose two players have two different dynamical rules from the class of rules which seek the good such that $dp(A_i)/dt$ is a continuous function of the expected utilities and probabilities of the A_i, which assumes the value zero only if $U(A_i) = U(SQ)$ or $p(A_i) = 1$ or 0, and suppose that it is common knowledge that the players have these rules. Then every completely mixed state of indecision converges to [Defect, Defect].[8]

This is a consequence of the fact that [Defect, Defect] is the unique rationalizable strategy. For each player, Defect strongly dominates Cooperate. So, at each point in the space the velocity toward Defect is positive for each player. Then, by an argument like that used regarding the lower left quadrant of Chicken, the players will converge to [Defect, Defect].

In a reversal of the analogy, the pure equilibria of Chicken each have a neighborhood in which the vector field looks qualitatively like that of Prisoner's Dilemma. They are *strong equilibria* in the sense of Harsanyi (1973a). At the equilibrium each player's strategy is her unique best reply. By continuity of expected utilities as a function of probabilities, a Harsanyi-strong equilibrium should have a neighborhood within which each player's equilibrium strategy is still her unique best reply. Then it should be strongly dynamically stable in any reasonable dynamics. By continuity of expected utilities as a function of utilities of pure strategies, it should be hyperstable. In fact, Harsanyi-strong equilibria appear to possess all the local stability properties that one might desire.[9]

Our three examples of this section illustrate common qualitative patterns in 2 × 2 two-person games. If we consider the space of all such games, as defined by their payoffs, the cases where two payoffs in the game matrix are exactly equal has Lebesgue measure zero. If we neglect these, there are—up to symmetry—essentially the four qualitative situations depicted in Figure 3.18. The first situation is illustrated by Matching Pennies, the second by Chicken and Battle of the Sexes, and the third by Prisoner's Dilemma.[10] We haven't met an example of the fourth situation, but it is much like Prisoner's Dilemma in that the game is solvable by iterated elimination of strictly dominated strategies. C1 strictly dominates C2. When C2 is eliminated, R2 strictly dominates R1. Thus the unique Nash equilibrium is the unique rationalizable strategy.

I do not want to claim that games with Lebesgue measure zero have probability zero of occurring in the real world. There are reasons why we do have games where some payoffs equal others, and so such games are of practical as well as theoretical interest. But the foregoing at least gives some reason to believe that the examples to which we have devoted so much attention are not completely atypical.

Stability and Rationality

In Chapter 2 we saw how the Nash equilibrium concept arises naturally in the context of games played by bounded Bayesian deliberators. A refinement of the Nash equilibrium concept also arises naturally, that of a joint deliberational equilibrium to which deliberation starting in a completely mixed state of indecision can converge. This concept is related to the notions of perfect and proper equilibrium discussed in the game-theoretic literature, but it is not identical with either. It does not depend

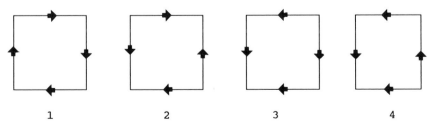

1	2	3	4

Figure 3.18.   Typical 2 × 2 games

for its interest on any irrationality on the part of the players, although it does depend on their limited computational resources.

In this chapter we surveyed various types of stability and robustness that arise naturally in the context of the dynamics of rational deliberation. These are related to game-theoretic notions of "strategic stability," which are often discussed in terms of a little irrationality on the part of the players. But I think that the types of stability we have surveyed can also be motivated without any presumed irrationality. In Chapters 4 and 5 I will examine just what rationality in these contexts entails.

In a situation where deliberation costs something, deliberation will often be terminated close to but short of a Nash equilibrium. The first theoretical question arising from this consideration concerns the dynamic stability of deliberational equilibria. It is at least arguable that interval-valued priors do not entail any irrationality (see Smith, 1961; Good, 1950; Levi, 1974; Kyburg, 1961), in which case robustness under imprecision is of interest even when rationality is common knowledge. Uncertainty and/or imprecise knowledge about the payoffs of the game is sufficient motivation for concern with the first kind of structural stability we have discussed. Structural stability under variations of the dynamical law are of obvious interest, since in our framework there is no unique rational dynamic law.

There are many interrelations between the various types of stability flowing from the deliberational dynamics, and between these and the many kinds of refinement of the Nash equilibrium that have been introduced in the game-theory literature. Some of these have been pointed out along the way, but we are far from having the whole story.[11] It appears that the framework of dynamic deliberation not only provides a rationale for the concerns of classical game theory, but also suggests fertile areas for new investigations.

4 The Value of Knowledge

Weight or the Value of Knowledge.

—F. P. Ramsey (n.d.)

Why is it better to know something rather than nothing? Perhaps because knowledge is an end in itself. But we also seek knowledge in order to make informed decisions. Informed decisions, we believe, are better than uninformed ones. What is the relevant sense of "better" and what basis is there for holding this belief? There is a Bayesian answer to these questions: coherence requires you to believe in the value of knowledge.

It is a theorem in the context of the decision theory of L. J. Savage (1954) and a standard treatment of learning by conditioning that the prior expected utility of making an informed decision is always at least as great as that of making an uninformed decision, and is strictly greater if there is any probability that the information may affect the decision. The proof is stated in a characteristically trenchant note by I. J. Good (1967). Good's treatment was set within a framework in which evidence comes packaged in *protokolsatze*: propositions (measurable sets) within the domain of one's personal probability measure. While such a model of learning is convenient and often a good enough approximation to reality, philosophers know how difficult it is to sustain as basic epistemology. And it is arguable whether it is realistic to represent the acquisition of knowledge in dynamic deliberation in this way.

This chapter will investigate the extent to which this account can be generalized to various models of learning, its import for the theory of deliberation, and its connection with payoff in the long run. I will develop an account of generalized learning processes and show that the theorem generalizes in a straightforward way to such learning processes.

Richard Jeffrey's (1965) "probability kinematics" and I. J. Good's (1983) "dynamic probability" can be thought of as special cases of generalized learning processes.

Good Thinking

You face a decision problem and you have the prior options of (1) deciding on your current information or (2) performing a cost-free experiment to obtain further information and then deciding. Here we model the results of the experiment simply as an observation sentence, one of an exhaustive set of mutually exclusive possible experimental results.

You can either choose between n acts, $A_1, \ldots, A_n$, now or perform a cost-free experiment, E, with possible results $\{e_k\}$ and then decide. For the sake of definiteness, let us suppose that you have been bitten by a dog you suspect may have been rabid. You must decide whether to take the (painful) Pasteur treatment or not. According to the standard expected utility model (as found in Savage), your value for an action is the weighted average of the possible payoffs of that action in different states of the world, K_i, weighted by your probabilities for those states of the world:

$$EU(A) = \Sigma_i p(K_i)U(A \& K_i)$$

Thus your current value for treatment will be a weighted average of your values for painful *useless* treatment and for painful *lifesaving* treatment; your current values for no treatment will be an average of your values for life without the painful treatment and for death from the disease.

Now suppose that you have to make the prior decision whether to act on your current degrees of belief or to seek further information by having a medical test performed. How do you apply expected utility analysis to this decision? Suppose that you know that you are an expected utility maximizer. Then the value of choosing now is just the expected value of the act with the greatest expected utility (the prior Bayes act):

$$U(\text{Choose now}) = \max_j \Sigma_i p(K_i)U(A_j \& K_i)$$
$$= \max_j \Sigma_k \Sigma_i p(K_i)p(e_k|K_i)U(A_j \& K_i)$$

Your value for undertaking the experiment (assumed to be cost-free) and then making your decision about treatment informed by the experimental results is your present expectation of the value of choosing that act after the experiment that has the highest expected utility after the experimental results are in (the posterior Bayes act). Let us assume that you know that upon getting the experimental results you will update by conditioning on it and then choose the act with greatest expected utility according to the updated probabilities.

Then we can calculate the value of making an informed decision in two stages. The value of making an informed decision conditional on experimental result e is the expected utility conditional on e of the act that has highest expected utility after assimilating the information e (the posterior Bayes act associated with e):

$$\max_j \Sigma_i p(K_i|e) U(A_j \,\&\, K_i)$$

Then your present value of making an informed decision is your present expectation of this quantity:

$U(\text{Learn now, choose later})$

$$= \Sigma_k p(e_k) \max_j \Sigma_i p(K_i|e_k) U(A_j \,\&\, K_i)$$

$$= \Sigma_k p(e_k) \max_j \Sigma_i \left[\frac{p(e_k|K_i)p(K_i)}{p(e_k)} \right] U(A_j \,\&\, K_i)$$

[by Bayes' theorem]

$$= \Sigma_k \max_j \Sigma_i p(e_k|K_i)p(K_i) U(A_j \,\&\, K_i)$$

The formulas for the present value of making an informed decision and of making an uninformed decision differ only in the order of the first two operations. But it is true on general mathematical grounds that $\Sigma_k \max_j g(k,j)$ is greater than or equal to $\max_j \Sigma_k g(k,j)$, with strict inequality if $\max_j g(k,j)$ is not the same for all k [QED]. This is the proof essentially as given by Good.

The situation is easy to visualize when there are only two possible experimental results, e_1 and e_2. Consider Figure 4.1. The expected utilities of the acts Treatment and No treatment graphed as a function of the probability of a positive experimental result are straight lines. The expected utility of the prior Bayes act is the convex function plotted in bold. The value of an informed decision is the straight dashed line. The vertical difference between the bold and dotted lines is the net gain in prior expected utility resulting from the determination to make an informed decision. This is zero only if both experimental outcomes lead to the same posterior Bayes act or if one is already certain of the experimental outcome; otherwise it is positive.

Moving to a continuum of possible acts (for example, setting a continuous control variable) does not materially alter the argument. This situation is diagramed in Figure 4.2 for the case where each different probability of positive result is associated with a different act. The expected utility of the prior Bayes act is here the upper envelope of the lines representing the expected utility of the acts.[1]

Let us recall here some of the assumptions under which this proof proceeds. In the first place, the expected utility theory assumed is statistical decision theory as found in Savage (1954): a distinction is made between states of the world, acts, and consequences; states of the world together with acts determine the consequences; and the relevant expectation is unconditional expected utility, $\Sigma_i p(K_i)U(A \ \& \ K_i)$. Second, by using the same notation for acts and states both before and after the

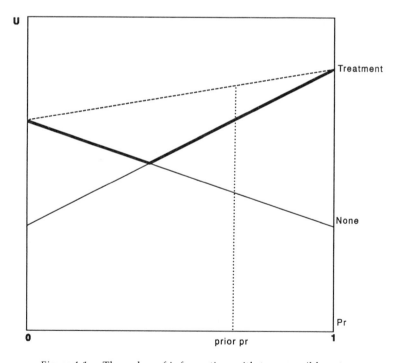

Figure 4.1. The value of information with two possible acts

experiment, we are assuming that in so far as they affect consequences the generic acts available after the experiment are equivalent to those available before it. And, third, it is assumed that the states are probabilistically independent of the performance of the experiment itself[2] (though not of particular experimental results): $p(K_i) = p(K_i|E)$. This assumption is not apparent in Good's treatment because he was interested in the case in which the experiment has already been done and the only decision is whether to utilize the experimental data in coming to one's decision.[3] The assumption can be violated when the performance of the experiment affects the state (as in destructive testing)[4] or when it is diagnostic of the state. Finally—as I have already emphasized—the proof implicitly assumes not only that the decisionmaker is a Bayesian but also that he knows that he will act as one. In particular, the decisionmaker believes with probability one that if he performs the experiment he will (1) update by conditioning and (2) choose the posterior Bayes act.[5]

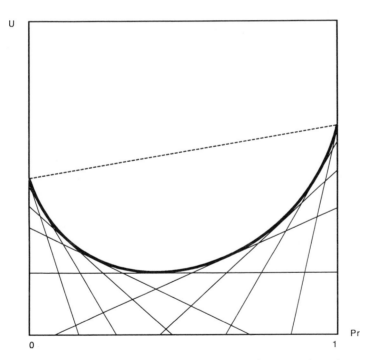

Figure 4.2. The value of information with an infinite number of acts

Probable Knowledge

Does knowledge always come nicely packaged as a proposition in one's subjective probability space? To attempt an affirmative answer would force one either to defend a form of "the myth of the given" of unprecedented strength or to relapse into skepticism. But the standard Bayesian theory of learning from experience by conditioning and, in particular, the analysis of the last section appear to include just this assumption. This is not because Bayesians have been ignorant of the problem, but rather because it is much easier to raise the difficulty than to suggest a constructive treatment.

One positive suggestion put forward by Richard Jeffrey (1965, 1968) is to generalize Bayes' rule of conditioning. Suppose that an observational interaction falls short of making proposition p certain but makes it highly probable. Suppose also that the only effect on the observer's subjective probability space is through the effect on p; the probabilities conditional on p and on its negation remain constant. Then we have what Jeffrey called belief change by *probability kinematics* on the partition $[p, -p]$. Conditioning on p and on its negation are extreme cases. Jeffrey extended the notion to any partition all of whose members have positive probability, in the obvious way. We have belief change by probability kinematics on that partition just in case posterior probabilities conditional on members of the partition (where defined) remain unchanged.

Does the analysis of the last section extend to the case of probable knowledge? Paul Graves (1989) has recently shown that it does. Here is a sketch of Graves' analysis: Suppose that you can either choose now among n acts or perform a cost-free experiment whose result will be a belief change by probability kinematics on partition Γ. There may be no proposition in your language capturing just the phenomenological "feel" of the possible observational inputs, but are there entertainable propositions that capture the possible effects on your probability space of the observational interaction? Well, you could just describe the possible final probability measures that could come about. There is no reason you could not think about these possible outcomes now, expanding your probability space to allow final probability, p_f, to enter as a random variable.

You believe now that your observational interaction is a legitimate way of acquiring information, and so you have now

$$p(q|p_f = p^*) = p^*(q) \qquad \text{(M)}$$

You believe that your belief change will be accomplished by probability kinematics on partition Γ, so for any final probability, p^*, any proposition, q, which is of the "first order" (that is, does not involve p_f), and any member γ of Γ, you have

$$p^*(q|\gamma) = p(q|\gamma) \tag{PK}$$

from the definition of probability kinematics on Γ. By (M) this is equivalent to:

$$p(q|p_f = p^* \ \& \ \gamma) = p(q|\gamma) \tag{S}$$

Since we are sure that the belief change is by probability kinematics on Γ, it is sufficient to specify the possible final probabilities that we specify just the final probabilities of members of the partition as

$$\bigwedge_i p_f(\gamma_i) = \alpha_i$$

since only one final probability can meet this specification and come from the initial probability by probability kinematics on Γ. So (S) becomes

$$p(q|\textstyle\bigwedge_i p_f(\gamma_i) = \alpha_i \ \& \ \gamma) = p(q|\gamma) \tag{M'}$$

The foregoing is all done in terms of what your present probabilities are about the way that your final probabilities will be after the ineffable observational interaction, without speculation as to the nature of that interaction. Nevertheless, it implies that your probabilities are structured as if your experimental result consisted in learning $\bigwedge_i p_f(\gamma_i) = \alpha_i$ and conditioning on the result. Then Good's theorem goes through just as in the last section, with these sentences in place of the different possible experimental results e_k.

Ramsey's Anticipation

Good made no great claims of originality. He cited treatments of the value of evidence by Lindley (1965) and Raiffa and Schlaifer (1961) as partial anticipations. To this list one must surely add L. J. Savage, who discussed the value of observation and indeed proved a form of the Good theorem in chapter 7 (and appendix 2) of *The Foundations of Statis-*

tics (1954). It would not be surprising if one could trace the basic idea back a little further. But it is worth reporting that Frank Ramsey had it back in the 1920s.

In two manuscript pages on "Weight or the Value of Knowledge" (n.d., pp. 005-20-01 and 005-20-03), Ramsey sketched a version of the theorem. He described a rich setting where one's act consists in choosing the values of a list, x_1, x_2, . . ., of "control variables." He supposed that there is an unknown proposition, a, such that the expected utility of x_i considered as a function of x_i [for a fixed value of $p(a)$] is continuous and twice differentiable, and he assumed its maximum at a nonextreme value of x_i so that at the maximum $dEU(x_i|a)/dx_i = 0$ with the second derivative negative. This situation is illustrated in Figure 4.3. It is also assumed that different acts are optimal for $p(a) = 1$ and $p(a) = 0$.

In this context Ramsey considered a function, $\phi(p)$, which he called the "expectation of advantage in regard to a if I expect it with probability p." This is what we called "the expected utility of the prior Bayes act." He argued that the second derivative of this function must be everywhere positive; that is, that the function must be strictly convex. I reproduce as Figure 4.4 Ramsey's own illustration of the situation. It can be compared with the case of a finite number of acts shown in Figure 4.1.

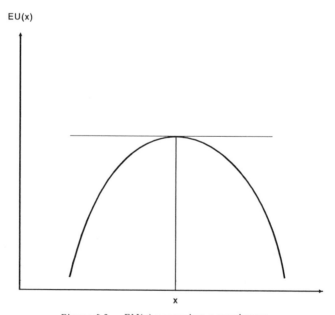

EU(x)

x

Figure 4.3.   EU(x) assuming a maximum

It follows immediately that the expected value of an experiment whose possible results are *a* and not-*a* is positive. If Ramsey had simply noted this, it would have been enough for the theorem. Instead, however, he did something much more interesting. He considered the case in which the experimental result was not the truth-value of *a* but the

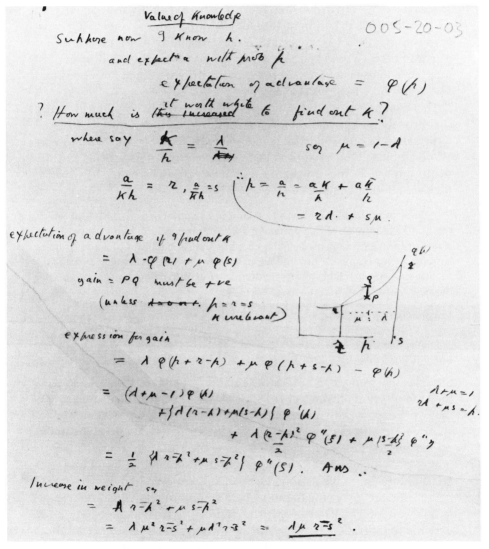

Figure 4.4. A page from Ramsey's manuscript

truth-value of another proposition, k, whose only effect on expected utility of the acts is in its alteration of the probability of the experiment. (In other words, the probability of a conditional on the experimental result considered as a random variable is a sufficient statistic for the experiment.) In Ramsey's illustration, r is the probability of a conditional on k (together with background knowledge) and s is the probability of a conditional on the denial of k. As Ramsey noted, it is evident (from the strict convexity of ϕ) that the gain in expected utility associated with undertaking the experiment (the length of the line segment PQ) must be positive unless k is irrelevant to the probability of a and $p = r = s$. This can be seen as a special case of the problem discussed in the last section, where belief was changed by probability kinematics on a and not-a with only two possible results.

This example is of special interest because we have other evidence that probability-kinematical ideas were not foreign to Ramsey. A partial anticipation of probability kinematics may be found in an 1851 paper by W. F. Donkin. Ramsey took a page of notes from this article, and the manuscript is in the University of Pittsburgh archives (n.d.). I quote Ramsey quoting Donkin:

> If there be any number of mutually exclusive hypotheses h_1, h_2, h_3—; of which the probabilities relative to a particular state of information are p_1, p_2, p_3—, and if new information is gained which changes the probabilities of some of them suppose of h_{m+1} and all that follow, *without having otherwise any reference to the rest*, then the probabilities of these latter have the *same ratios* to one another after the new information that they had *before*—

Emphasis is Ramsey's.

Dynamic Probability and Generalized Learning

Suppose that you are in a learning situation even more amorphous than the kind which motivates Jeffrey's ideas. There is no nontrivial partition that you expect with probability one to be sufficient for your belief change. Perhaps you are in a novel situation where you expect the unexpected observational input. Or, to bring the situation a little closer to home, perhaps there is to be no external observational input and you are in the realm of what Good (1983, chap. 10) called "dynamic probability." You are just going to think about some subject matter and update as a result of your thoughts. The role of "dynamic probability" in dynamic deliberation is of crucial importance for the sort of account explored in the preceding two chapters. How unstructured can the setting for belief change be while the Good theorem is retained? Here I will show that for a very general model of learning, the argument for the value of learning can be carried through. I will consider the learning situation a kind of "black box" and attempt no analysis of its internal structure. Nevertheless we must find some way to distinguish between the kind of situation we expect to be a learning situation and kinds we expect to be brainwashing, delusional, or otherwise epistemologically pathological. Fortunately we can do this in "behavioristic" terms. The key is condition (M).

Let us consider the mathematically simplest case, in which there are a finite number of states of nature and in which you believe now with probability one that your final probabilities will be one of a finite set, each member of which has some positive prior probability of being the one. You expect an upcoming change-of-belief situation to be a learning situation if your prior probabilities satisfy condition (M)—

$$p(K|p_f = p^*) = p^*(K) \tag{M}$$

—for each final probability and each state of nature, K.

The utility of electing the learning experience and then making a decision is

$$\Sigma_f p(p_f) \Sigma_i p(K|p_f) U(A_f^* \& K_i)$$

where A_f^* is the act performed if the final probability assignment is p_f. Under assumption (M), $p(K|p_f) = p_f(K)$. Assuming as well that you know that you will perform the posterior Bayes act, and that the states of nature are probabilistically independent of electing to undergo the learning experience, the utility of electing the learning experience is

$$\Sigma_f p(p_f) \max_k \Sigma_i p_f(K_i) U(A_k \& K_i)$$

which is the prior expectation of the posterior Bayes act. The value of acting now is

$$\max_k \Sigma_i p(K_i) U(A_k \& K_i) = \max_k \Sigma_f \Sigma_i p(K_i|p_f) p(p_f) U(A_k \& K_i)$$
$$= \max_k \Sigma_f \Sigma_i p(p_f) p_f(K_i) U(A_k \& K_i)$$

That is, the value of an act now is its prior expectation of posterior expected utility, and the value of the prior Bayes act is the maximum of those values. If we write $B(p)$ for the convex function representing the expected utility of the Bayes act on the basis of the probability assignment p,

$$B(p) = \max_k \Sigma_i p(K_i) U(A \,\&\, K_i)$$

and denote the prior expectation by E, then

$$U(\text{Act now}) = B[E(p_f)]$$

and

$$U(\text{Learn now, act later}) = E[B(p_f)]$$

That $U(\text{Learn now, act later}) \geq U(\text{Act now})$ is then an immediate consequence of the convexity of B by Jensen's inequality.

The forms of Good's theorem previously discussed are special cases. Here is Good thinking reduced to its bare essentials. Nothing at all about the nature of the event which is to occasion your belief change has been specified, excepting your belief in the epistemological legitimacy of the impending belief change as embodied in (M) and the probabilistic independence of the "black box learning experience" itself and the states of the world. Bayesians have found it difficult to say anything informative about belief revisions having so little structure, but in the presence of these minimal assumptions Good's theorem emerges intact.

Generalized Learning Generalized

One would like to generalize mathematically in two ways. In the first place, one would like to be able to consider the case where prior probability is not concentrated on a finite number of possible final probabilities but is perhaps continuously distributed over the space of all possible final probabilities over the space of states of nature. Second, one would like to be able to move from finite or countable spaces of states of nature to more general spaces. In this section I pursue both generalizations at once.

We assume that for our original decision problem, the space of states of the world, W, is Polish (metrizable as a complete separable metric space), and we form the measurable space $\langle W, X \rangle$ by letting X be the Borel σ-algebra for W. An act, A, will be taken to be a nonnegative bounded continuous real-valued random variable on the measurable space $\langle W,X \rangle$. Relative to a probability measure, P, on $\langle W,X \rangle$, the expected utility of the act is

$$EU[A,P] = \int_W A(w)dP$$

A set of acts, $\{A_i\}$, will be said to be *optimizable* relative to a probability, P, on $\langle W,X \rangle$ if (1) there is an upper bound to the expected utilities of all the acts in the set and (2) for every probability on $\langle W,X \rangle$ there is a member of $\{A_i\}$ with maximal expected utility. (We assume that in the case in which more than one act is maximal the decisionmaker can make an arbitrary choice.) Any finite set of acts is optimizable, but some infinite sets are not. (Descartes argued that God, in choosing which world to create, did not face a decision problem with an optimizable set of acts.) We assume an optimizable set of acts. Then the expected utility of the Bayes act exists and is

$$B[P] = \max_i EU[A_i,P]$$

Now our decisionmaker needs to think about the final probability of states of nature as a random variable. Let F be the set of all probability measures on $\langle W,X \rangle$. F may be very big, but it is nevertheless Polish in the weak* topology. Its Borel σ-algebra, V, is the smallest σ-algebra that makes the mappings $p_f \in F$ to $p_f(A)$ for arbitrary $p_f \in F$ and $A \in X$ measurable, so the natural higher-order measurable space is $\langle F,V \rangle$. We assume at the onset that the decisionmaker has a prior probability, P, on the product space $\langle W,X \rangle \times \langle F,V \rangle$.

A function, k, from $W \times F$ onto the reals is a Markov kernel of a regular conditional probability if: (1) for every $A \in X$, $k(\cdot,A)$ is a version of the random variable $P(A \| V)$ and (2) for any $p_f \in F$, $k(p_f,\cdot)$ is a probability measure on $\langle W,X \rangle$. Under our assumptions, such a Markov kernel exists and is unique up to a set of measure zero in P. (Indeed, the initial restriction to Polish state spaces was motivated to assure its existence.) The existence of the Markov kernel allows us to treat final probability measures as random variables and proceed essentially as before.

The generalized learning situation is again characterized by a form of condition (M) that equates final probability with conditional probability. Here it is the condition that there exists a Markov kernel such that $k(p_f,\cdot) = p_f(\cdot)$ for every $p_f \in F$. To state the same condition in a slightly different way, define the function $g(p_f,A) = p_f(A)$ for every $p_f \in F$ and every $A \in X$. Then by definition, g satisfies the second condition for the requisite Markov kernel. Condition (M) is then fulfilled if g satisfies the first condition: $p_f(A)$ with A fixed and p_f considered as a random variable is a version of $P(A \| V)$ for every $A \in X$.

For cost-free learning, the expected utility of Choose now is $B[P]$. Under condition (M), the expected utility of Learn now, choose later is $E[B(p_f)]$. Then, essentially as before, we can show that the expected utility of Choose now is less than or equal to the expected utility of Learn now, choose later:

> PROOF Let A^* be the Bayes act for P, the prior Bayes act. Let $S(p_f) = EU(A^*)$. For all values of p_f, $S(p_f) \leq B(p_f)$ and at $p_f = P$, $B(p_f) = B(P)$ by definitions of S and B. So:

> $B(P) = S(P)$ [by definition]

> $S(P) = S[E(p_f)]$ [by condition (M)]

> $S[E(p_f)] = E[S(p_f)]$ [S is a continuous affine functional]

> $E[S(p_f)] \leq E[B(p_f)]$ [since $S(p_f) \leq B(p_f)$ for all p_f]

Generalized Causal Decision Theory

I noted at the outset that Good's theorem is proved in the context of Savage-type expected utility theory, where states of the world together with acts jointly determine ultimate consequences. This is a kind of causal decision theory, in that the distinction between states, acts, and consequences is at bottom causal. Deterministic causal decision theory of the Savage type can be generalized to indeterministic causal decision theory,[6] where the state and act jointly determine probabilities of consequences: $p(C|K \& A)$. Then the expected utility of an act is defined by a double expectation:

$$U(A) = \Sigma_{ij} p(K_i) p(C_j | A \& K_i) U(C_j \& K_i \& A)$$

where $\{K_i\}$ is a partition of states interpreted as causal preconditions of the decision, $\{C_j\}$ is a partition of consequences, and A is the act.

What is the status of Good's theorem in this more general, indeterministic form of causal decision theory? The expected utility of A therein

$$\Sigma_{ij} p(K_i) p(C_j | A \& K_i) U(C_j \& A \& K_i)$$

can be thought of as an expansion of Savage's formula

$$\Sigma_i p(K_i) U(A \text{ \& } K_i)$$

wherein Savage's $U(A \text{ \& } K_i)$ is analyzed as

$$\Sigma_j p(C_j | A \text{ \& } K_i) U(C_j \text{ \& } A \text{ \& } K_i)$$

Accordingly, Good's analysis extends to this case provided that this quantity is independent on each experiment result. A sufficient condition for this is that we have both the following:

$$U(C_j \text{ \& } A \text{ \& } K_i \text{ \& } e_k) = U(C_j \text{ \& } A \text{ \& } K_i) \quad \text{for all } i, j, k \tag{1}$$

and

$$p(C_j | A \text{ \& } K_i \text{ \& } e_k) = p(C_j | A \text{ \& } K_i) \quad \text{for all } i, j, k \tag{2}$$

(1) is one precise way of saying in this context that information is really free. (2) may be thought of as saying that all the experimental results do is give information about the state of the world. They do not affect your belief about the conditional chance of a consequence of an act obtaining in a given state of the world. Given the intended interpretation where $\{K_i\}$ is a sufficient partition for conditional chance of consequence on act, and thus the state together with the act determine the chance of consequence, condition (2) will be fulfilled if the theory has been properly applied. [We also continue to assume as before that the performance of the experiment itself, E, which the experimental results, e_k, partition is probabilistically independent of the states.] Good's theorem then holds for the most general form of causal decision theory.

Deliberational Equilibrium Reconsidered

In causal decision theory the general validity of Good's theorem suggests that in the absence of substantial processing costs, one should assimilate whatever information is generated by the process of deliberation. Deliberation then becomes a dynamic process of moving toward the apparent optimal act under conditions of informational feedback. In such a decision process, a decisionmaker cannot choose a nonequilibrium act. As he gets close to choosing the act, informational feedback will make it appear less than maximally attractive and will point his deliberation in a different direction. In causal decision theory, a policy of selecting an equilibrium decision is almost a consequence of the expected utility principle.

Why almost? Well, in the first place there are real-world costs of computation that might be significant. But even if we idealize away these costs, there is a kind of fallacy of composition involved in assuming that one can justify a strategy of informational feedback by induction on the application of the Good theorem. Consider an artificial paradoxical situation in which there is always free information available, and the decision as to which act to perform could be postponed for any finite time. Under a strategy of always assimilating free information, the decision-maker would never act! When the strategy as a whole is evaluated against "Choose the prior Bayes act," we see that the conditions of the theorem are violated. There is no choice of a posterior Bayes act subsequent to the deliberational process.

A correct Bayesian treatment of deliberation must evaluate deliberational strategies as wholes. The question of optimum deliberational strategies for problems of the kind we have been discussing is a large and complex question, which I will not address in any detail here. A few qualitative points can, however, be made on the basis of the foregoing discussion.

Suppose that you are confronted with two opaque boxes, A and B, and you are to choose one and receive its contents. A mean demon, who you believe is a good predictor of your behavior conditional on either choice, has put money under the box she predicted you won't choose—let's say $1,000 if it is A and $1,100 if it is B, to make it interesting. Suppose you initially incline toward B, but when you are about to take B you recalculate and find that A is more appealing; but when you are about to take A you find B more appealing; and so on. You find your deliberations oscillating, converging toward indecision rather than decision. You are suffering from *Richter's complaint* (Richter, 1984). Richter's theory of the etiology of this problem was that there is something wrong with causal decision theory. Sharvy (1983) and Harper (1984) replied that you should consider mixed decisions, which do indeed include an equilibrium decision. Richter turned the screw: randomization costs something. In fact, let's say that the reason that this is a *mean* demon is that she will boil you in oil if she catches you using a nondegenerate mixed strategy.

In this case I would say that the cause of Richter's complaint is not a defect in causal decision theory but rather a misapplication of Good's theorem. The initial choice is not between "Decide now between A and B" and "Deliberate, generate free information, and then face essentially the same choice situation." Rather, if we take the story at face value, it is between the former and "Deliberate, choose A, B, or a mixed strategy, or fail to make any choice." If this is the only other sort of deliberational strategy open to you, and you assign any positive probability to deliberation getting you into the kind of trouble described, causal decision theory can recommend "Decide now between A and B," in accord with Richter's intuition.

The sort of pathology to which Richter called our attention is not simply the lack of an equilibrium decision, as is shown in the following example (Skyrms, 1984, p. 85):

You are to choose one of three shells $[A_1, A_2, A_3]$, and will receive what is under it. No mixed acts are allowed. (If you attempt to randomize, even mentally, the attempt will be detected and you will be shot.) A very good predictor has predicted your choice. If he predicted A_1 he put 10¢ under shell one and nothing under the others. If he predicted A_2, he put $10 under shell two and $100 under shell three. If he predicted A_3, he put $20 under shell three and $200 under shell two.

Suppose you start deliberation with a very small probability of choosing A_1 and equal probabilities of choosing A_2 or A_3. If you deliberate continuously, moving toward maximum expected utility with informational feedback, you will suffer from Richter's complaint, unable to decide between A_2 and A_3. Supposing that if you can't come to a decision you get nothing, the expected utility of choosing the prior Bayes act is higher than that of the deliberational strategy which cannot lead to a decision. From the standpoint of deliberational dynamics, Richter is dramatizing the question of convergence.

The example was designed to show something else as well. Suppose that you also have another deliberational strategy (Harper, 1984) under consideration: "Choose the equilibrium decision with highest prior expected utility." There is a unique equilibrium decision here, but the conditions for the Good theorem fail as before.

What can we say about the conditions under which the Good theorem will apply to a deliberational strategy? In the first place, the undertaking of dynamic deliberation should be independent of the states of nature. In game-theoretic situations, it should be neither a cause nor a symptom of the acts of other players. This calls for some care in application of models of dynamic deliberation.

In the second place, the process as a whole must be cost-free. If it is possible that the process does not lead to any decision, then there is an associated cost equal to the difference in payoff of the prior Bayes act and of no decision. For the process as a whole to be cost-free, the expected costs of not reaching a decision must be zero. (This may happen because a deliberational strategy has prior probability zero of leading to no decision, even though it may possibly lead to no decision.) Otherwise the costs of deliberation by that strategy must be balanced against its benefits. (One way of guaranteeing a decision is to adopt a strategy with a time limit, such that if no pure act has been selected by the time limit the mixed act corresponding to the decisionmaker's state of indecision about pure acts will be selected as a default.)

In the third place, the deliberational strategy as a whole must satisfy condition (M). Then, assuming the foregoing conditions, for any fixed act its initial expected utility must be equal to the initial expectation of its final expected utility. For deliberation to be nontrivial, one must be uncertain about where deliberation will lead. Since initial probability is the initial expectation of final probability, we have:

$$\text{If } p_i[p_f(p) = \alpha] = 1 \quad \text{then} \quad p_i(p) = \alpha$$

If you know where you're going, you're already there. Thus to the extent that deliberation generates information by computation, the results of computation must be initially uncertain.

Condition (M) can also give us some guidance regarding the internal structure of a deliberational strategy. Consider the deliberational strategy that computes expected utility; assigns probability one to the act with maximum expected utility (provided there is a unique one); revises probabilities of states of nature accordingly; and recomputes; and on and on. In the case of the mean demon hiding money under the two boxes, this strategy oscillates between assigning probability one to box *A* and probability one to box *B*. From the point of view of automatic control, some damping in the system would be desirable. Condition (M) provides a less *ad hoc* justification. Applying it now to stages of deliberation we have:

$$\text{If } p_i[p] = 1 \quad \text{then} \quad p_i[p_f(p) < 1] = 0$$

Or, by contraposition: If you think that you may change your mind, you're not certain. A strategy which expects informational feedback that may with some positive probability alter the Bayes act, and which proceeds stagewise in accordance with (M), will not leap immediately to the assignment of probability one to the prior Bayes act but will rather move some distance in the direction of attractive options. Condition (M) is thus the foundation and touchstone of the theory of Bayesian dynamic deliberation.

M Is for Martingale

The analysis of generalized Good thinking shows that condition (M) is of central importance. Fulfillment of condition (M) shows that a decisionmaker regards any impending belief change as a generalized learning experience. This applies even when the experience cannot be neatly summarized as being given a proposition in his probability space. Consider the example of Ulysses and the sirens. Prior to the encounter with the sirens, Ulysses has initial probabilities, p, about what his probabilities will be after hearing the siren song, p_f. The possible sensory inputs from the sirens cannot be easily summarized as propositions in his probability space. Ulysses believes that the sirens have the power and predilection to cloud men's minds so that they cease to believe that the rocks are dangerous (R). Condition (M) fails

$$p(R|p_f(R) < 0.1) > 0.1$$

and Ulysses believes that this sort of input can get him in deep trouble. Prudently, he makes arrangements (1) to prevent the input and (2) to prevent himself from acting effectively if (1) fails.

Can we say anything about the value of learning in the long run? Consider an infinite sequence of learning situations at times $t_1, t_2, \ldots$ and a corresponding sequence of probabilities[7] $p_1, p_2, \ldots$[8] that indicate respectively the upshot of these learning situations. The situations might, for instance, be observations of outcomes of flips of a coin in a trial with unknown bias and with updating by conditioning. Prior to the sequence, we suppose that you have a big probability space on which $p_1, p_2, \ldots$ are random variables. Suppose also that you have the appropriate version of condition (M) to assure the expectation principle:

$$E[p_{n+1} \| p_1, \ldots p_n] = p_n$$

(In our example, the random variable consisting of the expected value of the probability of heads after observing $n + 1$ tosses conditional on the probabilities after observing the first n tosses is identical to the probability after observing n tosses considered as a random variable.) Then the sequence of upcoming revised probabilities as random variables, p_1,

p_2, . . . forms a nonnegative martingale. With probability one, the sequence $p_1, p_2,$ . . . converges to a random variable p_{ff} with

$$E\ [p_{ff}]\ =\ E[p_1]\ =\ p$$

The random variable, p_{ff}, is final probability in the light of the whole learning sequence. In our example, p_{ff} is a reasonable facsimile of "the true chance that the coin comes up heads." The initial probability of heads, $p(H)$, is equal to your initial expectation of the "true chance of heads," $E[p_{ff}(H)]$. The example generalizes (Dynkin, 1978; Diaconis and Freedman, 1984). Almost everything we know about convergence to a limiting relative frequency—the strong law of large numbers, de Finetti's theorem, and generalizations of de Finetti's theorem for various versions of partial exchangeability—are special cases of this martingale convergence argument.

What can we say about the value of knowledge in the long run? Suppose that learning experiences were really free in terms of time and opportunity costs, so that one could undertake an infinite number of learning experiences in a finite time and then make a decision. By the martingale convergence theorem, the same argument used in the treatment of generalized learning for p_f applies here for p_{ff}, establishing in a general way the value of making a most informed decision.

5 Dynamic Coherence

Obviously, if p is the fact observed, my degree of
belief in q after the observation should be equal to my
degree of belief in p given q before, or by the
multiplication law to the quotient of my degree of
belief in p & q by my degree of belief in p. When my
degrees of belief change in this way we can say that
they have been changed consistently by my
observation.

—Frank Ramsey (1931)

Observation can only give us information capable of
influencing our opinion. The meaning of this
statement is very precise: it means that to the
probability of a fact conditioned on this
information . . . we can indeed attribute a different
value.

—Bruno de Finetti (1937)

The treatment of the expected utility of new information in the preceding chapter required certain principles governing the dynamics of belief change. In the classical form of the theorem, the requirement was that the decisionmaker update beliefs by conditioning on new information. We saw that the theorem remains valid under the more permissive requirement that the appropriate form of condition (M) hold. Is there a place for such dynamic conditions in the foundations of Bayesian methodology?

It is obvious from the epigraphs to this chapter that both Ramsey and de Finetti considered the principle of updating by conditioning a basic one.[1] It has, however, been vigorously maintained by Hacking (1967) and Kyburg (1978) that the principle is unsupportable. Kyburg (1978, pp. 176–177), for example, claimed that this was a grave deficiency in the theory of personal probability:

It might be maintained, and would be by anyone who regarded the theory of personal probability as providing insights into scientific inference, that its main function is dynamic: it is the changes in the probability function that are wrought by empirical evidence, through the mediation of Bayes' theorem (or a generalization thereof) that give the theory its philosophical importance . . . But the really serious problem is that there is nothing in the theory that says a person should *change* his degrees of belief in response to the evidence in accordance with Bayes' theorem. On the contrary the whole thrust of the subjectivistic theory is to claim that the history of an individual's beliefs is irrelevant to their rationality: all that counts at a given time is that they conform to the requirements of coherence.

Kyburg should not be understood to be overlooking the statements of de Finetti in a paper which he himself translated, but rather to be claiming that there is no appropriate dynamic coherence argument to back up the principle of belief change conditioning endorsed by de Finetti and Ramsey.

The same point of view had been put forth earlier by Hacking (1967, p. 315) in an essay examining Savage's system. Hacking called the rule of updating by conditioning on the evidence the "dynamic assumption of personalism" and argued that no dynamic coherence argument for this rule is possible:

A man knowing *e* would be incoherent if the rates offered on *h* unconditionally differed from his rates on *h* conditional on *e*. But no incoherence obtains when we shift from the point before *e* is known to the point after it is known . . . Since the man announces his post-*e* rates only after *e* is discovered, and simultaneously cancels his pre-*e* rates, there is no system of betting with him which is guaranteed success in the sense of a dutch book.

Since *consistency* is Ramsey's term for *coherence*, the epigraph strongly suggests that Ramsey held the opposite view. The same is true for de Finetti. Is there a dynamic coherence argument for updating by conditioning? Are there dynamic coherence arguments for the generalized learning situations considered in the last chapter? We will be able to find affirmative answers to both questions, and thus to both answer the skeptical doubts expressed by Kyburg and Hacking regarding conditioning and to extend the account of coherent updating to epistemological models more general than the conditioning model. But before proceeding to these topics, I would like to devote some space to a background discussion of the prior question of static coherence.

Pumping Gold

Ramsey (1931) noted that incoherence has a dramatic consequence—an incoherent bookie lays himself open to a "dutch book": "If anyone's condition violated these laws, his choice would depend on the precise form in which the option were offered him, which would be absurd. He could then have book made against him by a cunning bettor and would stand to lose in any event." Ramsey rightly treated the possibility of a dutch book as a symptom of deeper pathology. A bettor who violates the laws of the probability calculus leaves himself open to having book made against him because he will consider two different sets of odds as fair for an option, depending on how that option is described, with the equivalence of the descriptions following from the underlying Boolean logic.

The leading idea is simple enough. Suppose that a very rich and reliable bookie posts odds on a horse race. He values a contract which pays a pound of gold if Stewball wins at one ounce of gold. He values a contract which pays a pound of gold if Molly wins at one ounce of gold. He will buy or sell these contracts in any quantity at what he considers a fair price (his valuation) or better. Suppose that he also deals in disjunctive contracts which pay a pound of gold if either Stewball or Molly wins, and he values these at four ounces of gold. If you can buy separate contracts for Stewball and for Molly at a net outlay of two ounces of gold and sell back a disjunctive contract for four ounces of gold, leaving you at worst a net gain of two ounces of gold no matter which horse wins the race, you have made a dutch book against the bookie because his evaluation of the disjunctive contract does not cohere with his evaluation of the separate contracts on its disjuncts.

Coherence requires that if the bookie values the separate contracts at one ounce of gold each, he values the disjunctive contract—which pays off exactly as holding both separate contracts together would—at two ounces of gold. The disjunctive contract has two equivalent descriptions: (1) as a wager on the proposition that either Stewball or Molly wins, and (2) as two simultaneous wagers: one on the proposition that Stewball wins and one on the proposition that Molly wins. Coherence also requires that a contract which pays a pound of gold no matter what happens is worth a pound of gold, and that a contract that pays off a pound of gold in some circumstances and requires no payment otherwise has nonnegative value.

Coherent Expectations

De Finetti (1937, 1975) founded the theory of personal probability on the theory of coherent expectations. (We will pretend, for the moment, that utility is linear with respect to money.) Let A be a payoff function mapping each possible state of the world onto a real number which is the payoff associated with A in that state of the world. You may think of A as a gamble or as an act in the sense of Savage. A *prevision* or *expectation operator* evaluates such gambles. Formally, it is a functional which maps each A onto a real number $E(A)$, which the decisionmaker takes to be the fair price of the gamble or value of the act. In gambling terms, we assume that the decisionmaker prefers a payment of $E(A) + \varepsilon$ to A to a payment of $E(A) - \varepsilon$ for any positive epsilon and that the decisionmaker is indifferent between A and a sure payment of $E(A)$.

A prevision is incoherent if it is susceptible to a dutch book in the following sense. There are constants $c_1 \ldots c_n$ and random variables $A_1 \ldots A_n$ such that $\Sigma_i c_i \cdot [A_i - E(A_i)]$ is uniformly negative. That is, the least upper bound taken over possible states of the world is negative. One can think of $E(A)$ as the fair price that one pays for the unit gamble; A as the payoff; and c as the stakes. (Note that since there are only a finite number of gambles, A_i, involved and since the net payoff is bounded away from zero, the clever bettor can afford to offer each gamble at a better than fair price and still guarantee that the decisionmaker sustains a sure loss.) A prevision is coherent if it is not incoherent in this sense.

De Finetti showed that it is necessary and sufficient for coherence that (1) prevision is additive: $E(A_1 + A_2) = E(A_1) + E(A_2)$; and (2) greatest lower bound $A \leq E(A) \leq$ least upper bound A. It follows that coherent prevision is a linear functional.

The probability of an event (a set of states of the world) is then identified with its characteristic payoff function: the wager that pays off one at states of the world in the event and zero otherwise. Then a coherent prevision must give a finitely additive probability with probability of the null event being zero and probability of the sure event being one.

Utility

As we know, utility is not always linear with respect to money. This fact did not escape de Finetti or Ramsey. Ramsey proceeded from the dutch book to a deeper analysis in which this assumption is dispensed with and both finitely additive probabilities and utilities are extracted from coherent preferences over a rich system of gambles. To the 1964 translation of his 1937 article, "La Prevision," de Finetti added a new footnote: "I did not know of Ramsey's work before 1937, but I was aware of the difficulty of money bets. I preferred to get around it by considering sufficiently small stakes, rather than build up a complex theory to deal with it. I do not remember whether I failed to mention this limitation to small amounts inadvertently, or for some reason" (Kyburg and Smokler, 1980, p. 72). And in *Theory of Probability* de Finetti explicitly had recourse to the theory of utility to make good the mathematical assumptions of the dutch book argument (1975, pp. 74–80).

Prevision and Measure

The foregoing still leaves open an important measure-theoretic question. Is probability to be countably as well as finitely additive? Different approaches can be taken here. One can strengthen the notion of coherence by allowing the cunning bettor a countable number of bets and thus obtain countable additivity as a necessary condition for coherence. (See Adams, 1962; Heath and Sudderth, 1978, th. 6.) This passes on a greater debt on utility theory, which can be paid if utility theory imposes a continuity condition on preferences (see Villegas, 1964). But to some— including most definitely de Finetti—this line of thought appears to beg important questions.

In general, the restriction to finite additivity severs probability theory from the mathematical foundation in measure theory initiated by Kolmogorov and most probability theorists have been loath to follow de Finetti down this road. De Finetti stressed the conflicts between his approach and the standard measure-theoretic treatment, but it is also important to notice that there are substantial domains within which the two approaches are compatible. Under the right topological conditions—if we are interested in *nice* acts, A_i, on a *nice* space of states of nature—it turns out that previsions coherent in the sense of de Finetti mesh together perfectly with classical measure-theoretic foundations of probability.

What is *nice*? The generic answer is: A set of conditions under which you can prove an appropriate version of the Riesz representation theorem. Under such conditions you can regard de Finetti's prevision as a classical expectation operator arising from integration with respect to an underlying countably additive measure.

For example, suppose that the state space is a closed bounded subset of n-dimensional Euclidian space (as it would be if the relevant state consisted in an assignment of probabilities to acts of other players in finite games), and suppose that the acts are continuous random variables on this space. The space is a compact Hausdorff space, so by a version of the Riesz representation theorem (see Royden, 1968, p. 310) each bounded linear functional on the space of continuous real-valued functions corresponds to a unique underlying Baire measure. Since the space is also a metric space, this is also a Borel measure: a measure defined on the smallest σ-algebra containing the closed sets. The bounded linear functionals (the previsions) can be gotten by integration with respect to the underlying measure.[2]

The foregoing observation certainly does not answer all the philosophical questions that de Finetti raised with respect to countable additivity, but it does show that even in the context of a strict de Finetti version of coherence a subjective Bayesian has considerable territory within which classical countably additive measure theory can be applied in good conscience.

Coherent Preferences and Upper and Lower Probabilities

Suppose that a decisionmaker's preferences admit a probability-utility representation but are not defined over a set of acts rich enough to make that representation unique. Then the decisionmaker's preferences correspond to a set of probability-utility pairs such that for all acts for which her preferences are defined, preference goes by expected utility. Given a utility scale for ultimate consequences,[3] the indeterminacy is restricted to the subjective probabilities. Her belief state corresponds to a convex set of probability measures. (See Good, 1950; Smith, 1961; Dempster, 1968; Levi, 1974.)

Looking at things in opposite order, we can see that such an incomplete belief state may be perfectly adequate. The vast set of Savage acts will include only a few members which are actual options for our decisionmaker—that is, payoff functions that she can actualize by her decision. Well-defined preferences over her actual options are all she needs for decision. If for all probabilities in her convex set, expected utility (A) is greater than (equal to) expected utility (B), then she unambiguously prefers A to B (is indifferent between A and B). If her unambiguous preferences order her options, they are adequate for decision.

What if they don't? Suppose that the decisionmaker has a utility scale for ultimate consequences and a convex set of probability measures over states of the world. Suppose that the decisionmaker has a choice to make and that expected utilities figured with respect to different probability measures in her belief set disagree about what she should do. Is there anything intelligent to be said here except that she doesn't have unambiguous preferences over the relevant options and needs to acquire them?

Let us return to the special situation of the bookie and suppose—as is natural here—that the bookie can simply refuse to take either end of the proffered wager. She might buy bets on Stewball to win at 2-to-1 odds or better and sell at even money but refuse transactions at intermediate odds. Opting out gives a payoff of zero. In this sort of situation C. A. B. Smith was able to establish—at least in the finite case—that betting as if one had a convex set of probability measures, bounded by upper and lower probabilities, calculated expected utility according to each, and accepted a wager just in case it has positive expected value according to each, is sufficient for avoiding a dutch book in his sense. (See Smith, 1961, for details.)

As the decisionmaker's degrees of belief become more and more diffuse—as the convex set gets bigger—coherence is achieved at the expense of more and more opting out. In the degenerate case where the convex set includes all possible probabilities, coherence is achieved by the simple expedient of not betting, except on tautologies. This kind of coherence does not exactly come free. Opting out may have an opportunity cost. But is there any sensible way to think about the opportunity cost in the absence of the relevant probabilities of states of nature?

There is in the special case in which the opportunity cost is invariant over the states of nature. Suppose that Mr. U-L has probabilities between ¼ and ¾ that Stewball will win the race. Suppose that he is offered simultaneously these wagers: (1) $2 if Stewball wins, −$1 if Stewball loses; (2) $2 if Stewball loses, −$1 if he wins. Mr. U-L will decline both bets, assuring a nice safe payoff of $0. But if he had accepted both bets, he would have had a sure gain of $1. He has declined to make a dutch book against the bettor (or bettors)!

This aspect of the dutch book has been analyzed by Robert Buehler (1976). Mr. U-L prefers opting out to bet 1 and opting out to bet 2. If he reversed both preferences, he would be better off in each state of the world. Buehler calls a set of preferences "preference reversal (PR) incoherent" if there is some subset such that simultaneous reversal of that subset guarantees a higher payoff in each state of the world. Buehler shows that PR-coherent preferences are those which would arise if the ordering went by expected utility calculated according to some exact probability. The theory of upper and lower probabilities promises a more realistic modeling of decisionmakers and a generalization of Bayesian inference, but it is not without its own interpretational problems. These emerge when one asks what a decisionmaker should do when the probabilities in his convex set do not lead to the same recommendation. There are a number of possible answers to this question:

1. Can't say (Skyrms, 1984).
2. Choose according to some definite probability in that set (Good, 1950).

3. Opt out (Smith, 1961).
4. Anything goes.
5. Use maximin to decide (Wald, 1950; Levi, 1987).

Answer 5 leads to a decision theory that is incoherent in the sense of de Finetti, and answer 4 opens the door to incoherence. According to this view, a decisionmaker with degenerate [0,1] intervals would presumably be perfectly rational in making the transactions described at the beginning of this chapter that led to a dutch book. Answer 3 is Smith-coherent, but preference reversal incoherent in the special bookie situation. But what does "opting out" mean, if answer 3 is promoted to a general theory of rational decision?[4] Answer 2 is safe and is supported by the results of Buehler, but how do you do it? The theory doesn't say. The first answer is the most conservative position. If you don't have the preferences you don't have them, although you might like to narrow down your set of probability measures in such a way as to get them.[5]

My argument here does not mean that we should not develop models using upper and lower probabilities, but it does suggest that some care is called for in their interpretation. From the standpoint of those who favor answers 1 and 2 and to a large extent those who favor 3, the theory of exact probabilities is the touchstone for the correct treatment of upper and lower probabilities.

Dynamic Coherence

The foregoing gives some indication of the kind of static coherence results that are available. Can one find notions of dynamic coherence which give us consistency conditions for learning in the way that static coherence gives us pragmatic consistency conditions for degrees of belief at a given time? It appears that Ramsey and de Finetti thought that there is a unique, consistent way to update degrees of belief—that is, updating by Bayes' rule of conditioning:

$$p_2(Q) = p_1(Q|E)$$

where E is the evidence or data serving as the basis for the belief change. Why should they have thought that there was such a justification for Bayes' rule?

De Finetti established a coherence result for conditional probabilities which is not irrelevant. He considered conditional bets: bets which are called off if a condition is not fulfilled. The conditional probability of Q

on condition P can be defined in analogy with the unconditional case as the fair price of a characteristic bet with the modification that the price is returned if the condition, P, is false. In other words, I pay not in dollars but in units which are contracts to pay \$1 if P, nothing otherwise. We know already from earlier sections the rules of coherent currency conversion: one such contract is worth $p(P)$. Assuming that $p(P) > 0$, an unconditional price of \$$X$ is converted to \$$X/p(P)$ in conditional currency. Now the conditional probability of Q on condition P is defined as the fair price in conditional currency of a contract that pays \$1 if Q, nothing otherwise, and which is canceled if P is false. To find out the value of the conditional probability, all we need is the fair price for this contract in dollars, to which we will apply the rule of coherent currency conversion. But the contract just described has a simpler equivalent description: \$1 if $P \& Q$, nothing otherwise. The fair price of this contract is $p(P \& Q)$. Applying the currency conversion factor, $1/p(P)$, we get the familiar law:

$$p(Q|P) = \frac{p(P \& Q)}{p(P)}$$

It seems clear that, with this in hand, de Finetti thought he *had* a coherence argument for updating by conditioning. The discussion of called-off bets wears a temporal interpretation on its face. When E is observed, a reevaluation of bets conditional on E and on its denial will take place. It is almost analytic that in this reevaluation bets conditional on not-E are given a new value of \$0 since it is part of their definition that they are called off if E is not true. If the news is broadcast that E is true and the bookie then evaluates bets conditional on E at a value different from zero, it is obvious how one can then—after the news has come in—make a dutch book against him. And it is natural to assume that in this reevaluation, bets conditional on E that initially were judged fair will still be judged fair, and in general that the initial fair price in currency conditional on E will become the updated fair price in unconditional currency. If so, we have updating by conditioning.

But, the critics object, we are not entitled to make the natural assumption. This is what is to be established. Suppose that upon hearing the news that E, the bookie adopts new probabilities which make $p($not-$E)$ equal to zero but change the probabilities conditional on E in some unforeseen and totally wacky way. Can you exploit this behavior? It's too late. The old betting rates are gone and the new ones are in place. The wacky behavior was unforeseen, so there was no way to exploit it when the old betting rates were in place. This is, I believe, the way that Hacking and Kyburg see the epistemic situation. They conclude that de Finetti's result has a purely synchronic significance, that it speaks only to the coherence of conditional and unconditional bets made at the same time.

The problem of updating can, in various ways, be given more structure than we find in the foregoing picture. And with more structure, real dynamic coherence arguments are possible. One way of putting structure on the problem is to discuss the coherence of updating *rules*.

Bayes' Rule

Let us consider a model situation which Bayes' rule fits exactly. At time t_1, the bookie has a fixed prior probability assignment, p_1, over a probability space, and there is a finite partition $\{e_i\}$ of that space such that each member of the partition has positive prior probability. At time t_2 the true member of the partition is announced, and the bookie moves to a new probability, p_2, by a rule which treats the announced member of the partition as total input. More precisely, such a rule is a function, R, which maps members of the partition to posterior probability assignments. (Requiring final probability to be a function of members of the partition is a precise way of saying that to all intents and purposes the bookie learned nothing more than the true member of the partition. The bookie's strategy consists of the pair, $\langle p_1, R \rangle$.

We allow the cunning bettor to place a finite number of bets with the bookie at both times. He must make bets that the bookie considers fair or favorable at the time that they are made. He is allowed to know the bookie's probabilities at the times of the bets and is allowed to know the bookie's strategy. A bettor's strategy consists of a pair of functions $\langle f_1, f_2 \rangle$, where f_1 maps the pair consisting of the bookie's $\langle p_1, R \rangle$ onto a finite set of bets which for the bookie have nonnegative expected utility at t_1 and f_2 maps triples $\langle p_1, R, e_i \rangle$ onto finite sets of bets which for the bookie have nonnegative utility at t_2 if $p_2 = R(e_i)$. A bettor's strategy makes a dynamic dutch book against the bookie if there is a positive ε such that the bookie's winnings are at least ε in each state of the world. The bookie's strategy is dynamically coherent if there is no bettor's strategy which makes a dynamic dutch book against it.

With this much structure, we can get the coherence result that Ramsey and de Finetti envision:

(I) A bookie's strategy, $\langle p_1, R \rangle$, is dynamically coherent if and only if R is Bayes' rule. [Lewis]

The argument is the same sort of consistency argument used in the case of static coherence. In the presence of an epistemic rule R, the bettor has an additional way in which she can make a bet conditional on e. She can simply wait and bet at t_2 if e is the member of the partition announced, and not bet otherwise. The bookie's fair betting quotients for this sort of conditional bet are set by his rule R; they are set, that is, by the posterior probability onto which R maps e. If these are different from the fair betting quotients for conditional bets set by the bookie's prior probabilities, then the cunning bettor can exploit the difference to make a dutch book. Conversely, if the bookie's rule is Bayes' rule, then any payoff that the cunning bettor can achieve by betting at t_1 and t_2 could have been achieved by betting only at t_1 using conditional bets. Given these observations, de Finetti's (1937) result takes us the rest of the way.

The dutch book theorem I have described is essentially that of Lewis as reported by Teller (1973). Related dynamic coherence results for updating rules, in a slightly different setting, may be found in Cornfield (1969) and Freedman and Purves (1969). In each of these arguments, it is the updating *rule* which provides the link between the initial probability, the new evidence, and the final probability—and thus provides the structure which makes a dynamic coherence argument possible. Nothing quite this explicit appears in Ramsey or de Finetti, but this is a natural way in which to interpret their claims for conditioning.

The coherence argument for updating by conditioning can be carried through in more general settings. For instance, Lane and Sudderth (1985) considered the following situation: x and y are random quantities taking values in X and Y, to be observed in sequence. At time t_1 the bookie posts his fair price for characteristic bets on subsets of the product space according to function P and discloses his updating rule, $q(x)$, which gives updated fair prices for characteristic bets on subsets of Y upon observing a given value of X. Then a value of X is observed, and at t_2 the bookie accepts bets at the updated fair prices. The bettor is allowed at t_1 a finite number of bets on subsets of the product space and at t_2 a finite number of bets on subsets of Y. The definition of coherence is the same as before. They show:

> (II) The pair (P,q) is coherent if and only if P is a finitely additive probability measure and for every set, A, in the product space:
>
> $$P(A) = \int q(x) \{y: (x,y) \in A\} P_0(dx)$$
>
> where P_0 is the marginal of P on X.   [Lane and Sudderth]

In other words, P admits a disintegration into the marginal P_0 and a conditional probability distribution, q, for y given x. In this rather general sense, coherence requires updating by conditional probability. A number of related results which may be viewed as variations on this theme are to be found in Lane and Sudderth (1984).

Bayes' Method

Standard statistical contexts which involve conditioning may exhibit more structure. There is a set, θ, of states of the world and a set, X, of possible observations. States of nature are taken to determine chance probabilities, CH, for subsets of X, according to some mapping from X to the set of probability measures for subsets of X. On a minimal interpretation, states of the world are just chance hypotheses. The Bayesian starts with a prior (degree-of-belief) probability, DB, over θ. His prior degree of belief over X is the marginal determined by

$$ DB(B) = \int CH_\theta(B) DB(d\theta) $$

Upon observing a member of X, he updates by Bayes' rule using Bayes' theorem. This is Bayes' method. If a bookie is willing to post odds on all relevant sets before and after the observation, then the coherence arguments already rehearsed support Bayes' method.

Non-Bayesians may balk at using a degree-of-belief probability, or even at betting at all, prior to the observation, although they have no objections to chance hypotheses. Freedman and Purves (1969) considered a game with a bookie, a gambler, and a master of ceremonies. The master of ceremonies selects a state w in θ and then selects an observation x in X at random according to CH_w. The master of ceremonies reveals this observation to the bookie and the gambler, at which time the bookie posts odds on all subsets of θ and the gambler places a finite number of bets. Finally, the master of ceremonies reveals the true state, w, and the bookie and gambler settle up.

The bookie is assumed to have an inferential method: a conditional odds function which for each possible observation, x, determines odds to be posted on subsets of θ. A bettor's strategy maps observations, x, onto stakes at which to bet on subsets of θ. Thus the bookie's method together with the bettor's strategy determine for each state of the world a chance expectation of payoff. A bettor's strategy makes a *dutch book in chance* against the bookie's method if and only if the bookie's chance expectation of payoff is negative and bounded away from zero over states of the world. Let us say that the bookie's method is *chance coherent* if no bettor's strategy makes a dutch book in chance against it.

For the case where θ and X are finite and the bookie posts odds on all subsets of θ, Freedman and Purves (1969) showed that the bookie's inferential method is chance coherent if and only if it coincides with Bayes' method applied to some finitely additive prior defined over all subsets of θ. If the non-Bayesian wishes to be chance coherent his updating rule should be embeddable in a Bayesian framework.

Heath and Sudderth (1978) extended the analysis of Freedman and Purves to infinite sets, with essentially the same results. Under special topological conditions stronger results can be had. Lane and Sudderth (1983) considered the case where θ and X are separable metric spaces, the chance function and the bookie's updating function are both countably additive and weakly continuous, and either θ or X is compact. In this setting they showed that coherent inferential methods for the bookie coincide with the application of Bayes' method to a (proper) countably additive prior.

The epistemological models discussed in this and the previous section can be combined. There are states of the world determining chances, θ, and two observations in X and in Y. The gambler may be allowed to bet in different ways. A number of situations of this type were investigated by Lane and Sudderth (1984). This paper contains an explicit discussion of the role of time in the results and of the fact that it is the bookie's inferential method that is being judged coherent or incoherent.

Probability Kinematics

The model in which Bayes' rule was directly applicable assumed a nice meshing of (1) a well-defined prior and (2) neatly packaged experimental results. In the previous section I discussed weakening (1), and in this section and the next I will discuss weakening (2). The ideal story we sometimes tell about (2) is that an experiment is about to be performed, or an observation to be made, such that (a) the possible results form a finite partition of the space and (b) the act of observation tells the experimenter with certainty the true member of the partition. Jeffrey's probability kinematics is designed for the situation in which (a) holds but (b) doesn't.

Suppose that we have an initial probability, p_1, and a finite partition, $\{e_i\}$, such that each of its members has finite probability. We say, following Jeffrey (1965), that a probability, p_2, comes from p_1 by probability kinematics on $\{e_i\}$ if and only if in p_2 the probabilities conditional on members of the partition (where defined) are unchanged. Then, by definition, $\{e_i\}$ is a sufficient partition for the set of probabilities that can come from p_1 by probability kinematics on it. That set of possible final probabilities is a convex set whose extreme points are the probabilities which come from p_1 by conditioning on members of the partition.

Jeffrey's motivation was the reconciliation of Bayesian methodology with skeptical epistemology. How can one sensibly treat an uncertain observation—that is, an "observation" from which no proposition in the agent's language is learned for certain in the observational experience? Jeffrey's idea was that the learning situation might have enough structure so that one might know that what was learned was about a partition. For example, an observer seeing a jelly bean by candlelight may learn its color but not its flavor given color, or a physician may learn from an examination a partition of possible diagnoses but not a prognosis given a diagnosis.

In seeking a coherence argument for probability kinematics, we must find a precise way of saying that the bookie's strategy was only a decision about the partition, just as in the case of Bayes' rule we had to find a precise way to say that the proposition to be conditioned on is treated as the sum total of what the bookie learned. In the case of Bayes' rule the requisite modeling consists of making the final probability a function of the experimental result. Something more delicate is required for probability kinematics.

One approach is to introduce a third reference point at which the true member of the partition is observed with certainty (Skyrms, 1987e). Suppose that the bookie is shown a jelly bean under dim light and on the basis of this observation she must revise her probabilities on the finite space whose points are color-flavor pairs. Subsequently, she is told by the gamemaster the true color of the bean. She must post odds on the color-flavor space at three times: t_1, prior to any observation; t_2, after the uncertain observation; t_3 after the true color is announced. A gambler who knows the bookie's method can make a finite number of bets at any time for whatever stakes he chooses. In the end the gamemaster announces the flavor of the bean and all bets are settled.

What is the bookie's strategy? It is not a function, but rather a relation: a set of quadruples $\langle p_1, p_2, C, p_3 \rangle$, where C is the color announced. All members in the set have the same p_1, which gives each atom in the space positive probability. Each p_2 represents the probabilities that are allowed as upshots of the ineffable observational interaction. Since it is an uncertain observation, we do require that each observation give each atom positive probability. How do we specify that the interaction carries information only about the color; that, for instance, the bookie doesn't cheat and taste the bean? We require that her strategy be such that p_3 not depend on p_2, the thought being that the gamemaster's announcement of the true color should swamp out the effect of any uncertain information about color gotten from the uncertain observation. So we require that if two quadruples in the bookie's strategy agree on C, they agree on p_3; p_3 is a function of C. This is the qualitative sufficiency condition which identifies the partition of colors as the appropriate partition.

The leading idea for a coherence argument for probability kinematics is that then one can apply the arguments for Bayes' rule to show that p_3 should come from p_2 by conditioning on the announced color and p_3 should come from p_1 by conditioning on the announced color. But if probabilities conditional on members of the partition are equal for p_3 and p_1 and for p_2 and p_3 then they must be equal between p_1 and p_2, so the strategy must be one of belief change by probability kinematics on the partition of colors. One way of stating the conclusion is that if the bookie does not have a strategy which proceeds by probability kinematics in the partition of colors almost everywhere (in p_1) she is subject to a dutch book. This way of stating the dutch book for probability kinematics requires that the bookie have higher-order initial probabilities about the possible p_2's on the color-flavor space that may eventuate from uncertain observation. If one wants to avoid assuming the existence of these higher-order probabilities, then a stronger notion of coherence—that of a "bulletproof strategy"—can be formulated, such that coherence requires belief change by probability kinematics on the relevant partition. (See Skyrms, 1987c, for details.) The introduction of higher-order probabilities of the kind just mentioned carries with it further requirements for coherence, and it allows a slightly different approach to probability kinematics.

Black-Box Learning and Higher-Order Probabilities

Suppose that the bookie at t_1 has probabilities over some finite space, W, and anticipates an observational experience such that she cannot describe the possible observational results, or even specify a sufficient partition à la Jeffrey for the experiment. But she can think about how her probabilities at t_2 may have been modified by the observation, and we will suppose that at t_1 she also has prior probabilities over the possible posteriors that she may have at t_2—in other words, over the space of all probabilities on W. A gambler is allowed to make a finite number of bets at each time. Here the two times are linked not by a rule or method for updating, but rather by the *temporal reference* of the higher-order probabilities.

Arguments have recently been given by Goldstein (1983) and van Fraassen (1984) that in this situation coherence requires that the bookie's higher-order probabilities obey a version of principle (M). To take the simplest case, suppose that the bookie's higher-order probabilities are concentrated on a finite number of possible p_2's. Then, as van Fraassen pointed out, unless the bookie's prior higher-order probabilities satisfy $p_1[Q|p_2(Q) = b] = b$ for every Q contained in W and every b with positive prior probability of $p_2(Q) = b$, she is subject to a dutch book. Equivalently, we have as our coherence condition the form of condition (M) given in Chapter 4,

$$p_1(w|p_f = p^*) = p^*(w) \quad \text{[for each } w \in W]\tag{M}$$

The idea is straightforward. The gambler can make a bet on Q conditional on $p_2(Q) = b$ in two ways. He can make the conditional bet at t_1 in the standard way, or he can wait until t_2 and bet just in case $p_2(Q) = b$. If (M) is violated, these two ways carry different rates—and this fact can be exploited by the bettor. Thus the bettor can assure himself a sure win if $p_2(Q) = b$ and with no loss otherwise. Since $p_1[p_2(Q) = b] > 0$, this strategy can be transformed into a strategy which guarantees an unconditional sure win by a suitable small side bet against $[p_2(Q) = b]$. Thus, even in the epistemic situation with the least structure, dynamic coherence gives us the key condition for the generalizations of Good's theorem developed in Chapter 4.

Goldstein (1983) showed that essentially the same argument works when p_2 is not concentrated on a finite number of points to show that coherence requires:

$$p_1[Q|p_2(Q) \in I] \in I\tag{M'}$$

for every Q and every closed interval, I, such that $p_1[p_2(Q) \in I] > 0$. Some further generalizations are discussed in Gaifman (1988) and in the preceding chapter of this book.

In one sense this argument extends the theory of coherent belief change far beyond the bounds of classical Bayesian theory, but in another sense it does not. Where we have principle (M), belief change is formally consistent with a conditioning model; that is, the model in which we condition in the prior higher-order probability space on a specification of the final probability, $p_2 = p^*$. It is not that we think of final probabilities as *data* which we take into account to find out that they are indeed the final probabilities. It is just that the final probabilities *are* conditional probabilities in the prior higher-order space.

This means that if the bookie satisfies condition (M), any payoff the gambler could achieve by waiting until t_2 and betting at that time if a certain final probability pops up can just as well be achieved by making a bet at t_1 conditional on that being the final probability. So if the bookie in our model situation is statically coherent at t_1 and t_2 and satisfies condition (M), she is dynamically coherent. Once more, we are brought back to the theme that dynamic coherence is embeddability in a conditioning model.

Rules and Reference

Lewis (in Teller, 1973) and Freedman and Purves (1969) linked different times by considering the coherence of a rule or strategy. In the arguments of van Fraassen and Goldstein, the reference of higher-order probabilities does the job. Let us reexamine the question of belief change by probability kinematics from this point of view. We will begin with a variant of the dutch book theorem developed by Armendt (1980). Suppose at t_1 the bookie has degrees of belief over a finite color-flavor space, W, and has degrees of belief about what her degrees of belief will be at t_2 after a learning experience over W. In fact we suppose that at t_1 she has degrees of belief over the product space of W with the space of all probability measures over W. For simplicity, assume again that prior probability is concentrated on a finite number of possible p_2's and that each color has positive prior probability. We dispense with t_3.

We will say that the bookie's prior probability treats the partition of colors as sufficient if the following conditions hold.

> SUFFICIENCY 1 $p_1[Q|C \ \& \ \wedge_i p_2(C_i) = \alpha_i] = p_1[Q|C]$, for every C, every proposition $\wedge_i p_2(C_i) = \alpha_i$ with positive prior probability, and every Q a subset of W.

> SUFFICIENCY 2 Except for a set of p_1 zero, if two p_2's agree on the probabilities they assign to the partition of colors, they are identical.

The idea is that if the bookie learns only about color, then the new probabilities over the color partition should determine the new probabilities over the whole space and, as before, information as to the true color should swamp out the effects of partial information about the color.

Now suppose that for some possible p_2, Q, and C, $p_2[Q|C]$ is unequal to $p_1[Q|C]$. If p_2 were to eventuate, a gambler could make a profit by making a bet on Q conditional on C (for positive or negative stakes depending on the direction of the inequality) at t_1 and selling the bet back at a profit at t_2. In the presence of the sufficiency condition, the bet at t_1 can be made also conditional on the deviant p_2 appearing at t_2. If the deviant p_2 appears at t_2, the gambler proceeds to make his sure profit; if not the initial bet is canceled. If the deviant p_2 has positive prior probability, then a suitable side bet will transform the foregoing into an unconditional dutch book. (The gambler has taken advantage of the free bet against the set of measure zero referred to in Sufficiency 2.)

Notice that all reference to the bookie's method, rule, or strategy has now vanished and conditions on them have been replaced with conditions on the bookie's higher-order degrees of belief. *Rules have been traded for reference.*

This idea can be pressed. Suppose together with the foregoing that the bookie's prior is concentrated on the set of p_2's that give some C or other probability one. Then the bookie is open to an unconditional dynamic dutch book unless she moves from p_1 to p_2 by conditioning on some C. Finally, suppose that at t_2 the gamemaster announces the true color, as in the Lewis setup. Then if the bookie conditions on the wrong color at t_2, the gambler can insure a win simply by betting on the right one. So the bookie is safe from a dynamic dutch book only if she conditions on the color announced by the gamemaster. This is the Lewis result done without rules.

> MORAL Dynamic coherence is not a trivial result of being against method, providing that those who forego rules may still have beliefs.

Coherence and Deliberation

The theory of dynamic coherence is not a vacuum, but rather a field with a substantial number of fundamental results. In the classical case where priors exist and evidence comes nicely packaged so that updating by conditioning is well defined, there are straightforward coherence arguments for Bayes' rule. This model can be relaxed: the prior might not be well defined, or the learning situation might not have the structure assumed in the classical model. In both cases, there are a number of results with a common theme: coherence is embeddability in a classical Bayesian model.

It is of particular interest for the theory of deliberational dynamics that the principle of coherence in the black-box learning situation is the martingale principle, (M). It is this principle which is crucial for the most general form of the theorem that provides a justification for the feedback of pure cost-free information and dictates some of the most general qualitative features of dynamic deliberation.

The question of how learning should be modeled in dynamic deliberation is a delicate question, because it is computation, not perception, that generates the new information. This is the realm of what I. J. Good (1950, 1983) called "dynamic probability." The evidence could be modeled as data for conditioning in a very big space, but this does not square well with the emphasis of the approach on real-time computation and procedural rationality. It is possible—on the basis of such considerations—to doubt whether any sort of Bayesian approach to these situations is possible. Such worries should be eased by the coherence results for quite general black-box learning models. The qualitative features of generalized coherent updating can serve as a touchstone for dynamic deliberation, without imposing unrealistic excess structure on the model.

6 Good Habits

The knowledge of the psychology of the adversary
must at each instance be taken into account to modify
the rules of conduct that are adopted.

—Emil Borel (1924)

The rationality of economics is substantive rationality
while the rationality of psychology is procedural
rationality.

—Herbert Simon (1986)

We are creatures of habit for good reason. Whereas thought costs something, acting out of habit can be economical. A good habit is one which can be expected to save more in costs of reasoning than it is expected to lose by foregoing an extensive analysis of the decisions involved. In a sense, the notion of a good habit has already been introduced, in the discussion of bounded Bayesian deliberation found in Chapters 2 and 3, in that the deliberators' adaptive rules can be thought of as good habits. For the most part, however, it was assumed that implementing these rules had negligible cost and was in general unproblematic.

In this chapter I want to explore the possibility that decisionmakers may be even more bounded in that they may find it economical to substitute special-purpose habits of direct strategy selection for the Bayesian deliberation of Chapters 2 and 3. The possibility presents itself as one obvious direction to explore in weakening the extremely strong assumptions required to get classical game theory out of Bayesian dynamic deliberation.

Even if all the players in a game *are* Bayesian deliberators, they might each entertain this possibility about the others, or entertain the possibility that the others are entertaining this possibility about them. That is, it is plausible to suppose that in many situations *common knowledge* that the players are Bayesian deliberators may fail at some level or other. Even such an attenuated relaxation of the assumptions can lead to dramatically nonclassical results in games played by Bayesian deliberators.

On the Rational Stability of Good Habits

There is a tradition in ethics, going back to Aristotle, which analyses the virtues as good habits. In the *Nicomachean Ethics* (1976, book 3), Aristotle summarizes his analysis of the virtues

that they are mean states and dispositions; and that they of themselves enable their possessor to perform the same sort of actions as those by which they are acquired; and that they are under our control and are voluntary; and act as the right principle prescribes.

One finds various flavors of this sort of theory in Hobbes and Hume, as well as versions of implicit and explicit rule utilitarianism.[1] Here is a sample from the *Leviathan:*

Now the science of virtue and vice is moral philosophy; and therefore the true doctrine of the laws of nature is the true moral philosophy. But the writers of moral philosophy, although they acknowledge the same virtues and vices; yet not seeing wherein consisted their goodness; not that they came to be praised, as the means of peaceable, sociable, and comfortable living, place them in a mediocrity of passions.

Critics of such rule-based theories have often called into question the *stability* of the rules. If, in a particular case, the dictates of the rule conflict with the goal of maximizing expected utility among the possible acts, will the rational decisionmaker not abandon the rule in favor of the maximal act? (See, for example, Smart, 1956). And if so, is not any rule except the rule of maximizing expected utility inherently unstable?

The question is more complicated than it may at first appear. We can start with a qualification with which Aristotle followed the previously quoted passage:

But our dispositions are not voluntary in the same sense that our actions are. Our actions are under our control from beginning to end, because we are aware of the individual stages, but we only control the beginning of our dispositions; the individual stages of their development, as in the case of illness, are unnoticeable. They are, however, voluntary in the sense that it was originally in our power to exercise them in one way or another.

As one exercises a well-established habit, the question of alternative actions may not arise. The actor does not see the routine decisions governed by habit as candidates for serious deliberation. When you brush your teeth in the morning, you are flying on autopilot. This makes perfect sense if the habits are motivated, as we suppose in this chapter, by considerations of bounded rationality. One does not typically have a conflict between the exercise of the habit and choice of the action with highest expected utility, because one applies the habits in domains where it is infeasible or uneconomical to calculate expected utility.

But what about the atypical case where information comes free, a case that presents expected utilities for alternative actions such that maximizing expected utility conflicts with the exercise of the habit? Won't a rational decisionmaker in this case go against the habit? The answer is a qualified "yes," but the qualification is important. It is that the hypothesized expected utility must take account of "second-order" payoffs which arise from going against the habit, as well as the "first-order" payoffs attaching directly to the actions in question. In particular, I want to call attention to two important sorts of second-order payoffs.

In the first place, it costs some effort to establish a good habit. And, as Aristotle noted, a habit is strengthened by acting in accordance with it and weakened by acting against it. If a habit is good in the long run, then it may pay to incur costs to acquire it and to forego myopic "opportunities" to preserve it. I teach my son to brush his teeth not because I am worried about cavities in baby teeth, but because once established the habit is easy to maintain and may avoid nasty problems in the future. Once costs of learning and extinction are taken into account, good habits may have much more rational stability than a superficial examination of the problem would indicate. These second-order considerations will be especially dramatic in cases where a good habit is hard to establish and easy to extinguish—for example, the habit of not smoking for a heavy smoker.[2] For humans, the determination of such cost functions is a matter of empirical psychology.

In the second place, in certain situations of social interaction, it may be to one's advantage to have others believe that one has a good habit. The most convincing evidence that one has the habit may consist in exercising it, and acting against it may be the most convincing evidence that one doesn't have it. This is not meant to be a universal consideration—in some markets deception will sell better than truth, and in some crowds it may be better that one's good habits are not public knowledge—but it should be counted when it is applicable.[3] In matters of social convention or custom, acting in accordance with a rule may not only convince others that you follow it, but also may tend to cause them to follow it as well. In certain cases, this may be in your own interest as well as theirs. Specific models which illustrate this phenomenon will be discussed later in this chapter.

If all payoffs have been taken into account and it is still evident in a particular case that acting against the habit has higher expected utility than acting in accordance with it, then the rational decisionmaker will prefer to act against the habit. To say otherwise makes nonsense of the foundations of the theory of rational decision.[4]

Good habits are not compulsive neuroses; reasonable rules admit of exceptions. Does this mean that utilitarian habits and rules are inherently unstable? It does not. The foregoing considerations suggest that, all things considered, real exceptions to good habits may be quite rare. And then the reinforcement of routine application may far outweigh the exceptional nudge in the direction of extinction. If so, the habit or rule will be stable notwithstanding its defeasibility.

Finite Iterated Prisoner's Dilemma

Special-purpose habits apply when easily recognizable choices must repeatedly be made. Let us look at such a situation first from the standpoint of a model which assumes common knowledge of Bayesian rationality, and then in terms of models which weaken that assumption. Prisoner's Dilemma makes an interesting candidate for several reasons:

Prisoner's Dilemma

	Defect	Cooperate
Defect	$-5, -5$	$5, -10$
Cooperate	$-10, 5$	$0, 0$

In the first place, common knowledge of rationality alone singles out [Defect, Defect] as the unique solution. Since for each player, Defect yields strictly greater payoffs no matter what the other player does, [Defect, Defect] is not only the unique Nash equilibrium but also the unique rationalizable strategy. Second, Prisoner's Dilemma is a striking and popular model of conflict between the pursuit of individual self-interest and the pursuit of the common interest. The question as to how these might be brought into harmony is one of the most vexing problems in the utilitarian tradition.[5] Or, remembering the convergence of utilitarianism and justice-as-fairness discussed in Chapter 1, we can look at the problem as an example of the conflict between private interest and justice. Each player, choosing under the veil of ignorance, would prefer the joint strategy [Cooperate, Cooperate]. In fact, in this example, the veil of ignorance is irrelevant because of the symmetry of the pay-offs.

But let us suppose that the game is to be repeated a given finite number of times between two players and that this is common knowledge. This opens up the possibility that earlier plays may influence later ones and suggests that players may initially cooperate to establish a reputation for cooperation, induce the other player to cooperate later, and reap the rewards of [Cooperate, Cooperate]. There is some experimental evidence to suggest that subjects do just that. But a simple proof shows that if it is also common knowledge that the players are Bayesian expected utility maximizers, this cannot happen and both players will always defect.

On the last trial there is no question of influencing the other player's beliefs about what you may do on a later trial. And whatever your beliefs are about what the other player will do, it is better to defect. So you will defect on the last trial, and for the same reasons, your opponent will too. Both players know this, and each one knows that the other knows it. So on the next-to-last trial, there is no question of influencing the other player's beliefs about what you will do on the last trial. She knows that you will defect on the last trial. Then it is best to defect on this trial. So, by the process of what is called "backward induction" in the game-theory literature (see Kohlberg and Mertens, 1986, sec. 2.3), we are led to the conclusion that the only equilibrium has each player defecting on each trial.

Various commentators have viewed this conclusion with some repugnance. Luce and Raiffa (1957) found it "contrary to ordinary wisdom." There can be no doubt that the conclusion follows from the stated premises, but the premises deserve scrutiny.

Beyond Common Knowledge of Rationality

Should the theory of rational behavior in games of strategy be based on the assumption of common knowledge of rationality? Until quite recently the answer implicit in most game-theoretic theorizing has been "yes." But when the question is raised explicitly, there seems to be no real rationale for that answer save for the difficulty of formulating a more general theory.

Von Neumann and Morgenstern considered just this question at the beginning of *Theory of Games and Economic Behavior* and came to the conclusion that "the rules of rational behavior must provide definitely for the possibility of irrational conduct on the part of others" (1947, p. 32). The tenor of their discussion here makes a nice contrast to that of their indirect argument for the Nash equilibrium concept. They worried about whether irrationality might pay:

Imagine that we have discovered a set of rules for all participants—to be termed as "optimal" or "rational"—each of which is indeed optimal provided that the other participants conform. Then the question remains as to what will happen if some of the participants do not conform. If it should turn out to be advantageous to them—and, quite particularly, disadvantageous to the conformists—then the above "solution" would seem very questionable.   [p. 32]

The Nash equilibrium concept, especially in the context of non-zero-sum game theory, is inadequate in several ways to the concerns raised in this discussion. It addresses the question of whether a single player can profit from deviating from the equilibrium provided that none of the others do, but it does not address the question of multiple deviations, nor of the advantage or disadvantage of conformism given some deviation. Pursuit of such questions leads outside the confines of classical game theory and calls for a more general treatment of rational strategic choice. As von Neumann and Morgenstern concluded:

In whatever way we formulate the guiding principles and the objective justification of "rational behavior," provisos will have to be made for every possible conduct of "the others." Only in this way can a satisfactory and exhaustive theory be developed.   [p. 32]

In a famous computer tournament, Axelrod (1984) matched submitted computer programs against each other in runs of iterated Prisoner's Dilemma. The winner was a very simple program submitted by Anatol Rappoport: Tit-for-tat. Tit-for-tat begins by cooperating and thereafter plays against an opponent what the opponent played against it in the last move. It cooperates with cooperators, punishes defectors, and forgives defectors who have reformed. It provides a simple implementation of "ordinary wisdom." Tit-for-tat thus gives us an especially interesting kind of "nonconformity" to investigate infinite iterated Prisoner's Dilemma.

Suppose that you are going to play 100 iterations of Prisoner's Dilemma against Rappoport's program. What is your optimal strategy? A little thought will convince you that it is not to defect on every trial (for a total loss of -985), nor to try anything very fancy, but rather to cooperate on the first 99 trials and defect on the last for a net gain of $+5$. This is quite a change from the Nash equilibrium strategy of always defecting.

Let us reflect on the effects of the introduction of Rappoport's non-conformist player. If you were to continue to play your Nash equilibrium strategy, the nonconformist would indeed do worse than his Nash equilibrium strategy by being victimized on the first play. But if you respond optimally, the nonconformist gets a total payoff of -10, much better than the total payoff at the Nash equilibrium of $-1,000$. You do even better, but in order to rationally exploit the nonconformist's irrationality you have had to cooperate with him 99 times out of 100.

Suppose now that two rational players play 100 iterations of Prisoner's Dilemma, but that each believes the other to be a Rappoport nonconformist. Each, maximizing expected utility according to her beliefs, will do as you did and cooperate the first 99 times and defect on the last trial. We here have 99 percent cooperation between two rational players, in the absence of *common knowledge* of rationality. If the game continued for 1,000 trials, the figure would be 99.9 percent cooperation. As the number of trials increases the difference in average payoff per trial between our rational players and true tit-for-tat players goes to zero.

And we don't really need certainty that the other player is a nonconformist to get the effect. All we need is a degree of belief high enough that it is worth the risk for a player to start out by cooperating in order to try out the other player. (This probability can be small if the number of trials is great.) Then each player starts out by cooperating in order to test the other player, but each player's initial behavior is consistent with the hypothesis that she is indeed a tit-for-tat nonconformist. Thus they both cooperate until the final trial.

Failure of common knowledge of rationality at higher levels can also lead to cooperation. Suppose now that each player is rational and that each knows that the other is rational, but each is certain that the other is certain that he is a Rappoport nonconformist. Then each player will think that the other player will initially cooperate by the reasoning of the previous case. And each will perceive it in his interest to cooperate initially in order to fool the other player into thinking that he is a genuine tit-for-tat player. Each will expect the other to cooperate up to the last trial if he cooperates up to the next-to-last trial and to defect on the last trial no matter what he does. So each will cooperate up to the next-to-last trial and defect on the last two trials. Here again, certainty is not required for the effect. I presume it initially only to make the reasoning transparent. The doubts about rationality may be arbitrarily small if the number of trials is arbitrarily great.

A variety of models of this type are explored in path-breaking papers by Kreps, Milgrom, Roberts, and Wilson (1982), Kreps and Wilson

(1982a), and Milgrom and Roberts (1982).[6] They give game-theoretic analyses of the kinds of situation described here, using an idea of Harsanyi (1967). The *prima facie* problem in giving a game-theoretic analysis is that the players lack the strong common knowledge necessary to provide a rationale for the game-theoretic equilibrium concept. Harsanyi's idea is to embed the game in a larger game in which the strong common-knowledge assumptions are satisfied. This bigger game has an extra player, Nature, who makes the first move. Nature plays a mixed strategy, and all uncertainties about other players or the structure of the game tree are resolved by Nature's move. But the other players are not fully informed about Nature's move; this is a game of *imperfect* information. Common knowledge of a common prior and of rationality of the players are assumed to hold in *this* enlarged game. Using this sort of modeling, the authors demonstrated the existence of sequential equilibria (see Chapters 1 and 2), where all players cooperate for most of the game, such that for arbitrarily long sequences of iterated Prisoner's Dilemma the payoffs approach those which would come from always cooperating.

These papers should be required reading for all social philosophers, and indeed for all students of rational behavior. They show that if we make even the slightest move in the direction of von Neumann and Morgenstern's suggestion that rules of rational behavior provide for the possibility of irrational conduct on the part of others, entirely new phenomena—undreamt of in classical game theory—spring to life.

The weakening of the strong assumption of common knowledge of rationality is plausible on its face, but Reny (1987) and Bicchieri (1988a, b, c) came to a stronger conclusion. It may be forced by rational choice itself. The point is that in games like iterated Prisoner's Dilemma, it is *within the power of the players* to defeat the presumption of common knowledge of rationality by cooperating on a move. And depending on how one player thinks the other will revise her beliefs when confronted with such an action, *doing so may maximize expected utility*. For example, in 100-fold iterated Prisoner's Dilemma, if I believe that if I cooperate on round one you will come to believe that I am a tit-for-tat player and maximize expected utility on that assumption, then cooperating on round one maximizes expected utility for me. Since rational choice here defeats common knowledge of rationality, it follows that given common knowledge of the structure of the game and given my beliefs about how you would revise your beliefs, common knowledge of rationality is impossible.[7]

The new possibilities are, in fact, richer than the preceding discussion indicates, for so far I have considered only one type of nonconformist. Kreps and Wilson (1982a, p. 276) made the point this way:

> What is evident from our simple examples is that a very little uncertainty "destabilizes" game-theoretic analysis in games with a fairly large number of stages. The reader may suspect that something more is true: By cleverly choosing the nature of the small uncertainty (precisely—its support), one can get out of a game-theoretic analysis whatever one wishes. We have no formal proposition of this sort to present at this time, but we certainly share these suspicions. If this is so, then the game-theoretic analysis of this type of game comes down eventually to how one picks the initial incomplete information. And nothing in the *theory* of games will help one to do this.

Choosing Good Habits

I began this chapter with a defense of the rationality of choosing by habit when doing so is cost efficient, all relevant costs being taken into account. If a habit is thought likely to be exercised a large number of times, then it makes sense to devote some thought to the choice of the habit. So it is of some interest to examine situations where decisionmakers carefully deliberate about the choice of very simple habits.

Let us suppose that our decisionmakers are considering habits for finite iterated Prisoner's Dilemma and to start with let us suppose that they are willing to consider only extremely simple *Markov habits*: the action taken on each play depends only on the action taken by the opponent on the preceding play (if there was a preceding play). There are eight possible Markov habits:

	Initial move	Response if opponent did C	Response if opponent did D
1.	C	C	C
2.	C	C	D
3.	C	D	C
4.	C	D	D
5.	D	C	C
6.	D	C	D
7.	D	D	C
8.	D	D	D

Habit 1 is "Always Cooperate"; 2 is "Tit-for-tat"; 8 is "Always Defect."

We can consider the 8 × 8 two-person game where each player chooses a Markov habit to implement in *n*-fold iterated Prisoner's Dilemma with the other. For *n* greater than 2, there are two Nash equilibria in this game: at [2,2] both players play Tit-for-tat, and at [8,8] both players always defect. This focuses our attention on two types of nonconformist. Suppose in addition that the game was played by Bayesian dynamic deliberators with adequate common knowledge for deliberation, as in Chapters 2 and 3. Then, as the number of iterations, *n*, increases, the area of the space of indecision which is in the basin of attraction for Tit-for-tat rapidly increases. Figures 6.1–6.4 for simplicity show phase portraits for different values of *n* for 2 × 2 two-person games in which the choice is simply between Tit-for-tat and Always Defect. It is clear that an extraordinary degree of initial mutual distrust is required for Always Defect to be selected. If—and this is a big if—the possible nonconformists described by Kreps, Wilson, Milgrom, and Roberts were thought of as agents with Markov habits selected in some such way, then for large *n* deliberational dynamics would provide a reason for thinking it likely that a nonconformist would have a Tit-for-tat habit.

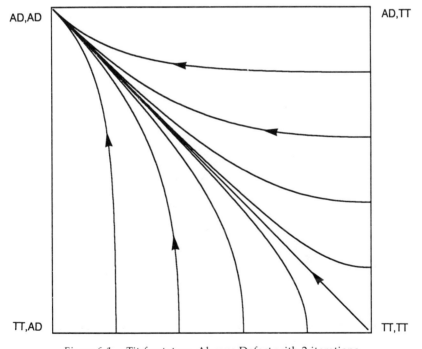

Figure 6.1. Tit-for-tat vs. Always Defect with 2 iterations

The foregoing model could be made more realistic in several ways. One would be to consider m-stage Markov habits, which define what a player does as a function of what his opponent has done in the last m trials. If n is large relative to m, both players playing Tit-for-tat should still arrive at an equilibrium with a large basin of attraction in the habit selection game. Another would be to make the habit selection game approximate the game of selecting an entrant to an Axelrod-style Prisoner's Dilemma tournament. There are k players, limited to m-stage Markov habits, such that each will play an n-stage iterated Prisoner's Dilemma against each other player.

In any event, as Borel emphasized, the psychology of the adversary or adversaries must be taken into account in the predeliberational probabilities. But even this oversimplified example shows that the dynamics of rational deliberation may exert a powerful influence on the outcome. In our example, the influence is salubrious—swamping all but the most extreme distrust—and promoting mutually beneficial habits.

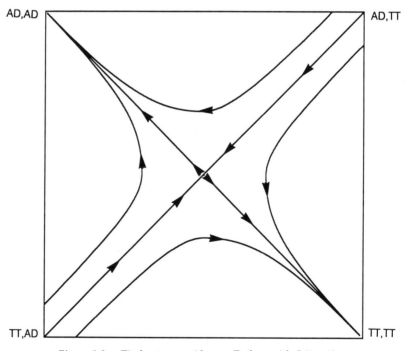

Figure 6.2.   Tit-for-tat vs. Always Defect with 3 iterations

Just Habits

Utilitarianism is profoundly transformed if we understand the utility concept as deriving its meaning not from some sort of nineteenth-century hedonometry but rather from representation theory for coherent preference. Then the utilitarian dictum "each shall count as one" is literally meaningless and, as Pareto suspected and Harsanyi proved, the ethical content of utilitarianism reduces to the Pareto principle: one state of the group is to be preferred to a second if the first state Pareto dominates the second. We will say that *utilitarian justice* requires the state of the group to be Pareto optimal.[8] We saw in Chapter 1 a considerable convergence between utilitarian justice and justice-as-fairness, but noted the possibility of disagreement in certain cases. This section is concerned directly with utilitarian justice.

In zero-sum games an equilibrium must be Pareto optimal, but in non-zero-sum games equilibria may not be Pareto optimal and Pareto optimal points may not be equilibria. Prisoner's Dilemma is a striking exam-

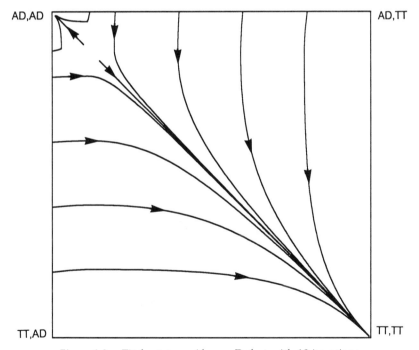

AD,AD

AD,TT

TT,AD

TT,TT

Figure 6.3.   Tit-for-tat vs. Always Defect with 10 iterations

ple of this situation: it has a unique Nash equilibrium at [Defect, Defect] which is Pareto dominated by a Pareto optimal point at [Cooperate, Cooperate]. It is perhaps this fact which accounts for "the hopelessness that one feels in such a game" (Luce and Raiffa, 1957, pp. 96–97). It is in the interests of both players to be at [Cooperate, Cooperate] rather than [Defect, Defect], but their individual optimizations drive them inexorably to the equilibrium point.

In an idealized game-theoretic setting, we might reformulate the problem of utilitarian justice as follows: "How is it possible, if at all, in games with equilibria that are not Pareto optimal for players to rationally secure the enhanced payoffs of nonequilibrium points which Pareto dominate equilibria?" The work of Kreps, Wilson, Milgrom, and Roberts suggests that the answer lies in the *Nicomachean Ethics*: "when people speak of justice we see that they all mean that kind of state of character that disposes them to perform just acts, and behave in a just manner, and wish for what is just" (book 5, i). It is therefore of some interest for social philosophy to ask to what extent their analysis of Prisoner's Dilemma

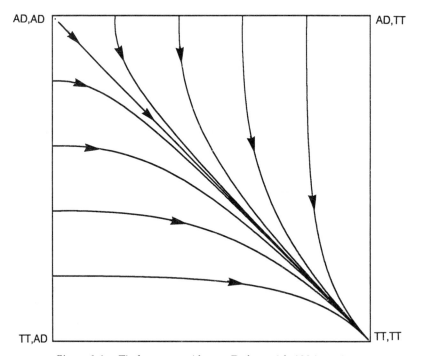

Figure 6.4. Tit-for-tat vs. Always Defect with 100 iterations

generalizes to finite iterations of other non-zero-sum games where equilibria are not Pareto optimal.

Suppose, for simplicity, that a finite n-person game has a unique Nash equilibrium, E, which is Pareto dominated by a Pareto optimal strategy, P, and that n players are going to repeat this game a large (and commonly known) number of times. We will say that a player plays her *just strategy* if she starts by playing her end of P on the first trial and continues by playing it if all other players have played their ends of P on the last move, but otherwise plays her end of E for the rest of the game. Playing one's just strategy is a Markov habit, *the habit of justice*. The just strategy in Prisoner's Dilemma is Tit-for-tat.

We wish to consider the analysis of repeated games in which instead of common knowledge of rationality there is some small probability that the players play by the habit of justice. Such a game of incomplete information can be embedded in a game of imperfect information using Harsanyi's device. As the number of repetitions becomes greater there are sequential equilibria wherein the players act justly most of the time and such that the payoffs approximate those which would come from players all playing by the habit of justice. *Utilitarian justice is rationally achievable in a context in which some players have (or may reasonably be thought to have some probability of having) just habits.*

Of course, one may not have a unique Nash equilibrium, and one may wish to consider the viability of "partially just" points that Pareto dominate a Nash equilibrium but are not Pareto optimal. Even here—as Fudenberg and Maskin (1986, theorem 3) showed—the fundamental analysis remains the same. Here the "partially just" players must agree on the "partially just" point at which they are aiming and on the default Nash equilibrium if the players are to reach "partial justice." But if they do, it is possible for rational play in a sequence of iterations to approximate the payoffs at the "partially just points."

The riches just disclosed may be viewed as an embarrassment by some game theorists but they should be welcomed as a revelation by social philosophers. What previously seemed like an impossibility has been replaced in the general case by a coordination problem.[9] With a little good luck, a combination of salience and rational deliberation can solve coordination problems, as we saw in the discussion of convention in Chapter 2. Thus one can glimpse the possibility of a rational modeling of Hume's view:

It has been asserted by some that justice arises from HUMAN CONVENTION and proceeds from the voluntary choice, consent and combination of mankind. If by convention be here meant a promise . . . nothing can be more absurd than this position. The observation of promises is itself one of the most considerable parts of justice; and we are not surely bound to keep our word, because we have given our word to keep it. But if by convention be meant a sense of common interest; which sense each man feels in his own breast, which he remarks in his fellows, and which carries him, in concurrence with others, into a general plan or system of actions which tends to public utility; it must be owned that, in this sense, justice arises from human conventions . . .

Thus, two men pull at the oars of a boat by common convention, for common interest, without any promise or contract; thus gold and silver are made the measures of exchange; thus speech, and words, and language are fixed, by human convention and agreement. Whatever is advantageous to two or more persons, if all perform their part—but what loses all advantage, if only one perform—can arise from no other principle.[10]

The Social Contract Revisited

A neo-Hobbesian theory of the social contract should explain why rational agents act in the way hypothesized in the state of nature without making it impossible for them to escape from the state of nature. And it must argue for the viability of the social contract without destroying the credibility of the state of nature. That is, both the "state of nature" and the civilized state under the social contract should be possible, natural, self-sustaining social states, with the latter being clearly preferable. Binmore (1988) suggested that if a theory of the social contract is to be more than a utopian fantasy, we should be interested in game-theoretic models for such a theory in which both the state of nature and the civilized state are portrayed as game-theoretic equilibria, with the civilized state perhaps being less robust but Pareto dominating the state of nature. Binmore argued that for the social contract to be accessible from the state of nature there must be a set of equilibria forming a path from the state of nature to the state implementing the social contract.

There are many possible "states of nature" and many possible social contracts. Here is a variation on Prisoner's Dilemma that illustrates the possibility of such a theory:

	C1	C2
R2	0,2	2,2
R1	1,1	2,0

[R1, C1] is the state of nature and [R2, C2] is the social contract. Both states are Nash equilibria. Each player would prefer the equilibrium at the social contract to that at the state of nature, but nevertheless the social contract is unstable and the state of nature is strongly stable.

The example raises another question for neo-Hobbesian theory, which should also explain how it is possible for rational agents to move from the state of nature to the social contract without invoking some *deus ex machina* to enforce the contract. The change must therefore be explained not by a change in the payoffs of the game, but rather by a change in the players' *beliefs*. In the example just given, however, deliberational dynamics runs in the opposite direction. It carries any perturbation off the social contract state to the state of nature.

The considerations presented in the last two sections show a way in which a neo-Humean theory can accommodate this game. Suppose that the game is iterated a large number of times, that it is not precluded that some player or players may play by habit some of the time, and that play by just habit is a possibility. We have seen that with common knowledge of Bayesian rationality weakened in this way it is possible for any "partially just" strategy to be approximated by an equilibrium in the associated Harsanyi game of imperfect information. Thus with each player having changing beliefs about the habits of other players, it is possible to have a path of temporary equilibria leading from the state of nature to the social contract. In this sense we can achieve Binmore's desideratum.

The requisite change in beliefs may not be irrational. As the game is iterated the players who do not play by habit have an opportunity to learn something about the possible habits of other players. Whether the whole process leads in the end to the social contract will depend on the nature of the players, on how players learn from experience, and on their prior probabilities. Such a theory would not argue that the evolution of the social contract is inevitable, but rather would investigate the conditions under which it is possible.

Taking Turns

In Chapter 2 I remarked that Prisoner's Dilemma was only one possible model for the Hobbesian state of nature and that Chicken models a rather different state. Consider the following variation on Chicken:

	Don't swerve	Swerve
Don't swerve	$-10, -10$	$5, -5$
Swerve	$-5, 5$	$-2, -2$

The point made in Chapter 2 was that rational deliberation can avoid conflict even in this sort of situation. It leads from most initial points of indecision to one of the pure Nash equilibria, [Row swerves, Column doesn't] or [Column swerves, Row doesn't], with the player initially most likely to swerve swerving and his initially more bellicose opponent "winning" the contest. If the players are initially equally likely to swerve, they converge to a mixed Nash equilibrium where each has equal probability of swerving or not. (The basic instability of this mixed Nash equilibrium might be tempered by nonzero satisficing levels.) The mixed equilibrium is in some sense more equitable than either of the pure equilibria, but it carries with it a rather undistinguished payoff of $[-3, -3]$, which is inferior to the payoff that the players would achieve if they both swerved.

What happens if we apply the kind of analysis to iterated Chicken that we applied to iterated Prisoner's Dilemma? To begin with, the possible Markov habits are:

	Initial move	Response if opponent swerved	Response if opponent didn't swerve
1.	Swerve	Swerve	Swerve
2.	Swerve	Swerve	Don't swerve
3.	Swerve	Don't swerve	Swerve
4.	Swerve	Don't swerve	Don't swerve
5.	Don't swerve	Swerve	Swerve
6.	Don't swerve	Swerve	Don't swerve
7.	Don't swerve	Don't swerve	Swerve
8.	Don't swerve	Don't swerve	Don't swerve

In the game where each player chooses a Markov habit for 100 iterations of Chicken, [1,8]—the habits [Always Swerve, Never Swerve]—and [8,1] are Nash equilibria corresponding to the Nash equilibria of the single-play game. But there are also other equilibria of interest, such as [4,5], [5,4], [2,6], and [6,2]. In cases of many iterations, [4,5] and [5,4] differ only minimally from [1,8] and [8,1]. Of real interest, however, are [2,6] and [6,2], which result in the players *taking turns* between the two Nash equilibria of the single-play game. These "taking-turns equilibria" yield an average payoff per trial of zero, which is rather more attractive for relatively equally aggressive opponents than the single-case mixed equilibrium payoff of -3.

Equilibrium selection between the taking-turns equilibria raises the delicate question of who goes first. This is a special coordination problem that arises for social contracts that resemble iterated Chicken but not iterated Prisoner's Dilemma.

The analysis of iterated Chicken-type situations can be developed in the same way as that for iterated Prisoner's Dilemma. That is, we could investigate the selection of Markov habits by dynamic deliberation, and we could generalize to situations where the players are not known to operate by Markov habits but are given some small probability of operating in this way. Other models could be analyzed in the same way. A comprehensive theory of rational social contracts should explore these questions of rational deliberation about good habits for not just one or two but a wide variety of game-theoretic models. Only the first steps toward such a theory have been taken.

Good Habits and Game Theory

Despite the explicit recognition by the founders of the subject that a theory of rational action in games should allow for rational play against irrational opponents, the theory of games has been developed under the assumption that all players are rational. In fact it has been developed under an (often tacit) assumption that is much stronger: the assumption of common knowledge of rationality. The role that this strong assumption plays in game theory has only recently been fully appreciated.[11]

The notion of common knowledge, that "everybody knows, and everybody knows that everybody knows, etc.", was introduced by Lewis (1969).[12] The inductive form leaves open the question of whether the "etc." is meant to cover transfinite induction or not, but for the examples we have discussed the difference is inessential. Aumann (1976) introduced a different definition of common knowledge. Each person's possible worlds are equipped with a *knowledge partition*. The interpretation is that in a world all the person knows is that she is in the cell of the partition that contains that world. She is assumed to know any proposition (or set of possible worlds) that is a superset of that cell. For any such world, w, and proposition, p, "she knows that p" is true in w. For the probability theorist this is just like probability conditional on a partition; for the modal logician it is the Kripke semantics for S-5. A considerable simplification of the treatment of knowledge is bought at the cost of begging some questions about the logic of "X knows that p."[13] For a group of people, we can think of a *group knowledge partition* as the finest common coarsening of the knowledge partitions of the members. Intuitively, what the group knows about the world that it is in is what all its members know. Then, according to Aumann, a proposition is common knowledge in world w for a group if it is a superset of the member of the group knowledge partition which contains w. The relationships between these different approaches are discussed in Barwise (1988), Brandenberger and Dekel (1985a,b), and Nielsen (1984).

The failures of common knowledge that we have examined are failures in all of these senses, since they are failures at finite levels. As we have seen, the failure of common knowledge of rationality can give results dramatically different from those of classical game theory, even when all the players are, if fact, rational. Does going beyond common knowledge of rationality open up a treasure chest or a Pandora's box for the game theorist? The answer depends on whether there is some way of carving out manageable classes of nonrational behavior so as to make possible a useful theory. One prime candidate for such a theory is a theory of good habits based on considerations of bounded rationality. Our Markov habits come at rather the low end of computational power. There are some studies at the high end, where habits may be implemented by arbitrary finite automata (Rubenstein, 1986; Meggido, 1988). The most realistic models are perhaps to be found in the unexplored middle region.

The idea of a theory of good habits came from ethics. The foregoing discussion of just habits suggests that a game-theoretic theory of good habits will contain much of interest to moral and social philosophers. Lest that discussion appear too rosy, however, I would like to emphasize that I have argued for the *possibility* of just habits, not their *necessity.* And there is more to ethics than utilitarian justice. The plain truth is that there are situations in which *nasty* habits are good habits—for essentially the same reason that relatively nice habits can be good habits in finite iterated Prisoner's Dilemma. These are situations in which it pays to acquire a reputation for being nasty.[14] What a theory of good habits has to offer ethics is not some sort of Pollyanna proof that rational decision theory requires one to be nice, but rather a more realistic framework and a richer set of possibilities within which ethical problems can be modeled.

7 Prospects for a Theory of Rational Deliberation

> We repeat most emphatically that our theory is thoroughly static. A dynamic theory would unquestionably be more complete and therefore preferable. But there is ample evidence from the other branches of science that it is futile to try to build one as long as the static theory is not thoroughly understood.
>
> —John von Neumann and Oskar Morgenstern (1947, p. 44)

The point of view that I have been advocating in this book is (1) that the theory of games should be embedded in the theory of expected utility maximization and (2) that the process of rational deliberation should be explicitly modeled and studied. I have outlined a research program rather than a finished theory. A few key questions have already been answered, but most of the territory remains to be explored.

Consistency Proofs

Is it *consistent* to embed the theory of games in the theory of expected utility maximization? Depending on the nature of the embedding, this general concern specifies to a number of consistency problems. The work of von Neumann, Morgenstern, and Nash gives a positive answer to one of these consistency problems. The root problem for the theory of the interaction of many rational agents for them lay not so much in considerations of free will or distinctions between "dead" and "live" variables, but rather in problems of implicit self-reference. What was required was a demonstration that it was consistent to suppose that all players had jointly maximized expected utility (see von Neumann and Morgenstern, 1947, sec. 2.2.3). Von Neumann offered such a consistency proof in his demonstration of the existence of an equilibrium for any finite zero-sum, two-person game with mixed strategies, a proof subsequently extended to the case of all finite, *n*-person, non-zero-sum games by John Nash. An essential element of the proof was the introduction of mixed strategies, which plays a role analogous to the introduction of truth-value gaps in the theory of semantical self-reference (see Martin, 1984).

For example, consider the two-stage Liar Paradox: Plato at time t_1 says "What Aristotle says at t_1 is false," and Aristotle at time t_1 says "What Plato says at t_1 is true." If we assume that each sentence is either true or false, we land in an inconsistency. If Plato speaks truly, then Aristotle's assertion is false and Plato must speak falsely. If Plato speaks falsely, then Aristotle's assertion must be true and therefore Plato speaks truly. Compare the game of Matching Pennies played with pure strategies. If Row plays R1 then Column maximizes payoff by playing C1, in which case Row must play R2 to maximize payoff. But if Row plays R2, Column maximizes payoff by playing C2 in which case Row must play R1 to maximize payoff.

If we introduce truth-value gaps, we can give a consistent semantics for a language containing the Liar Paradox. A partial valuation is an assignment of true or false to some of the sentences of the language. The *Tarski map* takes a partial valuation V into one V' according to the rules: (1) if a sentence is true according to V then the sentence that says it is true is true according to V'; (2) if a sentence is false according to V the sentence that says it is true is false according to V' and (3) V' respects the connectives. (For more detail, see Kripke's essay in Martin, 1984.) A consistent partial valuation is a fixed point of the Tarski map. There is a consistent partial valuation where what Aristotle and Plato say both have truth-value gaps, but there is no consistent valuation where both have truth values.

This analysis is analogous to Nash's consideration of the space of mixed strategies under the Nash map. A consistent solution is taken to be a fixed point of this map. For Matching Pennies, there is no consistent solution in pure strategies but there is a (unique) consistent solution in mixed strategies.

What are the assumptions that are shown to be consistent by the existence of the fixed point of a Nash map? The analyses of Bernheim (1984), Pearce (1984), Werlang (1986), Brandenberger and Dekel (1985a, b), and Binmore and Brandenberger (forthcoming) show that the Nash results constitute a consistency proof for assumptions that are considerably stronger than the assumption of joint maximization of expected utility on the part of the players. A Nash equilibrium corresponds not simply to a state where all players maximize expected utility, but rather to a state where it is common knowledge both that all players maximize expected utilities and what their actual (mixed) strategies are.

If we weaken the assumption to that of common knowledge that all players maximize expected utility alone, then the corresponding game-theoretic concept is broader: the *rationalizable strategic behavior* of Bernheim (1984) and Pearce (1984).[1] It is remarkable that for the general case of finite, n-person, non-zero-sum games treated by Nash, consistency of the assumption of common knowledge of maximizing expected utility does not here require mixed strategies. Any pure strategy which is a component of a rationalizable mixed strategy is also rationalizable as a pure strategy (see Bernheim, 1984, p. 1016). For example, in Matching Pennies every pure strategy is rationalizable. Every game that has a Nash equilibrium in mixed strategies has rationalizable pure strategies for each player.

If we require only that the players *are* all maximizing expected utility and drop the assumption of common knowledge of Bayesian rationality, an even wider class of possibilities is opened up. As we saw in the discussion of finite iterated Prisoner's Dilemma in Chapter 6, expected utility maximizers may choose even strictly dominated strategies in the belief that their opponents are not expected utility maximizers or in the belief that their opponents believe that they are not expected utility maximizers. In general, it takes the powerful assumption of common knowledge of expected utility maximization to rule out these possibilities—an assumption especially suspect in the theory of games in extensive form, where it may be within the power of a player to make a move which defeats the presumption of common knowledge of Bayesian rationality. (This point has been stressed by Reny, 1987, and Binmore, 1987.) A great array of possible rational behavior is thus opened up. Some of this new territory can be explored in an orderly way by pursuing a *theory of good habits*. It is becoming evident that the adoption of a thoroughly Bayesian viewpoint will lead to a richer and more realistic theory of the interaction of rational decisionmakers.

Causal Independence and Rationalizability

A thoroughly Bayesian viewpoint already has important implications for the static consistency proofs. In the case of two-person games, Pearce and Bernheim showed that the rationalizable strategies are just those that remain after iterated elimination of strongly dominated strategies. As they pointed out, the argument would extend in a straightforward way to n-person games if there were no special requirements on the beliefs involved. Their definition, however, does include the special requirement that a player's beliefs should treat the strategies of her several opponents as probabilistically independent. For example, player 1's degree of belief that player 2 does act *A* and player 3 does act *C* should be the product of her degrees of belief in the individual acts. Thus Bernheim (1984, p. 1014) reasoned: "A question arises here as to whether an agent's probabilistic conjectures can allow for correlation between the choices of other players. In a purely non-cooperative framework, such correlation would be nonsensical: The choices of any two agents are by definition independent events; they cannot affect each other. Consequently, I restrict players to have uncorrelated probabilistic assessments of their opponents' choices." (See also Pearce, 1984, p. 1035.)

This worry appears to be based on the assumption that knowledge of causal independence between events should be reflected as probabilistic independence in our degrees of belief about them. Counterexamples to this assumption are commonplace in Bayesian statistics. For instance, a coin of unknown bias is flipped a number of times, each flip being causally independent. In each possible chance probability, corresponding to a fixed value for the bias, we have probabilistic independence. But in a degree-of-belief distribution reflecting uncertainty as to the bias (the degree-of-belief expectation over the chance distributions), we do not get independence but rather a weaker symmetry: exchangeability. Mixtures of independent, identically distributed random variables are, in general, not independent but rather exchangeable.

In the case of 3 or more person matrix games, we are dealing with mixtures of independent but not necessarily identically distributed random variables. Let us suppose that all players played genuine mixed strategies and that the chance devices used by each player to implement his strategy are independent in a joint chance distribution, but that the players may be uncertain about the chances and get their degrees of belief by expecting over the chances. Thus, in a 101-person game where each player has two possible strategies, a player believes that the other players' acts will be determined by the flips of 100 biased coins, the flips being independent but the biases being the same only in quite extraordinary cases. Thus the mixture created by uncertainty about the biases of the coins need not display the symmetry (exchangeability) associated with mixtures of independent, identically distributed trials. What sort of restriction does the requirement of independence in the chance probabilities put on the degree-of-belief mixture?

Independence in the chance probabilities alone puts *no restrictions whatever* on the mixtures that can be gotten from them. The reason is that we can consider cases in which the chances are all zero or one. Such probability measures automatically satisfy the requirement of independence—

$$p(P \text{ \& } Q) = p(P) \cdot p(Q)$$

—and any probability over the plays of other players can be gotten by mixing them. Thus iterated deletion of strictly dominated strategies coincides with rationalizability in the n-person case.[2]

Nash Equilibrium Reconsidered

The foregoing considerations may affect not only the concept of rationalizability but also the von Neumann–Nash equilibrium concept. Whether they do or not turns on the interpretation of mixed strategies. The traditional way of thinking about mixed strategies has players' mixed acts being the choice of the chances of a chance device to which the choice of pure act is delegated. The equilibrium concept of von Neumann and Nash is motivated by the assumption that each player may have found out the chances chosen by the other players but cannot predict the outcome of the chance devices. If, in this situation, all players maximize expected utility then they are at a Nash equilibrium. If the number of players is greater than two, each player must have a joint probability over the acts of all the other players in order to calculate her expected utility. It is customarily assumed that the chances are independent, with the result that the joint probability is a product probability.

Another way of looking at mixed strategies was briefly mentioned in Chapter 2 (Aumann, 1987; Binmore and Brandenberger, forthcoming). The probabilities of acts in my "mixed strategy" are just the (shared) subjective probabilities of the other players that I do those acts. The reason that they have those shared probabilities might or might not be because the traditional story about randomizing devices that have been found out holds good. An equilibrium in mixed strategies is an equilibrium in beliefs. If we leave it at this, the players might have all sorts of correlations in their beliefs; anything goes. This conclusion, as Aumann (1974, 1987) showed, leads to spectacular changes in the equilibrium concept. It might be objected that in noncooperative game theory the *causal independence* of the players' choices should be common knowledge. The discussion of the previous section showed that this additional assumption places no additional restrictions on the kind of correlation that can occur in beliefs. This is true even if it is also common knowledge that all players implement mixed strategies in the classical way by choosing a chance device, and that the outcomes of different players' chance devices are probabilistically independent in the joint chance probability. If the chances have not been "found out," any kind of dependence can be created by uncertainties about the true chances.

Dynamics

A thoroughly Bayesian viewpoint, however, must include an analysis of the process of deliberation as well as its outcome. Once we drop the fiction that the mathematics of the interaction must be completely transparent to the decisionmaker, computation can generate new information and Bayesian analysis of the process of deliberation is possible. The analysis of optimal deliberation strategies for a given deliberator will depend on her particular cost functions and may be very complicated, but at a more general level connections with game theory can be established by considering broad categories of Bayesian deliberators.

We can then ask what conditions at the start of deliberation will lead, at the end of deliberation, to the strong common-knowledge conditions characteristic of the Nash equilibrium concept. If Bayesian deliberators have a common prior and a common adaptive rule which seeks the good, if they update by emulation, and if they *form their joint probabilities as product probabilities* (or in other words, assume independence), and if all this is initially common knowledge, then deliberation will preserve the essential common knowledge; *if* deliberation leads to a deliberational equilibrium it will correspond to a Nash equilibrium in mixed strategies. This last clause raises the question of convergence, which is suppressed in the approach that focuses on static consistency proofs. From the perspective of a theory of rational deliberation, the Nash equilibrium concept appears as even more of a special case.

Consideration of the deliberational process can motivate both weaker and stronger concepts. An example of the weaker concept would be the absence of common knowledge of the dynamical rule, the result being that common knowledge of the players' probabilities is not preserved during deliberation and deliberation may converge to rationalizable behavior which is not a Nash equilibrium. Examples of stronger concepts are dynamic *accessibility* and dynamic *stability*. These notions give one a different view of a number of examples prominent in the literature on refinements of the Nash equilibrium. Of particular interest is the sensitivity to timing in deliberation demonstrated in the examples of Samuelson and of Kohlberg and Mertens in Chapter 2. These show how delicate the dependence of the outcome on the process of deliberation can be. On the other hand, some phenomena are extremely robust over alternative dynamic deliberational rules. Considerations of stability and robustness come to the forefront in the theory of rational deliberation.

Fictitious Play by Carnapians

Two players play a 2 × 2 non-zero-sum game. They have both read Rudolf Carnap's (1950) *Logical Foundations of Probability* and decide to deliberate using Carnap's inductive logic. They both desire to maximize expected utility and all this is common knowledge. At each stage each calculates what pure act the other would do to maximize expected utility and counts that as the outcome of a virtual trial. (If there is a tie this stage is not counted as a trial.) Each then calculates a new set of probabilities according to Carnap as

$$p(A) = \frac{(\text{Number of times } A \text{ was chosen } + 1)}{(\text{Number of trials } + 2)}$$

Our players need not bring subjective priors to the deliberational situation. The probabilities when the number of "trials" is zero are prescribed by Carnap. Despite the rather dubious application of Carnap's inductive logic, these deliberators don't do too badly. For any 2 × 2 game they converge to a perfect Nash equilibrium.

From a Bayesian standpoint we see these Carnapians as modeling the stages of deliberation as a Bernoulli process and as putting a flat beta prior on the parameter of the process. Integration gives the Bayes-Laplace rule of succession. In a more general case, where each player has more than two acts, modeling as a multinomial with a symmetric Dirichlet prior gives Carnap's (1952) *Continuum of Inductive Methods*. If one objects to the use of symmetry assumptions to dictate a prior,[3] the general approach could be maintained if we assume the players bring arbitrary personal priors from the family of natural conjugate priors to deliberation. For example, in the two-act case, the players would each bring an arbitrary beta prior to deliberation and these priors would be assumed common knowledge at the beginning of deliberation. What is theoretically wrong with this approach?

In the first place, the stages of deliberation are not like flips of a coin with unknown bias or random sampling with replacement from an urn of unknown composition. One is not dealing with independent trials, since each trial modifies one's opponent's probabilities.[4] This fact is brought home by the kind of 3 × 3 game proposed by Shapley (1964). In this sort of game, Carnapians do not always converge (although in the specific example proposed by Shapley, Carnapians do converge because their *a priori* probabilities are at equilibrium). In the second place, what the other player would do if she has to decide now is not a *sufficient statistic* for the information generated at a stage of deliberation. It throws away information as to (1) the extent to which the utility of her most attractive act now exceeds that of her second most attractive act, and (2) the relative merits of other acts. The first datum is important because current expected utility is the expectation of final expected utility. If act 1 looks much better than its nearest competitor, it is judged (in reasonable general models) to be more likely to beat it in the end than if it looks only slightly better. Knowing the relative merits of other acts is important for the same reason. The currently third- or fourth-place acts carry utilities which are expectations of final expected utility. In some possible final probability distributions, they may win and their current expected utility magnitudes are influenced by, among other things, the likelihoods that they may finally win. I won't attempt to give specific models here, but these qualitative considerations will hold good for a wide range of plausible models.

More Sophisticated Deliberators

There is nothing in the nature of deliberational dynamics that requires that deliberators be simpleminded, but the illustrations I have chosen— the Nash, Darwin, and Carnap dynamics—are relatively unsophisticat- ed. These players follow their noses in the direction of the current apparent good, with no real memory of where they have been, no capa- bility of recognizing patterns, and no sense of where they are going. They do not model correlations in beliefs about other players. They assume independence wherever convenient, even though such assump- tions are unjustified. Nevertheless, even such simple rules may have some intrinsic interest and in many situations they are good enough.

Darwin dynamics has an implementation in the real world of evolu- tion. Its naivete derives from the fundamental biology being modeled (see Maynard Smith, 1982). The Nash dynamics has connections with the early game theory literature on fictitious play. The idea, due to Brown (1951), was that one considers a hypothetical series of plays such that in each round each player chooses a pure act with maximal expected utility, taking the other players' relative frequencies of play in the foregoing part of the series as his probabilities in calculating expected utility. Thus, the operative inductive rule here was Reichenbach's "straight rule" rather than Laplace's rule of succession. As inductive logic the technique is virtually incoherent, but in favorable circumstances the craziness washes out in the long run. Robinson (1951) showed that for any two-person zero-sum game the relative frequencies converge to a Nash equilibrium in mixed strategies and the result was subsequently extended to 2 × 2 two-person non-zero-sum games by Miyasawa (1961).

Convergence is, however, painfully slow and one is tempted to speed it up by discounting the past. This line of thought can lead easily to something like the Nash dynamics, and in fact a close relative of the Nash dynamics was suggested by Brown and von Neumann (1950).[5] Both fictitious play and the Brown–von Neumann differential equations appear to have been thought of as techniques for discovering equilibrium points, rather than as attempts to model deliberation. Their utility as general solution tools for games was called into question when Shapley produced an example of a 3 × 3 two-person non-zero-sum game for which neither fictitious play nor Brown–von Neumann dynamics converged.

It is perhaps no surprise that in the theory of coevolution we might have limit cycles rather than convergence to an equilibrium point. In the theory of rational deliberation this is a new complication, and it finds no static counterpart. Common knowledge of *procedural* Bayesian rationality in the sense developed in Chapter 2, even together with common knowledge of a common prior, may not guarantee common knowledge that the players will reach a deliberational equilibrium at which they have common knowledge of Bayesian rationality in the sense that the players' (mixed) acts all maximize their expected utilities.

In the examples just given, the deliberators lack the intellectual resources to see that they are getting into a cycle. This ignorance is, in a sense, just what keeps them in the cycle. If it dawned on a person that she was getting into such a cycle, she would surely change her probabilities for the other players' final acts on the basis of the total pattern she had recognized. It is plausible that she would do something like putting a uniform measure on the limit cycle and take the expectation. In the example in question this adjustment hits the equilibrium point, and there is perhaps a principled argument that, at least in the plane, it takes one in the right direction.[6]

We are thus led toward models where the deliberators have a memory and where the dynamics is not autonomous but rather depends on the whole past orbit of the system. Deliberators need either explicitly or implicitly to recognize patterns in past behavior and incorporate them into their updating procedures. There is a whole spectrum of models to be explored here, models that would vary according to the memory and computational resources of the deliberators. At the high end of the spectrum the latest work in inductive logic and in machine learning is clearly relevant. In at least some of these models problems of convergence may be serious. There is, however, one kind of deliberational model in the literature wherein—by definition—problems of convergence cannot arise.

The Tracing Procedure

Harsanyi and Selten (1988) have proposed a method of equilibrium selection for noncooperative games called the *tracing procedure*. It is possible to regard the tracing procedure as a kind of deliberational dynamics for computationally sophisticated players. The procedure always leads players having initial common priors to Nash equilibria, and a slightly modified version always leads to a unique Nash equilibrium.

It is supposed that at the beginning of the tracing procedure players have a common prior probability assignment over the possible pure acts of each player. A player, using this prior and the payoff matrix of the game, can calculate the expected utility of each of her acts. The tracing procedure begins by considering an auxiliary game, Game 0, with the same acts as the game in question but in which each player gets the payoff for an act equal to her prior expected utility for that act, no matter what the other players do.

For example, consider the Battle of the Sexes game with the following payoff matrix:

	C1	C2
R2	0,0	1,4
R1	4,1	0,0

and suppose that the common prior probabilities are (0.5,0.5) and (0.5,0.5). Then Row will assign R1 an expected payoff of 2 and R2 an expected payoff of 0.5; Column will assign C2 an expected payoff of 2 and C1 an expected payoff of 0.5. The auxiliary game will have the payoff matrix:

Game 0

	C1	C2
R2	2,0.5	2,2
R1	0.5,0.5	0.5,2

Game 0 has a unique Nash equilibrium at [R2, C2]. This is just the point that would result if each player chose the pure act that maximized expected utility according to the prior. Except in the case of ties in expected utility, Game 0 will have a unique Nash equilibrium.

The tracing procedure is now applied to the equilibria of a continuum of games as Game 0 is transformed into the original game, which we take as Game 1. For any X between zero and one, Game X is an average of these two games with payoffs equal to (X)(payoff of Game 1) + $(1 - X)$ (payoff of Game 0). A graph of the equilibrium points as X varies from zero to one will show a connected path from the equilibrium point of Game 0 to an equilibrium point of Game 1. This latter equilibrium is a solution for Game 1 according to the *linear tracing procedure*. The solution will almost always be unique. In our example, however, it is not, because the path trifurcates: the equilibrium of Game 0 is connected with all three equilibria of Game 1, as is shown in Figure 7.1. If, however, we had selected a prior which was off the diagonal, a unique equilibrium of Game 1 would have been selected. Harsanyi and Selten showed that the introduction of a small logarithmic term in the payoff function of the auxiliary games allowed the procedure to be modified so as always to give a unique result, and that this result agrees with the result of the linear tracing procedure in those cases where the latter gives a unique result. This *logarithmic tracing procedure* selects the mixed equilibrium of Game 1 in our example.

The image we may associate with the tracing procedure is of deliberators who are computionally adept but, initially at least, strategically naive. They can identify game-theoretic equilibria instantaneously. At time $t = 0$ each contemplates jumping to the conclusion that the act with maximum expected utility according to the common prior is the correct one. But at later times the hypothesis that the other players will make their best response gets stronger and stronger, until at time $t = 1$ only an equilibrium point of the original game will qualify as a solution.

Although this picture of deliberation is different in several respects from the one I have been developing in this book, it is striking that the

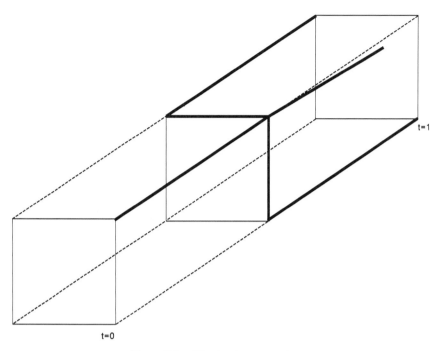

t=1

t=0

Figure 7.1.   The tracing procedure

results in this case are just those that would result from Nash or Darwin deliberational dynamics. Any initial point on one side of the diagonal goes to the pure equilibrium of Game 1 on that side, and any initial point on the diagonal goes to the mixed equilibrium point.

In games with less symmetry, however, differences in timing between various deliberational models can make a difference in which initial points go to which equilibria. Figures 7.2–7.4 compare the tracing procedure with the Nash and Darwin dynamics in this respect when applied to the following asymmetric Battle of the Sexes:

	C1	C2
R2	2,1	0,0
R1	0,0	1,4

This game has pure strategy equilibria at [R2, C1] and [R1, C2] and a mixed strategy equilibrium at $[p(R2) = \frac{4}{5}, p(C2) = \frac{2}{3}]$. In a rough qualitative sense, the dynamics agree. The pure equilibria are both strongly stable and their domains of attraction are bounded by a sepa-

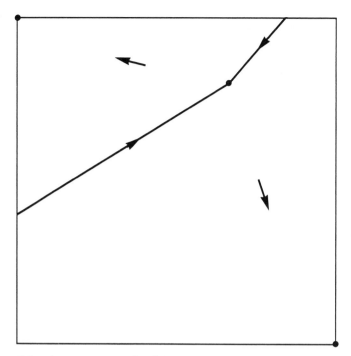

Figure 7.2. Asymmetric Battle of the Sexes with Harsanyi-Selten dynamics

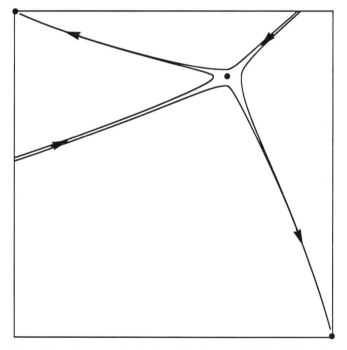

Figure 7.3. Asymmetric Battle of the Sexes with Nash dynamics

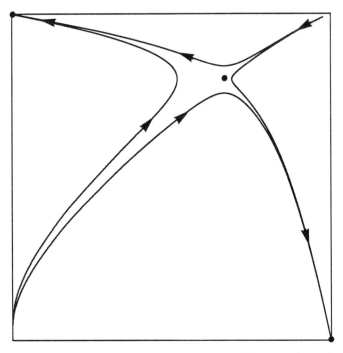

Figure 7.4.   Asymmetric Battle of the Sexes with Darwin dynamics

ratrix on which the mixed equilibrium point lies. Points on the separatrix go to the mixed equilibrium (assuming the logarithmic form of the tracing procedure). The mixed equilibrium is thus an unstable (saddle-point) equilibrium.

The figures show a real difference in the shape of the separatrix and in its intercepts on the X and Y axes. (The separatrix is drawn for the Harsanyi-Selten dynamics in Figure 7.2, but is to be inferred from the plots of orbits that circumscribe it in the Nash and Darwin dynamics shown in Figures 7.3 and 7.4.) One can, for example, find initial completely mixed points that are carried to the mixed equilibrium by the tracing procedure, to [R1, C2] by the Nash dynamics, and to [R2, C1] by the Darwin dynamics.

So far I have stressed the similarities between the tracing procedure and the kind of deliberational dynamics I have been investigating, but a difference in motivation and interpretation should be noted. Harsanyi and Selten supplemented the tracing procedure with a technique for defining an objective prior, based on the structure of the game. The two, taken together, are meant to define the equilibrium point which is *the correct solution of the game.* The point of view that I have been taking is more personalistic. Any prior is regarded as a legitimate starting point for deliberation. Furthermore, any of a wide class of deliberational rules is considered legitimate. Games might very well involve a number of players, each using a different deliberational rule. In this liberal setting, any notion of the correct solution must be relative to prior probabilities, deliberational rules, and assumptions of common knowledge.

Toward a Theory of Dynamic Deliberation

The idea that deliberators should seek out information and revise their probabilities accordingly during deliberation is hardly new. It follows from basic Bayesian principles. The new information may come from external experiment and observation, or it might come from the kind of information generated by computation itself. This latter kind of information and the attendant kinds of probability change have long been emphasized by I. J. Good (see Good, 1950, 1981; and also Hacking, 1967). A modest generalization of the Bayesian theory of learning allows the classical treatment of the economy of new information to be extended to cover Good's situations of "dynamic probability." Then classical Bayesian theory can be brought to bear on the questions of bounded or procedural rationality raised by Herbert Simon (1957, 1972, 1986). Here I have only sketched an idealized pure case. A rich variety of models with specific cost functions could be analyzed.

Models of dynamic deliberation make a natural home for Bayesian game theory. I take it as a virtue of this approach that the dynamic aspect of deliberation is not an *ad hoc* imposition on the theory of games, but rather is already a consequence of Bayesian first principles at the level of individual rationality. When applied to the theory of games it has three main consequences. The first is that under appropriate strong common-knowledge assumptions, the Nash equilibrium concept is grounded in joint deliberational equilibria. The second is that the deliberational context suggests natural strengthenings of the Nash equilibrium concept and provides a framework of dynamics in which such strengthenings can be systematically evaluated. The third, and perhaps the most important, is that in this context it is natural to explore the consequences of weakening the strong assumptions required to ground the Nash equilibrium. Some of these assumptions have already been questioned in the ground-breaking investigations of Harsanyi (1967), Aumann (1987), Bernheim (1984), Pearce (1984), Kreps and Wilson (1982a), Milgrom and Roberts (1982), and Reny (1987). Consideration of the process of deliberation adds a new dimension to these issues. It is not just a question of what common knowledge obtains at the moment of truth, but also how common knowledge is preserved, created, or destroyed in the deliberational process which leads up to the moment of truth. The strong common-knowledge assumptions behind the Nash equilibrium concept can be relaxed in a number of different ways, and each opens up a domain of phenomena unknown in classical game theory. Of particular interest is the possibility of a Bayesian theory of good habits. With regard to feasibility and costs of acquisition, execution, and possible extinction of habits, both the theory of computation and empirical psychology are relevant.[7]

In *Theory of Games and Economic Behavior* von Neumann and Morgenstern launched a theory of interacting rational decisionmakers. Many hoped and expected that this theory would lead to a new clarity in social thought and to powerful results in the behavioral sciences. These expectations have, at best, been only partially fulfilled. Part of the reason that this is so may have to do with inherent human irrationality, but another part of the reason is that von Neumann and Morgenstern tacitly built into their theory assumptions immensely stronger than just that of the rationality of the players. If these hidden assumptions are regarded as special cases and game theory is developed as part of a general theory of rational deliberation, the theory of games will become both a much richer theory and one more widely relevant to the real world.

Appendix

Notes

References

Index

Appendix:
Deliberational Dynamics
on Your Personal Computer

If you have an IBM personal computer with a color graphics adaptor, you can use the following BASIC programs to investigate the trajectories of initial points under different kinds of deliberation for a variety of simple games. These programs will run (slowly) in BASICA that comes with your DOS. They will run faster if compiled in TURBO BASIC (and still faster if you have a math coprocessor chip). The compiled version will also run on systems with a HERCULES monochrome graphics card. If you have no graphics, you must delete the graphics commands and add a command to print the probabilities to the screen rather than plotting them.

Nash Maps

In the following program for the family of Nash maps for 2 × 2 matrix games, the values in the payoff matrix are coded as follows:

	C1	C2
R2	R21,C21	R22,C22
R1	R11,C11	R12,C12

These programs can be modified in the obvious way for $n \times m$ matrix games.

```
1    REM Nash deliberator for 2 X 2 matrix games
5    DEFSNG A-Z  'all variables single precision
10   ON KEY (1) GOSUB 310  'function key 1 will start a
     new orbit
20   ON KEY (10) GOSUB 320  'function key 10 will end the
     program
30   KEY (1) ON
40   KEY (10) ON
45   CLS
50   INPUT "R11,R12,R21,R22,C11,C12,C21,C22";
     R11,R12,R21,R22,C11,C12,C21,C22
55   INPUT "Satisficing Level (Try .01)";SAT
56   INPUT "Index of Caution (Try 25)";ICAUTION
59   CLS
60   SCREEN 2
70   VIEW (200,0)-(600,140)
80   WINDOW (-.1,-.1)-(1.1,1.1)
90   LINE (0,0)-(1,1),,B
95   LOCATE 24,1
100  INPUT;"Pr(R2),Pr(C2)";PrR2,PrC2
101  LOCATE 24,1
102  PRINT SPACE$ (79);
110  PSET (PrC2,PrR2)
120  REM Calculate Expected Utilities
125  PrR1=(1-PrR2):PrC1=(1-PrC2)
130  UR1=(PrC1*R11+PrC2*R12)
140  UR2=(PrC1*R21+PrC2*R22)
150  RUSQ=(PrR1*UR1 + PrR2*UR2) 'R's utility for the
     status quo
160  UC1=(PrR1*C11 + PrR2*C21)
170  UC2=(PrR1*C12 + PrR2*C22)
180  CUSQ=(PrC1*UC1 + PrC2*UC2)
190  REM Calculate Covetabilities
200  IF UR1>RUSQ THEN COVR1=(UR1-RUSQ) ELSE COVR1=0
210  IF UR2>RUSQ THEN COVR2=(UR2-RUSQ) ELSE COVR2=0
220  IF UC1>CUSQ THEN COVC1=(UC1-CUSQ) ELSE COVC1=0
230  IF UC2>CUSQ THEN COVC2=(UC2-CUSQ) ELSE COVC2=0
240  REM Nash Dynamics
260  PrR2=((ICAUTION*PrR2 + COVR2)/(ICAUTION + COVR1 +
     COVR2))
270  PrC2=((ICAUTION*PrC2 + COVC2)/(ICAUTION + COVC1 +
     COVC2))
280  IF (COVR1>SAT OR COVR2>SAT OR COVC1>SAT OR
     COVC2>SAT) THEN GOTO 110 ELSE BEEP
290  LOCATE 24,1
300  PRINT PrR2;PrC2;" F1=ANOTHER ORBIT, F10=QUIT";
301  GOTO 301
310  LOCATE 24,1: PRINT SPACE$(79);:LOCATE 24,1:
     RETURN 100
320  END
```

The Darwin Flow

The following program approximates the Darwin flow for 2×2 matrix games. The accuracy of the approximation goes up (and the speed goes down) as the value of K goes up. Utilities must be nonnegative. A more elaborate program would include a subroutine to normalize the utilities, with maximum utility being set equal to one and minimum utility (if different) being set equal to zero.

```
1   REM Darwin deliberator for 2by2 Matrix games
5   DEFSNG A-Z 'all variables single precision
10  ON KEY (1) GOSUB 310   'function key 1 will start a
    new orbit
20  ON KEY (10) GOSUB 320   'function key 10 will end the
    program
30  KEY (1) ON
40  KEY (10) ON
45  CLS
50  INPUT "R11,R12,R21,R22,C11,C12,C21,C22 (>or=0)";
    R11,R12,R21,R22,C11,C12,C21,C22
55  INPUT "Satisficing Level (Try .01)";SAT
56  INPUT "Approximation constant,K (Try 100)";K
59  CLS
60  SCREEN 2   'for EGA graphics use SCREEN 9
70  VIEW (200,0)-(600,140)   'for EGA graphics use (20,0)-
    (600,320)
80  WINDOW (-.1,-.1)-(1.1,1.1)
90  LINE (0,0)-(1,1),,B
95  LOCATE 24,1
100 INPUT;"Pr(R2),Pr(C2)";PrR2,PrC2
101 LOCATE 24,1
102 PRINT SPACE$ (79);
110 PSET (PrC2,PrR2)
120 REM Calculate Expected Utilities
125 PrR1=(1-PrR2):PrC1=(1-PrC2)
130 UR1=(PrC1*R11+PrC2*R12)
140 UR2=(PrC1*R21+PrC2*R22)
150 RUSQ=(PrR1*UR1 + PrR2*UR2) 'R's Utility for the
    Status Quo
160 UC1=(PrR1*C11 + PrR2*C21)
170 UC2=(PrR1*C12 + PrR2*C22)
180 CUSQ=(PrC1*UC1 + PrC2*UC2)
190 REM Calculate Covetabilities
200 IF UR1>RUSQ THEN COVR1=(UR1-RUSQ) ELSE COVR1=0
210 IF UR2>RUSQ THEN COVR2=(UR2-RUSQ) ELSE COVR2=0
220 IF UC1>CUSQ THEN COVC1=(UC1-CUSQ) ELSE COVC1=0
230 IF UC2>CUSQ THEN COVC2=(UC2-CUSQ) ELSE COVC2=0
240 REM Darwin Dynamics
```

```
260 PrR2=PrR2+((1/K)*PrR2*((UR2-RUSQ)/RUSQ))
270 PrC2=PrC2+((1/K)*PrC2*((UC2-CUSQ)/CUSQ))
280 IF (COVR1>SAT OR COVR2>SAT OR COVC1>SAT OR
    COVC2>SAT) THEN GOTO 110 ELSE BEEP
290 LOCATE 24,1
300 PRINT PrR2;PrC2;" F1=ANOTHER ORBIT, F10=QUIT";
301 GOTO 301
310 LOCATE 24,1: PRINT SPACE$(79);:LOCATE 24,1:
    RETURN 100
320 END
```

Simple Extensive-Form Game with Perfect Information

Here we are dealing with a game in extensive form with the game tree:

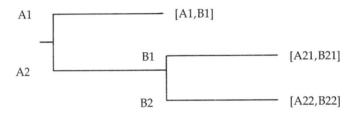

In this case the strategic normal form and the agent normal form are identical:

	B1 if A2	B2 if A2
A1	A1,B1	A1,B1
A2	A21,B21	A22,B22

Dynamic deliberation is just like deliberation on this normal-form game except that in computing her expected utilities, B uses probabilities conditional on her information set (that is, conditional on A2). We take $Pr(A2|A2) = 1$ and $Pr(A1|A2) = 0$. The requisite modification for the program for Nash dynamics for 2×2 games to fit this case is as follows.

```
1   REM Nash deliberator for extensive game
5   DEFSNG A-Z 'all variables single precision
10  ON KEY (1) GOSUB 310 'function key 1 will start a new
    orbit
20  ON KEY (10) GOSUB 320 'function key 10 will end the
    program
30  KEY (1) ON
40  KEY (10) ON
```

```
45 CLS
50 INPUT "A1,A21,A22,B1,B21,B22"; R1,R21,R22,C1,C21,C22
51 R11=R1:R12=R1:C11=C1:C12=C1
55 INPUT "Satisficing Level (Try .01)";SAT
56 INPUT "Index of Caution (Try 25)";ICAUTION
59 CLS
60 SCREEN 2
70 VIEW (200,0)-(600,140)
80 WINDOW (-.1,-.1)-(1.1,1.1)
90 LINE (0,0)-(1,1),,B
95 LOCATE 24,1
100 INPUT;"Pr(R2),Pr(C2)";PrR2,PrC2
101 LOCATE 24,1
102 PRINT SPACE$ (79);
110 PSET (PrC2,PrR2)
120 REM Calculate Expected Utilities
125 PrR1=(1-PrR2):PrC1=(1-PrC2)
130 UR1=(PrC1*R11+PrC2*R12)
140 UR2=PrC1*R21+PrC2*R22)
150 RUSQ=(PrR1*UR1 + PrR2*UR2) 'R's utility for the
    status quo
160 UC1=(0*C11 + 1*C21)
170 UC2=(0*C12 + 1*C22)
180 CUSQ=(PrC1*UC1 + PrC2*UC2)
190 REM Calculate covetabilities
200 IF UR1>RUSQ THEN COVR1=(UR1-RUSQ) ELSE COVR1=0
210 IF UR2>RUSQ THEN COVR2=(UR2-RUSQ) ELSE COVR2=0
220 IF UC1>CUSQ THEN COVC1=(UC1-CUSQ) ELSE COVC1=0
230 IF UC2>CUSQ THEN COVC2=(UC2-CUSQ) ELSE COVC2=0
240 REM Nash Dynamics
260 PrR2=((ICAUTION*PrR2 + COVR2)/(ICAUTION + COVR1 +
    COVR2))
270 PrC2=((ICAUTION*PrC2 + COVC2)/(ICAUTION + COVC1 +
    COVC2))
280 IF (COVR1>SAT or COVR2>SAT OR COVC1>SAT OR
    COVC2>SAT) THEN GOTO 110 ELSE BEEP
290 LOCATE 24,1
300 PRINT PrR2;PrC2;" F1=ANOTHER ORBIT, F10=QUIT";
301 GOTO 301
310 LOCATE 24,1: PRINT SPACE$(79);:LOCATE 24,1:
    RETURN 100
320 END
```

Simple Extensive-Form Game with Imperfect Information

This is the kind of extensive-form game with information set illustrated
in Figures 2.11 and 2.13. A has three acts: A1, A2, and A3. If A does A1
the game is ended. If A does A2 or A3, B knows that one or the other
has been done, but doesn't know which. In this case B must choose

between B1 and B2. Here B deliberates using his probabilities conditional on A2 or A3.

```
1  REM Darwin deliberator for extensive-form game with
   information set
5  DEFDBL A-Z 'all variables double precision
10 ON KEY (1) GOSUB 310 'function key 1 will start a new
   orbit
20 ON KEY (10) GOSUB 320 'function key 10 will end the
   program
30 KEY (1) ON
40 KEY (10) ON
45 CLS
49 REM Input payoffs
50 INPUT "A1,A21,A22,A31,A32,B1,B21,B22,B31,B32
   (>=0)";A1,A21,A22,A31,A32,B1,B21,B22,B31,B32
55 INPUT "Satisficing Level (Try .01)";SAT
56 INPUT "K (Try 100)";K
59 CLS
60 SCREEN 2 'for EGA graphics use SCREEN 9
70 VIEW (75,20)-(525,180)
75 ASPECT = 1.732
80 WINDOW (-1,ASPECT)-(1.1,-.1)
90 LINE (-1,0)-(1,0)
91 LINE (-1,0)-(0,ASPECT)
92 LINE (0,ASPECT)-(1,0)
95 LOCATE 24,1
96 INPUT;"PrA1,PrA2,PrA3 (All non-zero;sum to
   one)";PrA1,PrA2,PrA3
97 LOCATE 24,1:PRINT SPACE$(79);:LOCATE 24,1
98 INPUT; "PrB1cA2oA3,PrB2cA2oA3 (Non zero;sum to
   one)";PrB1cA2oA3,PrB2cA2oA3
101 LOCATE 24,1
102 PRINT SPACE$ (79);
110 PSET (PrA2-PrA1,ASPECT*PrA3) 'plot A's probabilities
   in triangle
111 PSET (1.1,ASPECT* PrB2cA2oA3)' plot B's conditional
   probability of B2
120 REM Calculate A's expected utilities
125 UA1=A1
130 UA2=(PrB1cA2oA3*A21+PrB2cA2oA3*A22)
140 UA3=(PrB1cA2oA3*A31+PrB2cA2oA3*A32)
150 AUSQ=(PrA1*UA1+PrA2*UA2+PrA3*UA3) 'A's Utility for
   the status quo
159 REM Calculate B's utilities conditional on the
   information set [A2 or A3]
160 UB1=((PrA2/PrA2+PrA3)*B21+(PrA3/PrA2+PrA3)*B31)
170 UB2=((PrA2/PrA2+PrA3)*B22+(PrA3/PrA2+PrA3)*B32)
180 BUSQ=(PrB1cA2oA3*UB1+PrB2cA2oA3*UB2)
190 REM Calculate Covetabilities
```

```
200 IF UA1>AUSQ THEN COVA1=(UA1-AUSQ) ELSE COVA1=0
210 IF UA2>AUSQ THEN COVA2=(UA2-AUSQ) ELSE COVA2=0
215 IF UA3>AUSQ THEN COVA3=(UA3-AUSQ) ELSE COVA3=0
220 IF UB1>BUSQ THEN COVB1=(UB1-BUSQ) ELSE COVB1=0
230 IF UB2>BUSQ THEN COVB2=(UB2-BUSQ) ELSE COVB2=0
240 REM Darwin Dynamics
250 PrA1=PrA1+(((1/K)*PrA1*((UA1-AUSQ)/AUSQ)))
260 PrA2=PrA2+(((1/K)*PrA2*((UA2-AUSQ)/AUSQ)))
265 PrA3=PrA3+(((1/K)*PrA3*((UA3-AUSQ)/AUSQ)))
270 PrB1cA2oA3=PrB1cA2oA3+((1/K)*PrB1cA2oA3*((UB1-
    BUSQ)/BUSQ))
275 PrB2cA2oA3=PrB2cA2oA3+((1/K)*PrB2cA2oA3*((UB2-
    BUSQ)/BUSQ))
280 IF COVA1>SAT OR COVA2>SAT OR COVA3>SAT OR COVB1>SAT
    OR COVB2>SAT THEN GOTO 110 ELSE BEEP
290 LOCATE 24,1
300 PRINT " F1=ANOTHER ORBIT, F10=QUIT";
301 GOTO 301
310 LOCATE 24,1: PRINT SPACE$(79);:LOCATE 24,1:RETURN 96
320 END
```

Notes

1. Principles of Rational Decision

1. See "Truth and Probability" in Ramsey (1931), de Finetti (1937), Savage (1954), and von Neumann and Morgenstern (1947).
2. In the paper Bernoulli forthrightly acknowledges his debt to Cramer, but Bernoulli often gets the credit.
3. Bernoulli's utility function gives the St. Petersburg game a finite expected payoff, but if utilities are not bounded above a super St. Petersburg game can nevertheless be constructed with infinite expected utility by letting the payoff for a head on toss n be $\exp(2^n)$. Thus, the St. Petersburg game shows that if utility theory is to avoid infinite utilities it must either bound utilities or not allow the unrestricted formation of gambles. In modern utility theories both approaches have been implemented.
4. Compare Alfred Marshall (1938, p. 135) on progressive taxation: "the systems of taxation which are now most widely prevalent follow generally the lines of Bernoulli's suggestion. Earlier systems took from the poor very much more than would be in accordance with that plan; while the systems of graduated taxation, which are being foreshadowed in several countries, are in some measure based on the assumption that the addition of one per cent to a very large income adds less to the wellbeing of the owner than an addition of one per cent to smaller incomes would."
5. Hutcheson's *Essay on the Nature and Conduct of the Passions and Affections with Illustrations on the Moral Sense* was first published in 1728. Here is a representative sample of his ideas taken from the third edition (1742), which is available in a facsimile (1969) that includes a useful introductory essay by Paul McReynolds:

In computing the *quantities* of Good or Evil, which we pursue or shun, either for ourselves or others, when the *Durations* are equal, the moment is the *Intenseness* or Dignity of the Enjoyment: and when the *Intenseness* of pleasure is the same, or equal, the moment is the *Duration*.

The Ratio of the *Hazard* of acquiring or retaining any Good must be multiplied into the Moment of the Good; so, also the *Hazard* of avoiding any evil is to be multiplied into the Moment of it, to find its comparative value.

Hence it is that the smallest certain Good may raise stronger Desire than the greatest Good, if the *Uncertainty* of the latter surpass *that* of the former, in a greater proportion that that of the greater to the less. Thus Men content themselves in all Affairs with *smaller,* but more probably successful Pursuits, quitting those of greater Moment but *less Probability.* [pp. 40–41]

The Pleasures of *Wealth* or *Power,* are proportioned to the Gratifications of the *Desires* or *Senses,* which the agent intends to gratify by them. [p. 156]

Concerning the Desires of *Wealth* and *Power,* besides what was suggested above to allay their Violence, from considering the small Addition commonly made to the *Happiness* of the Possessor, by the greatest degrees of them . . . [p. 195]

6. Harsanyi (1975a) writes:

As I tried to show in my 1955 paper, the ultimate logical basis for interpersonal utility comparisons, interpreted in this way, lies in the postulate that *preferences and utility functions of all human individuals* are *governed by the same psychological laws.* My utility function may be very different from yours. But since both of our utility functions are governed by the very same psychological laws, if I had your personal characteristics—and in particular, if I had your biological inheritance and had your life history behind me—then presumably I would now have a utility function exactly like yours. This means that any *inter*personal utility comparison I may try to make between your present utility and my own, reduces to an *intra*-personal utility comparison between the utility level *I* myself *do* now enjoy, and the utility level I *would* enjoy under certain hypothetical conditions, namely if I were placed in your physical, economic and social position, and also had my own biological and biographical background replaced by yours.

7. See "Truth and Probability" in Ramsey (1931).
8. In *Theory of Games and Economic Behavior,* von Neumann and Morgenstern had this to say about the general economic view of utility: "One may take the view that the only 'natural' datum in this domain is 'greater,' i.e. the concept of preference. In this case utilities are numerical up to a monotone transformation. This is, indeed, the generally accepted standpoint in economic literature, best expressed in the technique of indifference curves" (1947, p. 23).
9. Pareto (1927) made this comment in an appendix which was first included in the later French edition. The Schwier translation (1971) includes this appendix.
10. Of course, for problems more complicated than this simple distribution problem, these conceptions of personal justice may not agree.

11. In other words, her preference ordering is invariant with respect to permutations of truth-values of ethically neutral propositions. I leave open here what payoffs are, but one might as well think of them in the most general way as truth-values of propositions.

12. Roughly, that preference should be an order relation that obeys the sure-thing principle of Savage (1954).

13. If everyone's individual preference order is indifferent between two prospects, then so is the social preference order. If one prospect weakly Pareto dominates another, then it is socially preferred.

14. But, as Harsanyi (1955, footnote 5) pointed out, modern utilitarianism is compatible with additional normative content: "In view of consumers' notorious 'irrationality', some people may feel that these postulates go too far in accepting the consumers' sovereignty doctrine. These people may reinterpret the terms in the postulates as denoting, not certain individuals' actual preferences, but rather their 'true' preferences, that is, the preferences they *would* manifest under 'ideal conditions', in possession of perfect information and acting with perfect logic and care. With some ingenuity it should not be too difficult to give even some sort of 'operational' meaning to these ideal conditions, or to some approximation to them, acceptable for practical purposes. (Or, alternatively, these terms may be reinterpreted as referring even to the preferences that those individuals *ought* to exhibit in terms of a given ethical standard. The latter interpretation would, of course, deprive the postulates of much of their individualistic meaning.)"

15. Assumption (2) is not always stated explicitly, but it deserves careful consideration. Even if the categories were individuated finely enough so that preferences were *determined* (2) would not follow. The reason is that one's preferences *conditional on being in a category* may differ from the preferences *that one would have if one were in that category.* The village priest attaches greater utility to being a dead vampire at rest than to being a live and active one, but if he were a vampire he would prefer a good meal to a stake through the heart. For real-life examples, consider cases of addiction and "brainwashing." The slide from one kind of conditionality to the other is easy to make and in many cases harmless, but there are cases where clear thinking requires that the distinction be respected.

16. The interested reader should see the seminal works of Arrow (1951b), Harsanyi (1953, 1955), and Rawls (1957, 1958, 1971). Further commentary and development can be found in Arrow (1973), Broome (1987), Hammond (1981), Harsanyi (1975a), Rawls (1974), Resnik (1983, 1987).

17. See Aumann (1976), Barwise (1988), Binmore and Brandenberger (forthcoming), Brandenberger (forthcoming), Lewis (1969), Mertens and Zamir (1985), Werlang (1986). The concept will be discussed more in Chapter 6.

18. Column's act 1 *weakly dominates* his act 2 because he can do better with act 1 on one of Row's choices but does equally well with both acts on Row's other choice.

19. Pearce (1984) and Bernheim (1984) both argue that in noncooperative game theory, subjective probabilities over other players' acts should make the acts of different players independent, because their decisions are assumed to be causally independent. I believe that this identification of causal independence with independence in the subjective probabilities is incorrect, and that causal independence is here consistent with all kinds of subjective dependence. This issue will be discussed in Chapter 7.

20. Notice that if we change the payoffs for neither player swerving to [− 100, − 100], assuming that the crash will be rather serious, the mixed equilibrium will look worse to both players than either of the pure equilibria.

21. Nash's function is this: for any player, with possible acts A_i, the old probability, p, gets mapped into the new probability, p', by:

$$p'(A) = \frac{p(A) + \max\,[0,\,U(A)\,-\,U(\text{status quo})]}{1 + \Sigma_i \max\,[0,\,U(A_i)\,-\,U(\text{status quo})]}$$

22. This game is from Myerson (1978). The following discussion follows Myerson closely.

23. R2 is said to weakly dominate R1 since whatever Column does, R2 gives Row at least as great a payoff as R1, and for at least one of Column's possible acts, R2 gives Row a greater payoff than R1. Likewise C2 weakly dominates C1.

24. The *tracing procedure* of Harsanyi and Selten (1988) will be discussed in Chapter 7.

25. See also Aumann and Maschler (1972) and Selten (1975).

26. If I understand him correctly, Gauthier (1986) claims that it is nevertheless rational to carry out the threat.

2. Dynamic Deliberation: Equilibria

1. The Bayesian foundations for informational feedback will be discussed in detail in Chapter 4.

2. This is strictly true only if we neglect processing costs of deliberation. In general, a Bayesian deliberator will deliberate until the cost of another cycle exceeds the expected utility of further deliberation. If the expected utility of deliberation is not known, an estimate of it may be used as a kind of "satisficing level." In order to discuss limiting behavior at a general level, we will need to abstract from these considerations and proceed as if there were no processing costs. But in the real world there always are some processing costs. The computer programs given in the Appendix incorporate a satisficing level.

3. We will assume here that at the end of some specified time for deliberation, the existing state of indecision will automatically be converted to the corresponding default mixed act, whether or not the state of indecision has

reached an equilibrium. Thus the decisionmaker will always make a decision.

4. I am indebted to Michael Teit Nielsen for pointing out a flaw in an earlier formulation of "seeking the good."

5. A dynamics closely related to the Nash flow was proposed by Brown and von Neumann (1950):

$$\frac{dp(A)}{dt} = \text{cov}(A)^2 - p(A)\Sigma_j\text{cov}(A_j)^2$$

6. We are assuming here that the dynamics is autonomous. More general models with nonautonomous dynamics could be considered. See Chapter 7.

7. We assume here, and in subsequent updating, that the joint probabilities are product probabilities; each player views all other players as probabilistically independent. This simplifying assumption should ultimately be dropped. See the discussion in Chapter 7.

8. In this case joint probabilities are product probabilities, as specified in note 7, above.

9. Of course, if the given player also shares the inductive rule and shares the data that serve as input there seems no reason why her own beliefs about the action that she ultimately takes may not keep step with the beliefs of other players. But this additional story is not essential to the model, since her beliefs about other players are what she needs to calculate her expected utilities.

10. See Aumann (1987), Binmore and Brandenberger (forthcoming), Brandenberger and Dekel (1985a,b, 1986, 1987), and compare Harsanyi (1973a).

11. This position is consistent with the usual story of the first player flipping a coin, but does not require it.

12. If we consider the change in probability given by the discrete Bayes map, $B:$, and consider effortless processing by letting the time between updates go to zero, we get the *Bayes flow:*

$$\frac{dp(A)}{dt} = p(A)\frac{p(e|A) - \Sigma_i p(A_i)p(e|A_i)}{\Sigma_i p(A_i)p(e|A_i)}$$

13. These considerations are suggestive rather than definitive. One might take the position that where Nash dynamics raises zeros, the evidence itself has zero prior probability. Or one might hold that these are never really zero probabilities but rather infinitesimal ones, then conditioning on evidence whose *a priori* probability is infinitesimal can raise an infinitesimal probability to a standard one. Something similar can be done with lexicographically ordered probabilities. See Brandenberger and Dekel (1986).

14. The decisionmaker's current expected utilities are her expectation of the final expected utilities.

15. Since this dynamics is invariant under change of unit, there is no problem in shrinking the scale to one which would be appropriate for likelihoods. We assume some such sort of normalization procedure as part of the precise realization of the dynamics and as applying to all players using that dynamics.

16. This example differs from Myerson's original example in that values of -7 in Myerson's example have here been replaced with values of -4. In Myerson's original example, even the Nash dynamics "turns the corner." I am indebted to Mr. Kurt Norlin for a careful analysis of this example.

17. Samuelson's program of generalized evolutionary game theory is, in many ways, very close to deliberational dynamics.

18. Where a player may have different choices at different information sets in a tree, she may adopt Kuhn's (1953) metaphor and consider her future selves at information sets as her agents. This leads to Selten's (1975) *agent normal form*, which is a matrix game for all the agents of an extensive-form game, with each agent being equipped with the payoff of her player. Deliberational dynamics for a game in extensive form is defined as dynamic deliberation on its agent normal form, *with the modification that each agent use her player's probabilities conditional on being at that information set*. When players are in a completely mixed state of indecision, these conditional probabilities are defined in the usual way: $p(Q|I) = p(Q \& I)/p(I)$. Under the strong common-knowledge assumptions in force here, a deliberational equilibrium for a player consists of deliberational equilibria for all her agents.

19. The noncredible equilibrium is *subgame perfect* in the sense of Selten.

20. The treatment of second and third place may be crucial here if we start out in the vicinity of the "bad" equilibrium. In that case Nash deliberation would not lead to a reasonable revision of the relative probabilities of A2 and A3.

21. Marx to Engels, June 18, 1862, in *The Letters of Karl Marx*, selected and translated with explanatory notes and an Introduction by Saul K. Padover (Englewood Cliffs, N.J.: Prentice-Hall, 1979), 157.

3. Dynamic Deliberation: Stability

1. For every neighborhood, N, of e there is a neighborhood, N', of e such that the trajectories of points in N' at time zero remain in N for all positive time. See Hirsch and Smale (1974, chap. 9) for a detailed treatment.

2. The basin of attraction for [R1, C2] includes the interior of the whole space under the Darwin dynamics but, as we saw in the last chapter, it is somewhat smaller under the Nash dynamics.

3. It is also a strongly stable spiral attractor under the Darwin flow.

4. Kohlberg and Mertens (1986, p. 1004, n. 2): "Note that strategic stability is quite different from dynamic stability, which is a property usually associated with an adjustment process, or from evolutionary stability (in the sense of Maynard-Smith)."

5. This is true in the most general sense of structural stability, which is framed directly in terms of small perturbations in the vector field. See Hirsch and Smale (1974).

6. For the same sort of phenomenon in a close relative of the Darwin dynamics, see Zeeman (1980).

7. The field looks the same, that is, except that Bayesian dynamical rules make all combinations of pure strategies fixed points since zeros are not raised by conditioning. See the discussion in Chapter 2.

8. The question of what happens when we weaken the common-knowledge assumption will be discussed in Chapter 6.

9. See van Damme (1983) for a classification of various refinements of the Nash equilibrium concept, all of which are satisfied by Harsanyi-strong equilibria.

10. Of course, games which share this structure need not be a dilemma in any sense. The reader can verify that one can make up a game of this kind where the unique equilibrium outcome is optimal for all involved: "Prisoner's Delight."

11. There is much relevant game-theoretic literature. For instance, Moulin (1984) related solvability by iterated elimination of weakly dominated strategies to stability under the Cournot tâtonnement adjustment process. See also Selten (1975), Kohlberg and Mertens (1986), van Damme (1983), Kalai and Samet (1984).

4. The Value of Knowledge

1. If the experiment were not dichotomous but had n possible results, the expected utility of the prior Bayes act would graph as a convex surface in $(n + 1)$-dimensional Euclidian space lying below a hyperplane representing prior expectation of the expected utility of the posterior Bayes act.

2. See Maher (forthcoming) for a careful discussion.

3. But even here there is the assumption that the states are probabilistically independent of the determination to utilize the experimental results.

4. For instance, consider the Abbott and Costello example in my (1982) "Causal Decision Theory": Costello is charged with keeping a match dry until a crucial time. Abbott keeps asking Costello if the match is dry and Costello keeps replying "Yes." Finally it is time to light the match. "Are you sure it's dry?" Abbott asks for the final time. "Yes, I lit it a little while ago to make sure," Costello replies.

5. For an example where (1) fails, consider the case of the Wrath of Khan. You are a prisoner of Khan, who (you firmly believe) is about to insert a mindworm into your brain that will cause you to update by conditioning on the denial of the experimental result. For an example where (2) fails, consider the compulsive loser who conditions correctly on the experimental result but then proceeds to choose the act with smallest expected utility.

6. See Eells (1982), Lewis (1980), and Skyrms (1980a, 1982, 1984) for discussions of this generalization and its relation to evidential decision theory.
7. Assumed here to be countably additive.
8. On a Polish state space.

5. Dynamic Coherence

1. In *Theory of Probability,* de Finetti (1975, vol. 1) again was quite explicit on this point: "The acquisition of a further piece of information, *H*—in other words *experience,* since experience is nothing more than the acquisition of further information—acts always and only in the way that we have described: *suppressing the alternatives that turn out no longer to be possible . . .* As a result of this the probabilities are the $P(E|H)$ instead of the $P(E)$ . . ."
2. This sort of argument can be made in a much more general setting.
3. This scale may be constructed with the help of hypothetical gambles using hypothetical scaling probabilities.
4. In the accompanying discussion of Smith's (1961) paper, Lindley makes this comment: "Now it is obviously desirable to relax axioms so long as the essence of the situation being axiomatized is not lost, but my fear is that it has been lost this evening. We are trying to build up a description of real decisionmaking and in real decisionmaking everybody does decide, he never sits on the fence, for to do so is a decision to sit."
5. There is an interval-valued version of the theory of the economy of new information that remains to be investigated here. The preference for acquisition of new information may be unambiguous, although—perhaps because—preference for the acts is ambiguous.

6. Good Habits

1. See Kavka's discussion (1986, chap. 9) of Hobbes' "rule egoism," from which the passage from the *Leviathan* is quoted. An example from Hume's writing may be found in his *Treatise on Human Nature* (1888, book 3, part 3, sec. 1).
2. Sidgewick (1874, chap. 7) argued that "it is easier to tear down than build up," both with respect to our own habits and with respect to laws and customs of society. See also Schneewind (1977, chap. 12, sec. 4).
3. Hobbes relied heavily on such considerations in his reply to the Fool in chapter 15 of the *Leviathan.* See also Kavka's discussion (1986, 4-3, 9-5) of this topic.
4. Thus Gauthier's (1986) attempt to redefine rationality as "constrained maximization," and thus get the rationality of rule utilitarianism for free, appears to me ill conceived.
5. The three most widely discussed solutions make appeals to natural sympathy, education, or government.
6. See also Rosenthal (1981).

7. Note that the treatment I gave in Chapter 3 of dynamic deliberation for extensive-form games in terms of the agent normal form was based on the presumption of common knowledge of rationality. In the absence of such common knowledge the account is oversimplified because learning about whether the players are rational or not may take place during the course of the game.

8. This section employs the following form of Pareto dominance: S Pareto dominates S' for the group if and only if all members of the group prefer S to S'. This definition allows a little slippage from the utilitarian tradition. It guarantees a utilitarian representation in which no one has negative weight, but it does not guarantee that everyone has positive weight. A state is Pareto optimal if and only if it is not Pareto dominated by any other state.

9. The problem is one of coordinating on the target Nash equilibrium and the target point that Pareto dominates it.

10. Hume, "An Inquiry Concerning the Principles of Morals" (1881, app. 3). See also Hume, *A Treatise on Human Nature* (1888, book 3, part 2, sec. 2): "And this may be properly called a convention or agreement betwixt us, tho' without the imposition of a promise; since actions of each of us have reference to those of the other, and are performed upon the supposition, that something is to be performed on the other part."

11. See Aumann (1976, 1987), Barwise (1988), Binmore and Brandenberger (forthcoming), Brandenberger (forthcoming), Brandenberger and Dekel (1985a,b, 1986), Lewis (1969), Mertens and Zamir (1985), and Reny (1987).

12. See Lewis (1969, chap. 2). Lewis cited Schelling (1960) as a major influence, and less explicit forms of the idea are to be found in Schelling's book.

13. An example is the "KK-thesis": if X knows that p then X knows that X knows that p.

14. See the discussion of the chain-store paradox in Kreps and Wilson (1982a) and Milgrom and Roberts (1982).

7. Prospects for a Theory of Rational Deliberation

1. Roughly, a strategy is rationalizable for a player if she has a hierarchy of beliefs, beliefs about beliefs, and so on, such that her choosing that strategy together with the hierarchy of beliefs is consistent with the expected utility principle at every level.

2. I have argued that rationalizability, properly conceived, is what Brandenberger and Dekel (1987) call "correlated rationalizability." They prove that correlated rationalizability is equivalent to a kind of correlated equilibrium.

3. See Zabell (1988) for a delightful review and cautionary tale regarding symmetry assumptions in induction.

4. Richard Jeffrey tells me that Carnap was well aware that his inductive logic was modeling a special case, but he hoped to start with the simplest cases and eventually build up an inductive logic adequate to scientific inference.

Thus, Carnap might very well agree with these criticisms of "Carnapian deliberators."

5. That the Brown–von Neumann flow converges in the case studied by Miyasawa (1961) for fictitious play was established by Leal (1986). See also Rosenmuller (1971).

6. This argument would be based on the Poincaré-Bendixson theorem. See Hirsch and Smale (1974).

7. In the theory of computation where the "habits" are carried out by a machine. Some steps in this direction have been taken by Green (1982) and Rubenstein (1986).

References

Adams, E. 1962. "On Rational Betting Systems." *Archiv für Mathematische Logik and Grundlagenforschung* 6:7–18, 112–128.

———— 1988. "Consistency and Decision: Variations on a Ramseyian Theme." In *Causation in Decision, Belief Change, and Statistics,* ed. W. Harper and B. Skyrms, 49–69. Dordrecht: Kluwer.

Adams, E., and R. Rosenkrantz. 1980. "Applying the Jeffrey Decision Model to Rational Betting and Information Acquisition." *Theory and Decision* 12:1–20.

Aristotle. 1976. *The Nicomachean Ethics.* Trans. J. A. K. Thompson, rev. H. Tredennick. Harmondsworth: Penguin.

Armendt, B. 1980. "Is There a Dutch Book Theorem for Probability Kinematics?" *Philosophy of Science* 47:583–588.

———— 1986. "A Foundation for Causal Decision Theory." *Topoi* 5:3–19.

———— 1988. "Conditional Preference and Causal Expected Utility." In *Causation in Decision, Belief Change, and Statistics,* ed. W. Harper and B. Skyrms, 3–24. Dordrecht: Kluwer.

———— Forthcoming. "Impartiality and Causal Decision Theory." *PSA (1988),* vol. 1. East Lansing, Mich.: Philosophy of Science Association.

Arrow, K. 1951a. "Alternative Approaches to the Theory of Choice in Risk-Taking Situations." *Econometrica* 19:404–437.

———— 1951b. *Social Choice and Individual Values.* New York: Wiley.

———— 1973. "Some Ordinalist-Utilitarian Notes on Rawls's Theory of Justice." *Journal of Philosophy* 70:255.

———— 1986. "Rationality of Self and Others in an Economic System." In *Rational Choice,* ed. R. Hogarth and M. Reder, 201–215. Chicago: University of Chicago Press.

Aumann, R. J. 1974. "Subjectivity and Correlation in Randomized Strategies." *Journal of Mathematical Economics* 1:67–96.

———— 1976. "Agreeing to Disagree." *Annals of Statistics* 4:1236–1239.

———— 1987. "Correlated Equilibrium as an Expression of Bayesian Rationality." *Econometrica* 55:1–18.

Aumann, R. J., and M. Maschler. 1972. "Some Thoughts on the Minimax Principle." *Management Science* 18:54–63.

Axelrod, R. 1981. "The Emergence of Cooperation among Egoists." *American Political Science Review* 75:306–318.

———— 1984. *The Evolution of Cooperation.* New York: Basic Books.

Axelrod, R., and W. D. Hamilton. 1981. "The Evolution of Cooperation." *Science* 211:1390–1396.

Baillie, P. 1973. "Confirmation and the Dutch Book Argument." *British Journal for the Philosophy of Science* 24:393–397.

Banks, J. S., and J. Sobel. 1987. "Equilibrium Selection in Signaling Games." *Econometrica* 55:647–659.

Barwise, J. 1988. "On the Model Theory of Common Knowledge." Stanford, Calif.: CSLI/Philosophy, Stanford University.

Bernheim, B. D. 1984. "Rationalizable Strategic Behavior." *Econometrica* 52:1007–1028.

Bernoulli, D. 1783. "Specimen theoria novae de mensura sortis." *Commentarii Academiae Scientarum Imperialis Petropolitanae* 5:175–192. Trans. as "Exposition of a new theory of the measurement of risk" by L. Sommer in *Econometrica* 22 (1954):647–759.

Bicchieri, C. 1988a. "Common Knowledge and Backward Induction: A Solution to the Paradox." In *Theoretical Aspects of Reasoning about Knowledge,* ed. M. Vardi, 381–393. Los Altos, Calif.: Morgan Kaufman.

———— 1988b. "Self-refuting Theories of Strategic Interaction: A Paradox of Common Knowledge." *Erkenntnis* 11:1–17.

———— 1988c. "Strategic Behavior and Counterfactuals." *Synthese* 75:1–35.

Billingsley, P. 1979. *Probability and Measure.* New York: Wiley.

Binmore, K. 1987, 1988. "Modeling Rational Players I and II." *Economics and Philosophy* 3:179–214, 4:9–55.

———— 1988. "Game Theory and the Social Contract." Working paper, Department of Economics, University of Michigan, Ann Arbor, Mich.

Binmore, K., and A. Brandenberger. Forthcoming. "Common Knowledge and Game Theory." *Journal of Economic Perspectives.*

Blume, L. E., and D. Easley. 1982. "Learning to Be Rational." *Journal of Economic Theory* 26:340–351.

Bohnenblust, H. F., S. Karlin, and L. S. Shapley. 1950. "Solutions of Discrete Two-Person Games." In *Contributions to the Theory of Games,* vol. 1, ed. H. W. Kuhn and A. W. Tucker, 51–72. Annals of Mathematics Studies 24. Princeton: Princeton University Press.

Borel, E. 1924. "Sur les jeux où interviennent l'hasard et l'habileté des joueurs." In *Theorie des probabilités,* 204–224. Paris: Librairie Scientifique, J. Hermann. Trans. as "On Games that Involve Chance and the Skill of the Players" by L. J. Savage in *Econometrica* 21 (1953):101–115.

Brandenberger, A. Forthcoming. "The Role of Common Knowledge Assumptions in Game Theory." In *The Economics of Information, Games, and Missing Markets*, ed. F. Hahn.

Brandenberger, A., and E. Dekel. 1985a. "Common Knowledge with Probability." Research paper 796R, Graduate School of Business, Stanford University, Stanford, Calif.

———— 1985b. "Hierarchies of Beliefs and Common Knowledge." Research paper 841, Graduate School of Business, Stanford University, Stanford, Calif.

———— 1986. "On an Axiomatic Approach to Refinements of Nash Equilibrium." Economic theory discussion paper 4, Department of Applied Economics, Cambridge University, Cambridge, England.

———— 1987. "Rationalizability and Correlated Equilibria." *Econometrica* 55:1391–1402.

Broome, J. 1987. "Utilitarianism and Expected Utility." *Journal of Philosophy* 84:405–422.

Brown, G. W. 1951. "Iterative Solutions of Games by Fictitious Play." In *Activity Analysis of Production and Allocation*, ed. T. C. Koopmans, 374–376. Cowles Commission Monograph. New York: Wiley.

Brown, G. W., and J. von Neumann. 1950. "Solution of Games by Differential Equations." In *Contributions to the Theory of Games*, vol. 1., ed. H. W. Kuhn and A. W. Tucker, 73–79. Annals of Mathematics Studies 24. Princeton: Princeton University Press.

Buehler, R. J. 1976. "Coherent Preferences." *Annals of Statistics* 4:1051–64.

Carnap, R. 1950. *Logical Foundations of Probability.* Chicago: University of Chicago Press.

———— 1952. *The Continuum of Inductive Methods.* Chicago: University of Chicago Press.

Chihara, C., and R. Kennedy. 1979. "The Dutch Book Argument: Its Logical Flaws, Its Subjective Sources." *Philosophical Studies* 36:19–33.

Chipman, J. S. 1971a. "Non-Archimedean Behavior under Risk: An Elementary Analysis—with Application to the Theory of Assets." In *Preferences, Utility and Demand*, ed. J. S. Chipman et al. New York: Harcourt Brace.

———— 1971b. "On the Lexicographic Representation of Preference Orderings." In *Preferences, Utility and Demand*, ed. J. S. Chipman et al. New York: Harcourt Brace.

Cornfield, J. 1969. "The Bayesian Outlook and Its Application." *Biometrics* 25:617–658.

Crawford, V. 1974. "Learning the Optimal Strategy in Zero Sum Games." *Econometrica* 42:885–891.

———— 1985. "Learning Behavior and Mixed-Strategy Nash Equilibria." *Journal of Economic Behavior and Organization* 6:69–78.

Dalkey, N. 1953. "Equivalence of Information Patterns and Essentially Determinate Games." In *Contributions to the Theory of Games* vol. 2, ed.

H. W. Kuhn and A. W. Tucker, 217–245. Annals of Mathematics Studies 28. Princeton: Princeton University Press.

Danskin, J. M. 1954. "Fictitious Play for Continuous Games." *Naval Research Logistics Quarterly* 1:313–320.

de Finetti, B. 1937. "La Prévision: ses lois logiques, ses sources subjectives." *Annales de l'Institut Henri Poincaré* 7:1–68. Trans. as "Foresight: Its Logical Laws, Its Subjective Sources" in Kyburg and Smokler (1980).

———— 1970. "John von Neumann e Oskar Morgenstern." In *I Maestri dell'Economica Moderna.* Milan: Franco Agnelli.

———— 1975. *Theory of Probability,* vol. 1. New York: Wiley.

———— 1977. "Probabilities of Probabilities: A Real Problem or a Misunderstanding?" In *New Developments in the Applications of Bayesian Methods,* ed. A. Aykac and C. Brumat, 1–10. Amsterdam: North-Holland.

DeGroot, M. H., and J. B. Kadane. 1983. "Optimal Sequential Decisions in Problems Involving More Than One Decision Maker." In *Recent Advances in Statistics,* ed. M. H. Rizvi, J. S. Rustagi, and D. Siegmund, 197–210. New York: Academic Press.

Dempster, A. P. 1968. "A Generalization of Bayesian Inference." *Journal of the Royal Statistical Society,* ser. B, 30:205–247.

Diaconis, P., and D. Freedman. 1980. "Finite Exchangeable Sequences." *Annals of Probability* 8:745–764.

———— 1984. "Partial Exchangeability and Sufficiency." In *Statistics: Applications and New Directions,* ed. J. K. Ghosh and J. Roy, 205–236. Calcutta: Indian Statistical Institute.

Diaconis, P., and S. Zabell. 1982. "Updating Subjective Probability." *Journal of the American Statistical Association* 77:822–830.

Domotor, Z. 1980. "Probability Kinematics and the Representation of Belief Change." *Philosophy of Science* 47:384–404.

Donkin, W. F. 1851. "On Certain Questions Relating to the Theory of Probabilities." *Philosophical Magazine* 1:353–368, 2:55–60.

Dubins, L. E. 1975. "Finitely Additive Conditional Probabilities, Conglomerability and Disintegrations." *Annals of Probability* 3:89–99.

Dynkin, E. B. 1978. "Sufficient Statistics and Extreme Points." *Annals of Probability* 6:705–730.

Edgeworth, F. Y. 1881. *Mathematical Psychics.* London: C. Kegan Paul.

Eells, E. 1982. *Rational Decision and Causality.* Cambridge: Cambridge University Press.

———— 1984a. "Causal Decision Theory." *PSA (1984).* East Lansing, Mich.: Philosophy of Science Association.

———— 1984b. "Metatickles and the Dynamics of Deliberation." *Theory and Decision* 17:71–95.

———— 1985. "Weirich on Decision Instability." *Australasian Journal of Philosophy* 63:473–478.

Eells, E., and E. Sober. 1983. "Probabilistic Causality and the Question of Transitivity." *Philosophy of Science* 50:37–57.

——— 1986. "Common Causes and Decision Theory." *Philosophy of Science* 53:223–245.

Eibl-Eibesfeld, I. 1970. *Ethology: The Biology of Behavior.* New York: Holt, Rinehart and Winston.

Freedman, D. A., and R. A. Purves. 1969. "Bayes Method for Bookies." *Annals of Mathematical Statistics* 40:1177–1186.

Fudenberg, D., and E. Maskin. 1986. "The Folk Theorem in Repeated Games with Discounting and with Incomplete Information." *Econometrica* 54:533–554.

Gaifman, H. 1988. "A Theory of Higher Order Probabilities." In *Causation, Chance and Credence,* 191–219. ed. B. Skyrms and W. Harper. Dordrecht: Kluwer.

Gauthier, D. 1969. *The Logic of the Leviathan.* Oxford: Oxford University Press.

——— 1974. "Rational Cooperation." *Nous* 8:53–65.

——— 1975. "Coordination." *Dialogue* 14:195–221.

——— 1986. *Morals by Agreement.* Oxford: Clarendon Press.

Geanakoplos, J., and H. Polimarchakis. 1982. "We Can't Disagree Forever." *Journal of Economic Theory* 28:192–200.

Gibbard, A., and W. Harper. 1981. "Counterfactuals and Two Kinds of Expected Utility." In *Ifs: Conditionals, Beliefs, Decision, Chance, and Time,* ed. W. L. Harper, R. Stalnaker, and G. Pearce, 153–190. Dordrecht: Reidel.

Gilbert, M. 1981. "Game Theory and Convention." *Synthese* 46:41–93.

——— 1983. "Agreements, Conventions and Language." *Synthese* 54:375–404.

Goldstein, M. 1981. "Revising Previsions: A Geometric Interpretation." *Journal of the Royal Statistical Society,* ser. B, 43:105–130.

——— 1983. "The Prevision of a Prevision." *Journal of the American Statistical Association* 78:817–819.

——— 1986. "Exchangeable Belief Structures." *Journal of the American Statistical Association* 81:971–976.

Good, I. J. 1950. *Probability and the Weighing of Evidence.* New York: Hafner.

——— 1965. *The Estimation of Probabilities: An Essay on Modern Bayesian Methods.* Cambridge, Mass.: MIT Press.

——— 1967. "On the Principle of Total Evidence." *British Journal for the Philosophy of Science* 17:319–321.

——— 1974. "A Little Learning Can Be Dangerous." *British Journal for the Philosophy of Science* 25:340–342.

——— 1981. "The Weight of Evidence Provided by Uncertain Testimony or from an Uncertain Event." *Journal of Statistical Computation and Simulation* 13:56–60.

——— 1983. *Good Thinking: The Foundations of Probability and Its Applications.* Minneapolis: University of Minnesota Press.

Graves, P. 1989. "The Total Evidence Principle for Probability Kinematics." *Philosophy of Science* 56:317–324.

Green, E. 1982. "Internal Costs and Equilibrium: The Case of Repeated Prisoner's Dilemmas." Working paper, University of Pittsburgh, Pittsburgh, Penn.

Hacking, I. 1967. "Slightly More Realistic Personal Probability." *Philosophy of Science* 34:311–325.

Hammond, P. 1981. "Ex Ante and Ex Post Welfare Optimality under Uncertainty." *Economica* 48:135–150.

Harley, C. 1981. "Learning the Evolutionary Stable Strategy." *Journal of Theoretical Biology* 89:611–633.

Harper, W. 1984. "Ratifiability and Causal Decision Theory: Comments on Eells and Seidenfeld." *PSA (1984)*. East Lansing, Mich.: Philosophy of Science Association.

——— 1986. "Mixed Strategies and Ratifiability in Causal Decision Theory." *Erkenntnis* 24:25–36.

——— 1988. "Causal Decision Theory and Game Theory: A Classic Argument for Equilibrium Solutions, a Defense of Weak Equilibria, and a New Problem for the Normal Form Representation." In *Causation in Decision, Belief Change, and Statistics*, ed. W. Harper and B. Skyrms, 25–48. Dordrecht: Kluwer.

Harsanyi, J. C. 1953. "Cardinal Utility in Welfare Economics and the Theory of Risk Taking." *Journal of Political Economy* 61:343–345.

——— 1955. "Cardinal Welfare, Individualistic Ethics, and Interpersonal Comparisons of Utility." *Journal of Political Economy* 63:309–321.

——— 1967. "Games with Incomplete Information Played by Bayesian Players," parts 1–3. *Management Science* 14:159–183, 320–334, 486–502.

——— 1973a. "Games with Randomly Disturbed Payoffs: A New Rationale for Mixed Strategy Equilibrium Points." *International Journal of Game Theory* 2:1–23.

——— 1973b. "Oddness of the Number of Equilibrium Points: A New Proof." *International Journal of Game Theory* 2:235–250.

——— 1975a. "Can the Maximin Principle Serve as a Basis for Morality?" *American Political Science Review* 69:594–606.

——— 1975b. "The Tracing Procedure: A Bayesian Approach to Defining a Solution Concept for *n*-Person Noncooperative Games." *International Journal of Game Theory* 4:61–94.

——— 1976a. *Essays in Ethics, Social Behavior and Scientific Explanation*. Dordrecht: Reidel.

——— 1976b. "A Solution Concept for *n*-Person Noncooperative Games." *International Journal of Game Theory* 5:211–225.

——— 1977. *Rational Behavior and Bargaining Equilibrium in Games and Social Situations*. Cambridge: Cambridge University Press.

——— 1982a. *Papers in Game Theory*. Dordrecht: Reidel.

—— 1982b. "Solutions for Some Bargaining Games under the Harsanyi-Selten Solution Theory." *Mathematical Social Sciences* 3:179–191, 259–279.

Harsanyi, J. C., and R. Selten. 1988. *A General Theory of Equilibrium Selection in Games*. Cambridge, Mass.: MIT Press.

Heath, D., and W. Sudderth. 1972. "On a Theorem of de Finetti, Oddsmaking and Game Theory." *Annals of Mathematical Statistics* 43:2071–2077.

—— 1978. "On Finitely Additive Priors, Coherence and Extended Admissibility." *Annals of Statistics* 6:333–345.

Hill, B., and D. Lane. 1985. "Conglomerability and Countable Additivity." In *Bayesian Inference and Decision Techniques*, ed. P. K. Goel and A. Zellner. Amsterdam: North-Holland.

Hintikka, J. 1962. *Knowledge and Belief*. Ithaca: Cornell University Press.

Hirsch, M. W., and S. Smale. 1974. *Differential Equations, Dynamical Systems and Linear Algebra*. New York: Academic Press.

Horwich, P. 1985. "Decision Theory in the Light of Newcomb's Problem." *Philosophy of Science* 52:431–450.

Hume, D. 1881. "An Inquiry Concerning the Principles of Morals." In *Essays and Treatises on Various Subjects*, 109–177. Boston: J. P. Mendum.

—— 1888. *A Treatise on Human Nature*. Oxford: Clarendon Press.

Hutcheson, F. 1742. *An Essay on the Nature and Conduct of the Passions and Affections with Illustrations on the Moral Sense*, 3d ed. Facsimile ed., 1969; Gainsville, Fla.: Scholar's Facsimiles and Reprints.

Huxley, T. H. 1888. "The Struggle for Existence." *Nineteenth Century* 23:161–180.

Jackson, F., and R. Pargetter. 1976. "A Modified Dutch Book Argument." *Philosophical Studies* 29:403–407.

Jeffrey, R. 1965. *The Logic of Decision*. New York: McGraw-Hill. Rev. ed., 1983; Chicago: University of Chicago Press.

—— 1968. "Probable Knowledge." In *The Problem of Inductive Logic*, ed. I. Lakatos. Amsterdam: North-Holland.

—— 1970. Review of *A Paradox of Information*, by David Miller. *Journal of Symbolic Logic* 35:124–127.

—— 1981. "The Logic of Decision Defended." *Synthese* 48:473–492.

—— 1984. "Bayesianism with a Human Face." *Minnesota Studies in the Philosophy of Science* 10:133–156.

Jevons, W. S. 1871. *Theory of Political Economy*. London: n.p.

Kadane, J., and P. D. Larkey. 1982. "Subjective Probability and the Theory of Games." *Management Science* 28:113–120.

Kahn, H. 1984. *Thinking about the Unthinkable in the 1980s*. New York: Simon and Schuster.

Kalai, E., and D. Samet. 1984. "Persistent Equilibria in Strategic Games." *International Journal of Game Theory* 13:129–144.

Kalai, E., and W. Stanford. 1988. "Finite Rationality and Interpersonal Complexity in Repeated Games." *Econometrica* 55:303–328.

Kallenberg, O. 1983. *Random Measures*, 3d ed. New York: Academic Press.

Kavka, G. 1983. "Hobbes' War of All against All." *Ethics* 93:291–310.

——— 1986. *Hobbesian Moral and Political Theory*. Princeton: Princeton University Press.

——— 1987. *Paradoxes of Nuclear Deterrence*. Cambridge: Cambridge University Press.

Kemeny, J. 1955. "Fair Bets and Inductive Probabilities." *Journal of Symbolic Logic* 20:251–262.

Kohlberg, E., and J. Mertens. 1986. "On the Strategic Stability of Equilibria." *Econometrica* 54:1003–1037.

Kreps, D., P. Milgrom, J. Roberts, and R. Wilson. 1982. "Rational Cooperation in Finitely Repeated Prisoner's Dilemma." *Journal of Economic Theory* 27:245–252.

Kreps, D., and G. Ramey. 1987. "Structural Consistency, Consistency and Rationality." *Econometrica* 55:1331–1348.

Kreps, D., and R. Wilson. 1982a. "Reputation and Incomplete Information." *Journal of Economic Theory* 27:253–279.

——— 1982b. "Sequential Equilibria." *Econometrica* 50:863–894.

Kropotkin, P. 1902. *Mutual Aid*. London: n.p.

Kuhn, H. W. 1953. "Extensive Games and the Problem of Information." In *Contributions to the Theory of Games*, vol. 2., ed. H. W. Kuhn and A. W. Tucker, 193–216. Annals of Mathematics Studies 28. Princeton: Princeton University Press.

Kyburg, H. 1961. *Probability and the Logic of Rational Belief*. Middleton, Conn.: Wesleyan University Press.

——— 1974. *The Logical Foundations of Statistical Inference*. Dordrecht: Reidel.

——— 1978. "Subjective Probability: Criticisms, Reflections and Problems." *Journal of Philosophical Logic* 7:157–180.

——— 1980. "Acts and Conditional Probabilities." *Theory and Decision* 12:149–171.

——— 1988. "Powers." In *Causation in Decision, Belief Change, and Statistics*, ed. W. Harper and B. Skyrms, 71–82. Dordrecht: Kluwer.

Kyburg, H. E., Jr., and H. Smokler, eds. 1980. *Studies in Subjective Probability*. Huntington, N.Y.: Kreiger.

Lane, D. A., and W. D. Sudderth. 1983. "Coherent and Continuous Inference." *Annals of Statistics* 11:114–120.

——— 1984. "Coherent Predictive Inference." *Sankhya*, ser. A, 46:166–185.

——— 1985. "Coherent Predictions Are Strategic." *Annals of Statistics* 13:1244–1248.

Lave, L. 1962. "An Empirical Approach to Prisoner's Dilemma." *Quarterly Journal of Economics* 76:424–436.

Lay, S. 1982. *Convex Sets and Their Applications*. New York: Wiley.

Leal, C. I. S. 1986. "Topics in Non-cooperative Game Theory: Hyperstability of

Nash Equilibria, Brown–von Neumann Fictitious Play and Principle's Problem." Ph.D. diss. Princeton University, Princeton, N.J.

Lehman, R. 1955. "On Confirmation and Rational Betting." *Journal of Symbolic Logic* 20:251–262.

Levi, I. 1974. "On Indeterminate Probabilities." *Journal of Philosophy* 71:391–418.

—— 1975. "Newcomb's Many Problems." *Theory and Decision* 6:161–175.

—— 1978. "Confirmational Conditionalization." *Journal of Philosophy* 75:730–737.

—— 1980. *The Enterprise of Knowledge.* Cambridge, Mass.: MIT Press.

—— 1982. "A Note on Newcombmania." *Journal of Philosophy* 79:337–342.

—— 1983. "The Wrong Box." *Journal of Philosophy* 80:534–542.

—— 1984. *Decisions and Revisions.* London: Cambridge University Press.

—— Forthcoming. "The Demons of Decision."

Lewis, D. 1969. *Convention.* Cambridge, Mass.: Harvard University Press.

—— 1979. "Prisoner's Dilemma Is a Newcomb Problem." *Philosophy and Public Affairs* 8:235–240.

—— 1980. "Causal Decision Theory." *Australasian Journal of Philosophy* 59:5–30.

—— 1984. "Devil's Bargains and the Real World." In *The Security Gamble: Deterrence Dilemmas in the Nuclear Age,* ed D. MacLean. Totowa, N.J.: Rowman and Allenheld.

Lewis, D. K., and J. S. Richardson. 1966. "Scriven on Human Unpredictability." *Philosophical Studies* 17:69–74.

Lindley, D. V. 1965. *Introduction to Probability and Statistics,* part 2. Cambridge: Cambridge University Press.

Lipman, B. 1988. "How to Decide How to Decide How to . . .: Limited Rationality in Decisions and Games." Working paper, Carnegie-Mellon University, Pittsburgh, Penn.

Loeve, M. 1963. *Probability Theory,* 3d ed. New York: van Nostrand.

Lorenz, K. 1966. *On Aggression.* London: Methuen.

Luce, R. D., and H. Raiffa. 1957. *Games and Decisions.* New York: Wiley.

Maher, P. Forthcoming. "Symptomatic Acts and the Value of Evidence in Causal Decision Theory." *Philosophy of Science.*

Marshak, J. 1975. "Do Personal Probabilities of Probabilities Have an Operational Meaning?" *Theory and Decision* 6:127–132.

Marshall, A. 1938. *Principles of Economics,* 8th ed. London: Macmillan.

Martin, R. L. 1984. *Recent Essays on Truth and the Liar Paradox.* Oxford: Oxford University Press.

Maynard Smith, J. 1982. *Evolution and the Theory of Games.* Cambridge: Cambridge University Press.

Maynard Smith, J., and G. R. Price. 1973. "The Logic of Animal Conflict." *Nature* 146:15–18.

McKelvey, R., and T. Page. 1986. "Common Knowledge, Consensus, and Aggregate Information." *Econometrica* 54:109–127.

Meggido, N. 1988. "On Computable Beliefs of Rational Machines." Working paper, IBM Almaden Research Center, Almaden, Calif.

Mertens, J. F., and S. Zamir. 1985. "Formulation of Bayesian Analysis for Games with Incomplete Information." *International Journal of Game Theory* 14:1–29.

Milgrom, P. 1981. "An Axiomatic Characterization of Common Knowledge." *Econometrica* 49:219–222.

Milgrom, P., and J. Roberts. 1982. "Predation, Reputation, and Entry Deterrence." *Journal of Economic Theory* 27:280–312.

Miyasawa, K. 1961. "On the Convergence of a Learning Process in a 2 × 2 Non-Zero-Sum Two-Person Game." Research memorandum 33, Princeton University, Princeton, N.J.

Moulin, H. 1984. "Dominance Solvability and Cournot Stability." *Mathematical Social Sciences* 7:83–102.

––––––– 1986. *Game Theory for the Social Sciences*, 2d ed. New York: New York University Press.

Moulin, H., and J. P. Vial. 1978. "Strategically Zero Sum Games." *International Journal of Game Theory* 7:201–221.

Myerson, R. 1978. "Refinements of the Nash Equilibrium Concept." *International Journal of Game Theory* 7:73–80.

Nash, J. 1951. "Non-Cooperative Games." *Annals of Mathematics* 54:286–295.

Nielsen, L. 1984. "Common Knowledge, Communication and Convergence of Beliefs." *Mathematical Social Sciences* 8:1–14.

Nozick, R. 1969. "Newcomb's Problem and Two Principles of Choice." In *Essays in Honor of Carl G. Hempel*, ed. N. Rescher. Dordrecht: Reidel.

Orcutt, G. H. 1952. "Actions, Consequences, and Causal Relations." *Review of Economics and Statistics* 34:305–313.

Ore, O. 1960. "Pascal and the Invention of Modern Probability Theory." *American Mathematical Monthly* 67:409–416.

Pareto, V. [1927] 1971. *Manual of Political Economy*. Trans. A. S. Schwier. New York: Augustus S. Kelley.

Parker, G. A. 1974. "Assessment Strategy and the Evolution of Fighting Behavior." *Journal of Theoretical Biology* 47:223–243.

Pearce, D. G. 1984. "Rationalizable Strategic Behavior and the Problem of Perfection." *Econometrica* 52:1029–1050.

Perlman, M. 1974. "Jensen's Inequality for a Convex Vector-Valued Function on an Infinite Dimensional Space." *Journal of Multivariate Analysis* 4:52–65.

Putnam, H. 1975. "Probability Theory and Confirmation." In *Mathematics, Matter and Method*. Cambridge: Cambridge University Press.

Quine, W. 1936. "Truth by Convention." In *Philosophical Essays for A. N. Whitehead*, ed. O. H. Lee. New York: Longmans.

Rabinowicz, W. 1983. "On Ratificationism: A Critique of Jeffrey's New Logic of Decision." Unpublished manuscript.

———— 1985. "Ratificationism without Ratification." *Theory and Decision* 19:171–200.

Radner, R. 1975. "Satisficing." *Journal of Mathematical Economics* 2:253–262.

Raiffa, H. 1968. *Decision Analysis*. Reading, Mass.: Addison-Wesley.

Raiffa, H., and R. Schlaifer. 1961. *Applied Statistical Decision Theory*. Boston: Harvard Graduate School of Business Administration.

Ramsey, F. P. 1931. *The Foundations of Mathematics and Other Essays*. Ed. R. B. Braithwaite. New York: Harcourt Brace.

Ramsey, F. P. n.d. Unpublished manuscripts 005-20-01; 005-20-03; 003-13-01 in the Archives for Scientific Philosophy in the Twentieth Century at the Hillman Library of the University of Pittsburgh, Pittsburgh, Penn.

Rawls, J. 1957. "Justice as Fairness." *Journal of Philosophy* 54:653–662.

———— 1958. "Justice as Fairness." *Philosophical Review* 67:164–194.

———— 1971. *A Theory of Justice*. Cambridge, Mass.: Harvard University Press.

———— 1974. "Some Reasons for the Maximin Criterion." *American Economic Review* 64:141–146.

Reny, P. 1987. "Rationality, Common Knowledge and the Theory of Games." Working paper, University of Western Ontario, London, Ontario.

Resnik, M. 1983. "A Restriction on a Theorem by Harsanyi." *Theory and Decision* 15:309–320.

———— 1987. *Choices*. Minneapolis: University of Minnesota Press.

Richter, R. 1984. "Rationality Revisited." *Australasian Journal of Philosophy* 62:392–403.

———— 1986. "Further Comments on Decision Instability." *Australasian Journal of Philosophy* 64:345–349.

Robbins, L. 1932. *An Essay on the Nature and Significance of Economic Science*. London: Macmillan.

———— 1938. "Interpersonal Comparisons of Utility." *Economic Journal* 48:635–641.

Roberts, A. W., and D. E. Varberg. 1973. *Convex Functions*. New York: Academic Press.

Robinson, J. 1951. "An Iterative Method of Solving a Game." *Annals of Mathematics* 54:296–301.

Rosenmuller, J. 1971. "Über Periodizitätseigenshaften spieltheoretischer Lernprozesse." *Zeitschrift für Wahrscheinlichkeitstheorie und verwandte Gebiete* 17:259–308.

Rosenthal, R. W. 1981. "Games of Perfect Information, Predatory Pricing and the Chain Store Paradox." *Journal of Economic Theory* 25:92–100.

Royden, H. L. 1968. *Real Analysis*, 2d ed. London: Macmillan.

Rubenstein, A. 1986. "Finite Automata Play the Repeated Prisoner's Dilemma." *Journal of Economic Theory* 39:83–96.

—— 1987. "The Complexity of Strategies and the Resolution of Conflict: An Introduction." Working paper, Suntory Toyota International Centre for Economics and Related Disciplines, London School of Economics and Political Science, London, England.

Samuelson, L. 1988. "Evolutionary Foundations for Solution Concepts for Finite, Two-Player, Normal-Form Games." In *Proceedings of the Second Conference on Theoretical Aspects of Reasoning about Knowledge,* ed. M. Vardi, 211–226. Los Altos, Calif.: Morgan Kaufmann.

Sanghvi, A. P., and M. J. Sobel. 1976. "Bayesian Games as Stochastic Processes." *International Journal of Game Theory* 5:1–22.

Savage, L. J. 1954. *The Foundations of Statistics.* New York: Wiley.

—— 1967. "Difficulties in the Theory of Personal Probability." *Philosophy of Science* 34:305–310.

Schelling, T. 1960. *The Strategy of Conflict.* London: Oxford University Press.

—— 1978. *Micromotives and Macrobehavior.* New York: Norton.

Schick, F. 1986. "Dutch Books and Money Pumps." *Journal of Philosophy* 83:112–118.

Schneewind, J. 1977. *Sidgewick's Ethics and Victorian Moral Philosophy.* London: Oxford University Press.

Seidenfeld, T. 1984. "Comments on Eells." In *PSA (1984).* East Lansing, Mich.: Philosophy of Science Association.

Seidenfeld, T., and Schervish, M. J. 1983. "A Conflict between Finite Additivity and Avoiding Dutch Book." *Philosophy of Science* 50:398–412.

Selten, R. 1965. "Spieltheoretische Behandlung eines Oligipolmodells mit Nachfragetragheit." *Zeitschrift für die gesamte Staatswissenschaft* 121:301–324, 667–689.

—— 1975. "Reexamination of the Perfectness Concept of Equilibrium in Extensive Games." *International Journal of Game Theory* 4:25–55.

—— 1978. "The Chain Store Paradox." *Theory and Decision* 9:127–159.

Selten, R., and U. Leopold. 1982. "Subjunctive Conditionals in Decision and Game Theory." In *Philosophy of Economics,* ed. W. Stegmuller, W. Balzer and W. Spohn. Berlin: Springer-Verlag.

Selten, R., and R. Stoecker. 1986. "End Behavior in Sequences of Finite Prisoner's Dilemma Supergames." *Journal of Economic Behavior and Organization* 7:47–70.

Sen, A. 1970. *Collective Choice and Social Welfare.* San Francisco: Holden Day.

Shapley, L. S. 1964. "Some Topics in Two Person Games." In *Advances in Game Theory,* ed. M. Dresher, L. S. Shapley, and A. W. Tucker, 1–28. Princeton: Princeton University Press.

Sharvy, R. 1983. "Richter Destroyed." Unpublished manuscript.

Shimony, A. 1955. "Coherence and the Axioms of Confirmation." *Journal of Symbolic Logic* 20:1–28.

—— 1967. "Amplifying Personal Probability." *Philosophy of Science* 34:326–333.

Shin, H. S. 1988. "Logical Structure of Common Knowledge." Working paper, Nuffield College, Oxford University, Oxford, England.

Shubik, M. 1982. *Game Theory in the Social Sciences.* Cambridge, Mass.: MIT Press.

Sidgewick, H. 1874. *The Methods of Ethics.* London: Macmillan.

Simon, H. 1957. *Models of Man.* New York: Wiley.

—— 1972. "Theories of Bounded Rationality." In *Decision and Organization,* ed. C. B. McGuire and R. Radner. Amsterdam: North-Holland.

—— 1986. "Rationality in Psychology and Economics." In *Rational Choice,* ed. R. M. Hogarth and M. W. Rader, 25–40. Chicago: University of Chicago Press.

Skyrms, B. 1980a. *Causal Necessity.* New Haven: Yale University Press.

—— 1980b. "Higher Order Degrees of Belief." In *Prospects for Pragmatism,* ed. D. H. Mellor. Cambridge: Cambridge University Press.

—— 1982. "Causal Decision Theory." *Journal of Philosophy* 79:695–711.

—— 1984. *Pragmatics and Empiricism.* New Haven: Yale University Press.

—— 1985. "Ultimate and Proximate Consequences in Causal Decision Theory." *Philosophy of Science* 52:608–611.

—— 1986. "Deliberational Equilibria." *Topoi* 5:59–67.

—— 1987a. "Coherence." In *Scientific Inquiry in Philosophical Perspective,* ed. N. Rescher, 225–242. Pittsburgh: University of Pittsburgh Press.

—— 1987b. "Dynamic Coherence." In *Foundations of Statistical Inference,* ed. I. B. MacNeil and G. J. Umphrey. Dordrecht: Reidel.

—— 1987c. "Dynamic Coherence and Probability Kinematics." *Philosophy of Science* 54:1–20.

—— 1987d. "On the Principle of Total Evidence with and without Observation Sentences." In *Logic, Philosophy of Science and Epistemology: Proceedings of the 11th International Wittgenstein Symposium,* 187–195. Vienna: Holder-Pichler-Tempsky.

—— 1987e. "Updating, Supposing and MAXENT." *Theory and Decision* 22:225–246.

—— 1988a. "Conditional Chance." In *Probability and Causality: Essays in Honor of Wesley Salmon,* ed. J. Fetzer, 161–178. Dordrecht: Reidel.

—— 1988b. "Deliberational Dynamics and the Foundations of Bayesian Game Theory." *Philosophical Perspectives,* no. 2, *Epistemology,* ed. J. E. Tomberlin. Atascadero, Calif.: Ridgeview.

—— 1988c. "Probability and Causation." *Journal of Econometrics* 39:53–68.

Smale, S. 1980. "The Prisoner's Dilemma and Dynamical Systems Associated to Non-cooperative Games." *Econometrica* 48:1617–1634.

Smart, J. J. C. 1956. "Extreme and Restricted Utilitarianism." *Philosophical Quarterly* 6:344–354. Reprinted in *Theories of Ethics,* ed. P. Foot (Oxford: Oxford University Press, 1967).

Smith, C. A. B. 1961. "Consistency in Statistical Inference and Decision." *Journal of the Royal Statistical Society,* ser. B, 23:1–37.

Sobel, J. H. 1983. "Expected Utilities and Rational Actions and Choices." *Theoria* 49.

——— 1986. "Notes on Decision Theory: Old Wine in New Bottles." *Australasian Journal of Philosophy* 64:407–437.

——— 1987. "Self-Doubts and Dutch Strategies." *Australasian Journal of Philosophy* 65:56–81.

Spohn, W. 1982. "How to Make Sense of Game Theory." In *Studies in Contemporary Economics,* vol. 2: *Philosophy of Economics,* ed. W. Stegmuller et al. Heidelberg and New York: Springer-Verlag.

Teller, P. 1973. "Conditionalization and Observation." *Synthese* 26:218–258.

——— 1976. "Conditionalization, Observation, and Change of Preference." In *Foundations of Probability Theory, Statistical Inference, and Statistical Theories of Science,* ed. W. Harper and C. Hooker. Dordrecht: Reidel.

Tversky, A., and D. Kahneman. 1986. "Rational Choice and the Framing of Decisions." In *Rational Choice,* ed. R. Hogarth and M. Reder, 67–94. Chicago: University of Chicago Press.

Uchii, S. 1973. "Higher Order Probabilities and Coherence." *Philosophy of Science* 40:373–381.

van Damme, E. 1983. *Refinements of the Nash Equilibrium Concept.* Berlin: Springer-Verlag.

van Fraassen, B. 1980. "Rational Belief and Probability Kinematics." *Philosophy of Science* 47:165–187.

——— 1984. "Belief and the Will." *Journal of Philosophy* 81:235–256.

——— 1986. "A Demonstration of the Jeffrey Conditionalization Rule." *Erkenntnis* 24:17–24.

——— 1987. "Symmetries of Personal Probability Kinematics," with an appendix by John Collins. In *Scientific Inquiry in Philosophical Perspective,* ed. N. Rescher, 183–220. New York: University Press of America.

Vickers, J. 1976. *Belief and Probability.* Dordrecht: Reidel.

——— 1988. *Chance and Structure.* Oxford: Clarendon Press.

Villegas, C. 1964. "On Qualitative Probability σ-algebras." *Annals of Mathematical Statistics* 35:1787–1796.

von Neumann, J. 1928. "Zur Theorie der Gesellschaftespiele." *Mathematische Annalen* 100:295–320.

von Neumann, J., and O. Morgenstern. 1947. *Theory of Games and Economic Behavior,* 2d ed. Princeton: Princeton University Press.

Wald, A. 1950. Statistical Decision Functions. New York: Wiley.

Weirich, P. 1985. "Decision Instability." *Australasian Journal of Philosophy* 63:465–472.

——— 1986. "Decisions in Dynamic Settings." In *PSA (1986),* ed. A. Fine and P. Machamer, 438–449. East Lansing, Mich.: Philosophy of Science Association.

——— 1988. "Hierarchical Maximization of Two Kinds of Expected Utility." *Philosophy of Science* 55:560–582.

Werlang, S. R. 1986. "Common Knowledge and Game Theory." Ph.D. diss., Department of Economics, Princeton University, Princeton, N.J.

Williams, P. M. 1980. "Bayesian Conditionalization and the Principle of Minimum Information." *British Journal for the Philosophy of Science* 31:131–144.

Zabell, S. L. 1988. "Symmetry and Its Discontents." In *Causation, Chance and Credence*, ed. W. Harper and B. Skyrms, 155–190. Dordrecht: Kluwer.

Zeeman, E. C. 1980. "Population Dynamics from Game Theory." In *Global Theory of Dynamical Systems: Lecture Notes in Mathematics*, ed. Z. Niteck and C. Robinson, 819. Berlin: Springer-Verlag.

Index